Manston's Travel Key Europe

Also in the Travel Key Guide Series:

Manston's Antique Fairs and Auctions of Britain

Manston's Antique Fairs and Auctions of France

*is for information.
Throughout Europe, the lower-case "i" is used
as the international symbol direct travelers to
information offices.*

Manston's Travel Key Europe

How to Make a Phone Call, Do Your Laundry, Find a Chemist, and Much More

by
Peter B. Manston

A Travel Key Guide
Published by B.T. Batsford, Ltd.
London

Copyright © 1985, 1987, 1988, 1989 by
Peter B. Manston
All rights reserved. No part of this work may be reproduced or utilized in any form by any means, whether electronic or mechanical, including photocopying, recording, or information retrieval system or data base, without the express written permission of B.T. Batsford (the publisher), except in the case of brief quotations embodied in critical articles and reviews.

Published in the United Kingdom by
  B.T. Batsford
  4 Fitzhardinge St.
  London W1H OAH
  Telephone 01-486 8484

Published in a different edition in the United States by
  Travel Keys
  P.O. Box 160691
  Sacramento, California 95816 U.S.A.
  Telephone (916) 452-5200

Designed by Peter B. Manston
Edited in the U.S. by Robert C. Bynum and in
  the U.K. by Alison Bolus
Type galleys by Lithographics, Sacramento,
  California U.S.A.
Printed and bound by Interpress
Manufactured in Hungary
First Printing January 1989

ISBN 0-7134-6236-1

Contents

Acknowledgements 6
Disclaimer 6
Introduction 7
Before You Go 8
Passports 16
Visas 25
Getting to Europe 34
Travelling Light 43
Clothes 47
Camera and Film 57
Money 60
Guarding Your Health 69
Did You Forget Anything? 84
Crossing the Language Barrier 87
Transport in Europe 90
Public Transport 112
Cars and Driving 143
Letters and Packages 164
Using European Telephones 174
Telephone Keys—Country by Country 184-248
Finding Public Toilets 249
Lodging 258
Food and Drink 278
Laundry 293
Security 302
Your Embassy 311
Open and Closed 322
Shopping 338
Value Added Tax Refunds 342
Flea Markets and Street Markets 361
Cultural Pursuits 671
Reading in Europe 375
Returning Home 400
Index 406
Will You Help? 427
Weights and Measures 430-431
About the Author 432 (inside back cover)

Acknowledgements

Between the day this book was just a gleam in my mind's eye and the day you get this book into your hands, dozens of people urged me on and generously helped. A few helped immeasurably by asking a single crucial question which significantly improved the final product. Others shared information and experiences. Others shared their years of experience living in Europe, checking the foreign language words and lending their knowledge. Thanks also to officials of the various national tourist offices, transit authorities, European embassy staff in Europe, and the European staff of the United States Department of Commerce Foreign Commercial Service, and Ortrud Alderman and Bernadette Meauzé for translation assistance. Thanks also to David Jones.

There are three people who deserve special thanks. Robert C. Bynum followed this project from its genesis, proving to be not only the book's godfather but also a perceptive and patient editor. Paula R. Mazuski provided encouragement and unstinting support when the work got hard and its completion kept receding into the distance like a mirage on a desert road. Alison Bolus helped greatly in adapting this book to its (almost entirely new) British edition.

My thanks to all.

Disclaimer

Don't forget that times change! In the everyday world, what we do today isn't necessarily what we'll have to do tomorrow. Prices go up, and very occasionally down. This guide will be updated in future editions as Europe changes.

This book is as complete and accurate as possible. Facts have been exhaustively checked and rechecked. Information had to be sifted and weighed. Therefore, though the information and prices are deemed to be accurate, they may not always be what you find. Neither the author nor the publisher can be responsible if you are inconvenienced by the information contained in the book.

The persons, companies, and institutions named in the book are believed to be reputable and engaged in the business or service they purport to. Any questions should be directed to them rather than the publisher. Inclusion or exclusion of mention of a firm or organization is not a reflection on the suitability of their servicer or product.

When you find differences, please let us know. Fill out the "Will You Help?" form section at the end of the book. What *you* find and suggest can make the next edition even more complete and more useful to those who follow your path.

Introduction
Why This Book, Too?

Simple things you take for granted at home can become incredibly difficult in a foreign country. How and where to buy a ticket for a bus or underground can be confusing and even frustrating. Once you have your ticket, what do you do next?

Doing the laundry (or having it done for you) is not always easy when you're abroad.

Using the telephone is so complex that many travellers won't even try.

The traveller simply needs help.

This book can eliminate many irritations and frustrations of travel, leaving you free to enjoy your vacation or concentrate on your business.

There are dozens of other guides to Europe. You can get them about theatres in London, cathedrals in any country, and dozens listing hotels and restaurants. "Manston's Travel Key Europe", however, is a guide to *travelling* in Europe, emphasizing specific nuts-and-bolts information such as:
- how to keep clothes clean.
- how to find a toilet when you need it and what to expect when you do.
- how to find and use a telephone.
- how to mail a letter or postcard.
- how to use public transport.
- how to get tax refunds on purchases of items you'll bring home.
- where to find a chemist.
- where to get help, including embassy and consulate locations, phone numbers, and what they can do for you.

This book, which will slip into your pocket or handbag, provides this information and much, much more. A concise, instant reference, it is indexed by subjects as well as by countries.

You may not need all of this information at once—or some of it ever—but think about how essential it will be when you need it right away. You'll have instant access to facts not readily available elsewhere in a single easy-to-use form. You'll feel more secure.

It is to every traveller who, far from home, has felt uneasy facing the unknown that this book is dedicated.

Before You Go

Information Sources

You will probably gather information from many sources: libraries, bookshops, national tourism promotion offices, travel agents, Sunday travel sections, and friends and relatives. Some sources offer general information, while others offer quite specialized information. Some brochures, events calendars, guidebooks, and city maps will only be available when you get to your destination.

Libraries

Libraries will have the largest quantity of information but it is not always current. Most public libraries have the common travel books. Guides a few years old are still useful as a general reference, though not for making reservations or determining current prices.

Libraries also have books about European history, politics, and culture. To get a better idea of the variety of travel books, look at the "Books In Print" subject volumes for paperbacks and hardbacks.

A good library will have European magazines and newspapers. University and college libraries usually contain the most complete selections. Even if you can't read the language, the pictures and advertisements will give you some flavour of the country.

Before You Go

By using the library, you'll get lots of ideas to plan your trip. The only drawback to library books is that you can't take them with you, unless you're going on a short trip.

Bookshops

Current information is best found in the most recent books available in bookshops. By nature, however, most material on the shelves will be produced for the mass market. More specialized books listed in "Books in Print" (available for reference at most bookshops) can be special ordered either through the bookshop or directly from the publisher.

A few bookshops with particularly large travel sections, or entirely devoted to travel books, maps, guides, etc. offer greater depth. The following bookshops all welcome mail and telephone orders and some offer free book lists or catalogues:

London

Chapter Travel Ltd.
126 St. John's Wood
High Street
London NW8 7ST
Tel. 01-586 9451
Fax 01-586 5517
Telex 263820 CHAPTR G

Compendium Bookshop
234 Camden High St.
London NW1
Tel. 01-485 8944

Foyle's (W. &. G.)
Ground Floor   113/119
Charing Cross Road
London WC2H 0EB
Tel. 01-437 5660

Robertson-McCarta Ltd.
122 King's Cross Road
London WC1X 9DS
Tel. 01-278 8276
Fax 01-837 9788
Telex 8951182 GECOMS G
Offers book and map lists.

The Travel Bookshop 13 Blenheim Crescent London W11 2EE Tel. 01-229 5260	Waterstone 121-5 Charing Cross Road London WC2H Tel. 01-434 4291 and other locations.

Outside London:

B.H. Blackwell Ltd. 50 Broad St. Oxford OX1 3BQ Tel. (0865) 792792 Fax (0865) 791438 Telex 83118 BWELOX G	Heffer 20 Trinity St. Cambridge CB2 3BG Tel. (0223) 358 351
Whiteman's Bookshop 7 Orange Grove Bath BA1 1LP Tel. (0225) 64029	Robert Humm & Co. Station House Stamford, Lincs. PE9 2JN

European Government Tourist Offices

Tourism is considered a nonpolluting national resource to be carefully nurtured, and European nations—except Albania—want you to come and visit. Almost all—except a few tiny countries—have government tourist offices or representatives in Britain.

To encourage you to visit, they put out volumes of material, mostly free for the asking. It ranges from carefully designed books to lush, four-colour glossy brochures to typewritten hotel lists. All entice you. Some nations shower you with more information than others: West Germany will send volumes of free information, while some Eastern countries have only a brochure or two. Italy and Greece put out free books designed for prospective tourists. East Germany's embassy has been known to send out a free, several hundred-page four-colour book about the country as well as tourist-oriented booklets.

You'll get a rich harvest for the price of a few postcards or letters. If you have special interests, such as fishing, churches, or music festivals, be sure to mention them in your request for information.

You should remember that the information you receive isn't unbiased: no tourist office will allude to political or social problems, polluted beaches, slag heaps, or slums. Neither will they mention smog-eaten monuments, or, for that matter, monumental traffic jams. Further, the focus may be where the particular nation wants the tourists to go: for example, the free Italian book devotes an equal amount of space to every single region, interesting or not to the traveller.

A list of European national tourist offices in the United Kingdom is below. European nations also have offices in other European countries' capitals and other major cities. You can find these offices in phone books or any local tourist information office. These offices have much of the same literature and offer much the same advice. However, some of the brochures may only be available in the language of the country you're in.

European Government Tourist Offices in Great Britain

Albania
Albturist
c/o Regent Holidays
13 Small Street
Bristol BS1 1DE
Tel. (0272) 211711
Telex 444606 REGENT G

Andorra
Andorra Delegation—
Tourism and
Information
63 Westover Road
London SW18 2RF
Tel. 01-874-4806

Austria
Austrian National
Tourist Office
30 St. George Street
London W1R 0AL
Tel. 01-629 0461
Fax 01-499 6038
Telex 24709 OESLTN G

Belgium
Belgian National Tourist
Office
38 Dover St.
London W1X 3RB
Tel. 01-499 5379
Fax 01-491 7577
Telex 296358 BELTO G

Bulgaria
Bulgarian Tourist Office
18 Prince's Street
London W1R 7RE
Tel. 01-499 6988
Telex 296467

Czechoslovakia
Cedok (London) Ltd.
Czechoslovak Travel
Bureau
17-18 Old Bond St.
London W1X 4RB
Tel. 01-629 6058
Fax 01-493 7841
Telex 21164 CEDOKL G

Denmark
Danish Tourist Board
Sceptre House
169 Regent St.
London W1R 8PY
Tel. 01-734 2637
Fax 01-494 2170
Telex 24682 DANTUR G

Finland
Finnish Tourist Board
Greener House
66-68 Haymarket
London SW1Y 4RF
Tel. 01-839 4048
Fax 01-321 0696
Telex 295960 FTBUK G

France
French Government
Tourist Office
178 Piccadilly
London W1V 0AL
Tel. 01-499 6911
(recording)
or 01-491 7622 (direct)

Germany, East (GDR)
c/o Berolina Travel Ltd.
22a Conduit St.
London W1R 9TB
Tel. 01-629 1664
Telex 263944 BTLLON G

Germany, West (BRD)
German National
Tourist Office
Nightingale House
65 Curzon St.
London W1Y 9PE
Telephone
01-495 3990/1
Fax 01-495 6129

Gibraltar
Gibraltar Tourist Office
4 Arundel Great Court
179 The Strand
London WC2R 1EH
Tel. 01-836 0777 or
01-240 6611
Fax 01-240 6612
Telex 266303 GIBTUR G

Greece
Greek National Tourist
Organization
195/197 Regent St.
London W1R 8DL
Tel. 01-734 5997

Hungary
Danube Travel
6 Conduit St.
London W1R 9TG
Tel. 01-493 0263
Fax 01-493 6963
Telex 23541

Before You Go 13

Ireland
Irish Tourist Board
Ireland House
150 New Bond St.
London W1Y 0AQ
Tel. 01-493 3201
or 629 7292
Fax 01-493 9065
Telex 266410

Luxembourg
Luxembourg National
Trade & Tourist Office
36 Piccadilly
London W1V 9PA
Tel. 01-434 2800
Telex 940-16933

Monaco
Monaco Government
Tourist & Convention
Office
50 Upper Brook St.
London W1Y 1PG
Tel. 01-629 4712
Fax 01-629 0425
Telex 889130 PPLUS G

Northern Ireland
Northern Ireland
Tourist Board
11 Berkeley St.
London W1X 6BU
Tel. 01-493 0601
Fax 01-499 3731
Telex 21839

Italy
Italian State Tourist
Office (ENIT)
1 Prince's St.
London W1R 8AY
Tel. 01-408 1254
Fax 01-493 6695
Telex 22402 ENIT G

Malta
Malta National Tourist
Office
207 College House
Wrights Lane
London W8 5SH
Tel. 01-938 2668
Fax 01-376 2273
Telex 266083

Netherlands
Netherlands Board of
Tourism
Eggington House
25-28 Buckingham Gate
London SW1E 6LD
Tel. 01-630 0451
Fax 01-828 7941
Telex 269005 HOLLND
G

Norway
Norwegian Tourist
Board
20 Pall Mall
London SW1Y 5NE
Tel. 01-839 6255 (Public
line)
Tel. 01-839 2650 (Travel
trade only)
Fax 01-8390 4180 Att.
NTB
Telex 265635 EXNOR G
ATT NTB

Poland
Polorbis Travel Ltd.
82 Mortimer St.
London W1N 7DE
Tel. 01-580 8028
Telex 8812232 POLORB G

Portugal
Portuguese National Tourist Office
New Bond St. House
1 New Bond St.
London W1Y 0NP
Tel. 01-493 3873
Telex 265653

Romania
Romanian Tourist Office
29 Thurloe Place
London SW7 2HP
Tel. 01-584 8090
Telex 262107

Soviet Union (U.S.S.R.)
Intourist Moscow
292 Regent St.
London W1R 6QL
Tel. 01-631 1252
or 580 4974

Spain
Spanish National Tourist Office
57 St. James's St.
London SW1A 2LD
Tel. 01-499 0901
Telex 888138

Sweden
Swedish National Tourist Office
3 Cork St.
London W1X 1HA
Tel. 01-437 5816
Fax 01-287 0164
Telex 22296 SWETUR G

Switzerland
Swiss National Tourist Office
Swiss Centre
New Coventry St.
London W1V 8EE
Tel. 01-734 1921
or 734 4576
Fax 01-437 4577
Telex 21295 SNTO G

Turkey
Turkish Tourist Office
Egyptian House
170 Piccadilly
London W1V 9DD
Tel. 01-734 8681

Yugoslavia
Yugoslav National Tourist Office
143 Regent St.
London W1R 8AE
Tel. 01-734 5243 or 439 0399, fax 01-437 0599
Telex 21454

Travel Agents

Travel agents offer useful and valuable information about where and how to travel. A good agent can conveniently provide important services at no direct cost to you, including package tours, fly-drive combinations, car rentals, tickets, rail-passes, and visa information. Most of their income comes from commissions from airlines, hotels, and other service sellers. Travel agents may have biases in favor of scheduled airlines, major tour operators and large hotel chains. They are less likely to want to deal with bucket shop and charter flight operators, budget-range small hotels, etc., because those organizations and establishments offer small (or no) commissions. Many travel agents will bill you directly if they receive no commission, or what they consider a substandard one.

Select travel agents on the basis of referrals, their knowledge and trustworthiness. You may wind up dealing with a single agent, or, particularly if you use charter flights, one for the flights and another for other purposes.

Sunday Travel Sections

Partly as a service and partly as an advertising vehicle, many Sunday newspapers have extensive travel sections. These are somewhat scattered in coverage, depending on which writers have been where and which advertisers are aiming for business.

They provide you with the most current information about where to go, what you'll find when you get there, and sometimes how much it will cost. You'll also read articles enticing you to places you hadn't thought about visiting. Some of them you may want to visit—or revisit. The positive is stressed: except for the rare article and letter to the editor, you'll sometimes need to read between the lines to get a balanced view.

Remember

Above all, you're in control. You can decide intelligently where you want to go, what you want to see, and how to get there.

Passports

You need to have a passport for all travel to the Continent. Passports are required by Immigration (both when arriving at foreign borders and also when returning home) and serve as identification when changing money, registering at hotels and other lodgings, and various other purposes.

There are two kinds of British passport: the full 10-year Standard British Passport, valid in all countries, and the one-year Visitor's Passport, valid for short stays in Western Europe, Greece, Turkey, Tunisia, Iceland, Bermuda, and sometimes Yugoslavia, but not in Eastern Europe (or much of the rest of the world).

At any one time, you can only have *one* passport: either a Standard British Passport *or* a Visitor's Passport. You must turn in the passport you have whenever you apply for another (or renew a passport).

If you could be considered a citizen or national of another country besides the U.K., be sure that by receiving a British passport, you're not inadvertently losing your non-British nationality.

Who is Entitled to a Passport

A number of varying categories of people are entitled to British passports: British citizens by birth or naturalisation (includes England, Scotland, Wales, Northern Ireland, the Channel Islands, and the Isle of Man), British Dependent

Territories citizens, British Nationals (non-British residents, mainly from Hong Kong), British Subjects, and British Protected Persons.

A request for a passport for children born after December 31, 1982 may require additional proof of nationality since not all children born in the U.K. after that date have British nationality.

Passport Photos

Two photos are required for every passport application, whether Standard and Visitor's. Photos may be in either black and white or colour, and must be 45mm high by 35mm wide (1.77 inches by 1.38 inches). Remember not to wear a hat or head covering when the photo is taken.

Children

Children under the age of 16 may be included on their parent's Standard or Visitor's passport and travel with them, but may not take their parent's passport to travel alone.

Children may, as an alternative, have passports of their own (except that children under 8 years of age may not have their own Visitor's Passport), but in all cases must have the parent's or guardian's permission to apply.

The Standard British Passport

Standard passports are issued by Home Office's regional Passport Offices. After the date you submit your application, allow at least one month to receive your passport during most of the year, and up to 3 months from February through August (when most applications are made).

Where and How to Apply

You may apply by mail or apply in person at the Passport Offices. You must be able to prove your British nationality with specific documents, which you must show or submit along with your application for a new passport or to make changes on your present passport. Addresses of Passport Offices are found at the end of this section.

Required Forms

There is a specific form for each type of application or change to the passport. All forms are issued by the Home Office and are available from Passport Offices. Use only the one form you need.

Home Office Form A: United Kingdom Passport Application. Use this form to apply for a new Standard British Passport for anyone over age 16.

Home Office Form B: Application for a United Kingdom Passport for a Child under 16. Use this for a Standard British Passport for children.

Home Office Form C: Application to Add Children or Make Changes to a United Kingdom Passport. Use this form to change your passport (change of name, photograph, or of personal details) or to add children under 16.

Home Office Form D: Application for the extension of a United Kingdom Passport. Use this form to add more time if your passport was issued before your sixteenth birthday or for another reason was issued for less than 10 years.

Home Office Form R: Application to replace a United Kingdom Passport. Use this form to obtain a new a Standard Passport when your current Standard Passport expires.

How Many Pages in a Passport?

Standard British Passports are issued with either 32 pages (enough for most people's travel) or 94 pages (if you expect to travel extensively in countries which stamp visas in passports, such as Eastern Europe). State your choice on your application.

Passport Costs

Standard 32-page passports cost £15. Standard 94-page passports cost £30. Payment may be made by a cheque or postal order payable to the Passport Office. It should be crossed "A/C Payee." If paying by Giro Transfer, add "Passport Fee" immediately after the amount written in words. Send the transfer document with your application.

If you want your passport returned by Registered Post, add £1.25 to cover the additional postage.

Proof of Nationality

In order to prove British nationality, you must provide documentation. All documentation must be original, *not* photocopies. If born before January 1, 1983, you must provide a birth certificate, certificate of naturalisation, and documentation of name changes (statutory declaration or change of name deed, and if a woman, marriage and or divorce documents).

If born abroad before January 1, 1983, contact the Passport Office for exact information.

If born in the U.K. on or after January 1, 1983, birth certificates must be provided. If the parents were not born in the U.K., proof of their U.K. nationality must also be provided.

If born in the U.K., you can obtain your birth certificate from the office of Registration of Births, Deaths, and Marriages in the locality of birth.

If born abroad, your documentation requirements may vary but you'll have to prove that your father was a British national.

Declaration and Signature

You must read and understand the Declaration before signing it. Sign and date it; unsigned forms will be returned.

Countersignature

To obtain a passport, you must be endorsed by someone (not a relative) who has known you two or more years. The classes of person must be licensed or professional, such as bank officers, doctors, lawyers, judges, minsters, permanent civil servants, police officers, or judges or even Members of Parliament.

If, because you have recently moved, you don't have anyone who has known you for two years and can countersign your application, contact the Passport Office for instructions.

The person who provides the countersignature must also sign the back of the one of the passport photographs and state that it is a true likeness.

Index Card and Mailing Labels

Each form comes with an Index Card, to acknowledge the receipt of your application and to provide mailing labels. Complete it and return it with your application.

Extending or Renewing a Standard Passport

If for any reason, your passport was issued for less than 10 years (usually because issued to a child), you may apply to extend it for the rest of the 10-year period. Use Home Office Form D, and send it with your passport to the Passport Office listed on the form for residents of your county.

There is no fee to extend your passport up to the 10-year maximum.

If you are extending a Blue passport, the passport will be amended and returned. If you have a Burgundy Red passport, a new document will be issued.

When extending a passport you must send new passport photographs.

Adding Children or Making Changes

You can make changes on your British Standard Passport by completing Home Office Form C and sending it in with your current passport. You may, if you wish, have a new photograph included; send two prints.

If you are adding one or more children to the passport, send payment for £4. If you are amending it to reflect a name change or have a new photograph included, the charge is £3.

When Your Current Passport Expires

You may replace an expired Standard British passport (to be issued in the same name) by completing Home Office Form R. (Otherwise use Home Office Form A.)

You will also need to send in your expired passport, two passport photographs, and the fee of £15 for a 32-page passport, or £30 for a 94-page passport.

Where to Apply

Each application form includes a list of the Passport Offices, and the counties which they serve. The offices in England and Wales are:

Passport Office
5th Floor
India Buildings
Water Street
Liverpool L2 0QZ
Tel. (051) 237 3010

Passport Office
Clive House
70 Petty France
London SW1 9HD
Tel. 01-279 3434

Passport Office
Olympia House
Upper Dock Street
Newport,
Gwent NPT 1XA
Tel. (0633) 244500
or 244292

Passport Office
55 Westfield Road
Peterborough
PE3 6TG
Tel. (0733) 895555

In Scotland, apply to:
Passport Office
3 Northgate
96 Milton Street
Cowcaddens
Glasgow G4 0BT
Tel. (041) 332 0271

In Northern Ireland,
apply to:
Passport Office
Hampton House
47-53 High Street
Belfast BT1 2QS
Tel. (0232) 232371

In Guernsey, apply to:
Passport Office
White Rock
St Peter Port
Tel. (0481) 26911

In Jersey, apply to:
Passport Office
Victoria Chambers,
Conway Street
St Helier
Tel. (0534) 25377

On the Isle of Man, apply to:
Passport Office
Douglas
Tel. (0624) 26262

Enter the Date Your Travel Begins

Each application includes a block to enter the first date of travel. Allow at least one month for a Standard British Passport, though from February to August (inclusive) it may take as long as 3 months.

Emergency: If You Need a Passport Quickly

If you need a passport quickly, complete the application, provide all required information, and contact the Passport Office. Explain your need and the reason. In these cases, quicker service is possible, though proof of the emergency may be required.

You may also apply in person at the Passport Office, though this will not itself guarantee quicker issuance of the passport than if you post your application.

Also, if you're traveling for a year or less, and only in Western Europe, Greece, and Turkey, it is much faster to obtain a Visitor's Passport than a Standard Passport.

If You Live Outside of the U.K.

If you need to replace an expiring passport while outside the U.K., contact the nearest British consulate for further information. Some procedures may be different but the fees are the same as in the U.K.

Visitor's Passport

Visitor's passports are valid for one year, and are quickly issued.

You will need to provide 2 photographs (as above).

You will also need to provide documents proving nationality, which can be:
- a Standard British Passport in your name
- a birth or adoption certificate, an uncancelled (but possibly expired) British Visitor's Passport, a certificate of naturalisation, or a retirement pension book or pension card, *and* an identification card, such as a driving licence, National Health Service card, bank cheque card, credit card, bus pass, or utility bill.

Applications must be made on "Form VP: Application for a British Visitor's Passport", which is available from Main Post Offices and Passport Offices. Note that application in England, Wales, and Scotland is through main Post Offices only—not through Passport Offices. However, in Northern Ireland, the Channel Islands, and the Isle of Man, Visitor's Passports are issued from Passport Offices (addresses in the Standard Passport section above).

Cost

The cost is £7.50 for a single person and £11.25 if the passport includes a spouse.

Changing, Extending, or Renewing a Visitor's Passport

A Visitor's Passport cannot be renewed, extended, or changed in any way once it has been issued.

Where to Apply for a British Visitor's Passport

England, Scotland, and Wales

Apply in person at Main Post Offices. You cannot apply for them by mail or obtain them from Passport Offices.

Northern Ireland, Channel Islands, and Isle of Man

Apply in person at Passport Offices as given in the Standard Passport section.

If You Already Have a Standard British Passport

You can only have one British Passport. While you may apply for and receive a Visitor's Passport even though you already have a Standard Passport, you must hand the Standard Passport in to the Post Office when you apply.

If you want the Standard Passport returned, you must apply in writing to the Passport Office where it was issued, give its number, and send in the Visitor's Passport.

Visas

A visa is a formal permit to cross a country's border. A government is not required to give you a visa or provide a reason for denying one. Separate visas are required for entry into each Eastern (Socialist) bloc country, and getting them can be a minor hassle. You can get them either in Britain or on the Continent. When your visa is issued, your passport is usually stamped, and frequently you are given forms you must keep with you while in that country.

You must have a full and current passport before beginning to apply for visas. Many countries require the passport to remain valid for at least six months after the visa is issued. Visas come in several forms: transit visas, issued merely for quick passage across a country; tourist visas; and others. For these other types, such as long-term stays and permanent residence, contact the nearest embassy or consulate of the country concerned. Conditions and costs are subject to change.

If you were born in or could be claimed as a citizen of an East European country, you should without fail obtain your visa in advance of arrival at the border. Otherwise you could be claimed as a national of that country and kept there.

How to Get Visas in Britain

There are two ways to get visas in Britain: either directly by yourself or through a visa service. Visa services are easier to deal with but charge for their services. Often, if travel agencies obtain visas for you they use a visa service.

1. *Do it yourself.* You can apply either in person (preferred) or by mail. To obtain a visa issued by mail, you'll have to call or write for a visa application. Send it, your passport, any fee, and any required photographs to the embassy or consulate. A key to Eastern European embassies and consulates in the United Kingdom is below.

2. *Use visa services.* You can avoid much of the frustration of getting the visa yourself by using a visa service. The visa requirements remain the same, but the service's familiarity with the system and its arcane processes ensures more rapid issuance. Generally they offer expedited service to obtain visas quickly. These agencies charge the visa cost plus a service fee. You will have to give them your passport, too.

Countries Requiring Visas for British Nationals

Visa Requirements Key

Note: These countries usually require a *full* British passport. A visitor's passport is not acceptable.

Albania

Visas are usually arranged by the official tour operator (Regent Tours, the Albturist representative in the U.K.), and cost £11, which is usually added to the tour price. There are no Albanian embassies or consulates in the U.K. There are Albanian embassies in Paris at 131 rue de la Pompe, 75016 Paris, tel. (1) 45.53.51.32; also in Rome, Italy at via Asmara 9,

Rome, tel. (06) 8380725, or any Eastern European capital. For information, contact:

Regent Tours
13 Small Street
Bristol BS1 1DE
Tel. (0272) 211711
Telex 444606

Bulgaria

Visas are not issued at the border; tourist visas cost £20, requires one photo. Takes 7 to 10 working days. Available through the embassy's consular office. Transit visas also available, same cost, also not available at the border. For information, contact:

Embassy of People's Republic of Bulgaria
186-188 Queen's Gate
London SW7 5HL
Tel. 01-584 9400

Czechoslovakia

Visas are not issued at the border; single entry tourist or transit visas cost £9, requires two photos. Note that the visa application form has four leaves without carbon paper; either supply your own paper or fill each section out by hand. Transit visas cost the same as a tourist visa.

Visas must be used within five months of issuance. You must prepay your journey, or exchange a minimum amount of money for each day you'll be there when you arrive at the border. For information contact:

Czechoslovak Embassy
25-30 Kensington Palace Gardens
London W8 4QY
Tel. 01-229 3966 or 727 3966

Germany, GDR (East)

Tourist visas are the current Sterling equivalent of 5 Mark (M) for transit, and 25M for tourist or camping visas, plus prepaid accommodation vouchers or 25M per day. (1 GDR Mark is valued at 1 West German Deutsche Mark.)

Tourist visas are only issued after you have prepaid your accommodations to the Reisebüro der DDR, the official state travel agency. This agency, either directly or through its authorized representatives in other countries, will provide you with hotel vouchers and a visa entitlement certificate (Visumberechtigungschein). Only then will a visa be issued at GDR embassies, consulates, and border crossings. All costs must be paid in Western currency. The West German Deutsche Mark (DM) is the standard. The GDR is not very accommodating to spur-of-the-moment travellers. Travellers can also try to obtain lodging at the Reisebüro der DDR offices at most frontier crossings, but hotel space is scarce and if hotels are full, you may not be able to enter the country. Unless applying for a transit visa (see below), you should allow three weeks to obtain the voucher and visa. In an emergency, you will still need at least ten days to two weeks, and pay all telex charges (50 Marks per telex).

If you are visiting friends or relatives, you must follow similar procedures but allow eight to 10 weeks to complete them. You are not required to pay for accommodation but must exchange the equivalent of 25 Marks per person per day (7.50 Marks for children 6 to 15 years old).

The representative of the Reisebüro der DDR in Britain is:

Berolina Travel, Ltd.
22 Conduit St.
London W1R 9TB
Tel. 01-629 1664
Telex 263944

You can also contact the Reisebüro directly at:
Reisebüro der DDR
Alexanderplatz 5, Postschliessfach 77
DDR 1026 Berlin
German Democratic Republic
Tel. 21 50 (main desk)
Telex 114648, 114651, and 114652

Transit visas (except to West Berlin) and tourist visas require a visa entitlement certificate or voucher, an application, and two photographs.

Transit visas, valid for no more than three days cost DM5 (West German Deutsche Marks) and are issued at consulates, embassies, or road border crossings. If you are going through East Germany to either Poland or Czechoslovakia, you must have your Polish or Czech visa before arrival at the East German border. You will have to make reservations and pay for lodging at the border Reisebüro der DDR office.

Visas for car travel between West Germany and West Berlin are available instantly at road crossings. No photos are required, but you must pay DM5 for one-way and DM10 for two-way passage. Transit visas on trains and busses are free, no photos required. No visa is required to fly from West Germany to West Berlin's Tegel airport.

One-day visas to East Berlin cost 5 Deutsche Marks. In addition, you must exchange at least 25 West German Deutsche Marks for East German Marks, which you have to spend before the end of the day, since they can't be reconverted and can't be taken out. You must return to West Berlin by midnight. These visas are issued while you wait at border crossings between East and West Berlin.

Note: no border crossings into East Germany by bicycle or moped are permitted.

For information, contact:

Embassy of the German Democratic Republic
34 Belgrave Square
London SW1X 8PZ
Tel. 01-235 6991 and 235 4465

Hungary

Tourist visas and transit visas are available at border crossings on roads, at the Vienna dock, and at the airport in Budapest, but not available at railway border crossings, or from Hungarian embassies. Tourist visas are £9 for a single-entry visa and £18 for a double-entry tourist visa. Requires two photos. For information, contact:

Hungarian Embassy
35b Eaton Place
London SW1X 8BY
Tel. 01-235 2664 and 235 4462

Poland

Tourist visas are available at Polish embassies and consulates, but not at border crossings, and are valid up to 6 months, cost £15, and require two photographs. The minimum required daily currency exchange is £10, or £4.40 for students or campers with a caravan or campervan (car and/or tent won't do). Transit visas valid for 48 hours are available at slightly lower cost if you have a visa for the onward country. For information, contact:

Embassy of the Polish People's Republic
47 Portland Place
London W1N
Tel. 01-580 4324

Romania

Tourist visas, valid up to 30 days, cost £20, no photos required, take 48 hours at consular offices in London, and are also available at road but not railway border crossings. A minimum daily hard-currency exchange of £8 per day per person is required. Visas must be used within 6 months of issuance. Transit visas valid for 27 hours are also available at the same cost. For information, contact:

Embassy of the Socialist Republic of Romania
4 Palace Green
London W8 4QD
Tel. 01-937 9666

Soviet Union, U.S.S.R.

Tourist visas are free, require four photographs, but are not issued until you provide the Intourist tour or travel arrangement number.

Tourist visas are only issued after you have paid for your expenses to Intourist, the official Soviet travel agency (which can be done through a travel agency at home).

You need a completed visa application, which you will receive as part of your travel arrangements confirmation, or upon request from the consulate. Travel agents usually handle obtaining the visa if you take a tour.

The U.S.S.R. is not very accommodating or flexible for the individual traveler. If you take a tour and arrange for the visa yourself, you will need the Intourist Reference Number and the Voucher Registration Number before a visa will be issued. If you are not on a tour, you must still reserve and pay for all accommodations in advance through an authorized agent of Intourist; you will also receive an Intourist Reference Number. You should allow two weeks to obtain a Soviet visa, or at the minimum, at least six working days to obtain a Soviet visa in Europe.

Information is available from Intourist in London, or

Embassy of the U.S.S.R.
Consular Section
5 Kensington Palace Gardens
London W8 4QS
Tel. 01-229 3215 and -16

Yugoslavia

Tourist visas are issued free at border crossings, or at embassies and consulates.

Note: In summer 1988, for a limited period, Yugoslavia accepted Visitor's Passports as well as full passports. Whether this will be repeated in future years is unknown.

For information, contact:

Yugoslav Embassy
7 Lexham Gardens
London W8 5JU
Tel. 01-370 6105

Getting Visas on the Continent

Eastern European visas are available from embassies in capital cities throughout Europe. Other major cities often have visa-issuing consulates. Check the yellow or classified pages of phone books. In many languages the word for embassy is a variant of "embassy", but look under "Représentations diplomatiques" in French and "Botschaft" in German or contact tourist information offices for addresses. Make your application in person.

Western European capitals such as Vienna, Paris, and Brussels are excellent places to apply, since they have both embassies and offices of the official travel agencies of the Eastern nations. West Germany and the Netherlands are less satisfactory because the official tourist agencies are not in the same cities (Frankfurt and Amsterdam) as the embassies (Bonn and The Hague).

Because of long queues, visa issuance may take a couple of hours. It takes longer for visas to East Germany and the Soviet Union because all travel must be arranged before visas will be issued (see above).

Once you're in Eastern Europe, visas are most easily obtained in other Eastern European capitals, because there are few if any queues, and the visa can be issued in as little as 15 minutes.

Embassies and consulates are often open for visa issuance only from 9 a.m. to noon or 1 p.m. You'll need passport photographs and cash (either sterling or other Western currency). Bring your own pen to complete the application, which will include instructions in the native language, plus English, French, and German. You can answer the questions on any form in English. Most ask your occupation. The consular staff will stamp your passport (except for the Soviet Union) and endorse your visa form. Take good care of the form, since you will have to produce it wherever you stay, whenever you change money, and when you leave the country.

Getting to Europe

You have only two ways to get to the continent: by boat and by planes, at least until the Chunnel is finished. Each choice has its special pleasures and its drawbacks.

In addition, you can often combine train and boat passage into tickets purchased together.

International Ferry Service

A large number of ferries link Britain to the Continent and to Ireland. The most frequent service is between England and France; the main English ports are Dover and Folkestone. The main Continental ports are Calais and Boulogne, France, and Oostende, Belgium.

During most of the year, there are dozens of ferries plying these routes with a frequency of as little as half an hour to one hour. However, vehicles need reservations at peak summer seasons. In off-peak seasons and at night, reservations aren't usually needed.

The shortest distance and time between England and the Continent is between Dover and Calais; regular ferries take about 1 to 1-1/2 hours, plus another hour for immigration and customs.

The Hovercraft and Jetfoils actually ride above the water, and take about half as long as regular ferries, but cost more. The Hovercraft take vehicles, too, but the Jetfoils do not.

Getting to Europe

Other international ferry lines leave from Harwich to several points in the Netherlands, Denmark, Norway, and Sweden, from Plymouth to Santander, Spain, from Portsmouth to Cherbourg and Le Havre, France, and Holyhead, Liverpool, Milford Haven and Fishguard to Ireland.

Ferry Costs

Ferry fares vary greatly, and depend on several variables. In all cases, there is the minimum per-passenger fare on each route, which does not vary by season. An exception is the cheap fares offered for same-day returns to Calais and Boulogne.

Because of the large number of ferries and frequency of crossing, it is extremely rare that there are too many passengers on a particular ferry.

There is an additional charges for each motor vehicle. Vehicle charges depend on the day, time of day (or night), and season as well as the route chosen and size of vehicle.

Cheap short-break returns, including vehicles, are available on some lines for those who want only to make a 24-hour to 1-week holiday on the Continent.

The least expensive and fastest ferry crossings are usually from Folkestone and Dover to Boulogne and Dunkerque in France, and to Oostende in Belgium. The longer passages, such as to Scandinavia and Spain cost substantially more.

In general, summer crossings are the most expensive, especially at the beginning and end of school holidays, and on Bank Holidays, and winter crossings are the least expensive.

If you book your vehicle on a late-night, inexpensive ferry crossing, but arrive several hours early at the dock, you can go on an earlier ferry if there is space available.

How to Find Out Which Line(s) Go Where You Want to Go

Every travel agency and travel desk at the auto clubs (AA and RAC) will be happy to make reservations and sell tickets. Every British Rail ticket office can make reservations and sell tickets for travelers without vehicles.

You can also contact, reserve, and pay for tickets directly with the ferry lines, either at their terminals, or through their offices.

The main ferry companies are listed below, along with the headquarters or reservation address, and the major ports they link.

B & I Line
P.O. Box 19
12 North Wall
Dublin 1
Ireland
Tel. Ireland (01) 788 266
Service between Holyhead Wales, Liverpool, and Dublin, Ireland.

British Channel Island Ferries	British Channel Island Ferries
40 Great Portland Street	P.O. Box 315
London W1N	Poole, Dorset BH15 4DB
Tel. 01-636 6070 or	Tel. (0202) 681 155
	Fax (0202) 679 828

Ferry service between Portsmouth, Weymouth, and Cherbourg (France) and the Channel Islands of Guernsey and Jersey.

Brittany Ferries	Brittany Ferries
The Brittany Centre	Millbay Docks
Wharf Road	Plymouth PL1 3EW
Portsmouth PO2 8RU	Tel. (0752) 221321
Tel. (0705) 827701 or	

Service between Portsmouth to Caen and St-Malo, France, between Plymouth and Roscoff, France and Santander, Spain, and between Poole and Cherbourg, France.

DFDS Seaways
Scandinavia House
Parkeston Quay
Harwich, Essex CO12 4QG
Tel. (0255) 554 681
Services between Harwich and Newcastle, and: Goteborg, Sweden, Esbjerg, Denmark, and between Harwich and Hamburg, Germany.

Emeraude Ferries
Albert Quay
St Helier, Jersey, Channel Islands
Tel. (0543) 74458
Service between Jersey or Guernsey and St-Malo, France.

Fred Olsen Lines
Victoria Plaza
111 Buckingham Palace Road
London SW1W 0SP
Tel. (01) 630 0033
Service between Harwich and Kristianstad and Oslo, Norway and Hirtshals, Denmark.

Hoverspeed Ltd.
Maybrook House
Queen's Gardens
Dover, Kent CT17 9UQ
Tel. (0304) 240 241
or 01-554 7061 (London), (021) 236 2190 (Birmingham), or (061) 228 1321 (Manchester)
Service between Dover and the French ports of Calais and Boulogne.

Isle of Man Steam Packet Company Limited
P.O. Box 5
Imperial Buildings
Douglas, Isle of Man
Tel. (0624) 72468
Service between Heysham, Liverpool, Fleetwood, Stranraer, Belfast (Northern Ireland) and Dublin (Ireland) to the Isle of Man.

Norway Line
Tyne Commission Quay
Albert Edward Dock
North Shields (Newcastle)
Tyne and Wear NE29 6EA
Tel. (091) 258 5555
Service between Newcastle the Norwegian ports of Stavanger and Bergen.

Norfolk Line
Atlas House
Southgates Road
Great Yarmouth, Norfolk NR30 3LN
Tel. (0943) 856 133
Service between Great Yarmouth and Scheveningen, the Netherlands.

North Sea Ferries
King George Dock
Hedon Road
Hull, Humberside HU9 5QA
Tel. (0482) 795141
Reservations only tel. (0482) 796145
Service between Hull and Rotterdam/Europoort, Netherlands and Zeebrugge, Belgium.

Olau Line U.K. Ltd.
Sheerness, Kent ME12 1SN
Tel. (0975) 666 666
Service between Sheerness (Kent) and Vlissingen, the Netherlands.

P & O European Ferries
Regent Street
London W1R 8LB
Tel. 01-734 4431   or

P & O European Ferries
Channel House
Channel View Road
Dover, Kent CT17 9TJ
Tel. (0304) 203 388

(Also offices in Portsmouth and Felixstowe.)
Service between Dover, and Zeebrugge and Oostende, Belgium, Calais and Boulogne, France; between Felixstowe and Zeebrugge, Belgium; Portsmouth and Cherbourg and Le Havre, France; between Cairnryan, Scotland and Larne, Northern Ireland.

Getting to Europe

P & O Ferries/Smyril Line
P.O. Box 5
P & O Ferries Terminal
Aberdeen, Grampian AB9 8DL, Scotland
Tel. (0224) 572
Service between the Shetland Islands and Bergen, Norway, and between Aberdeen and the Orkney and Shetland Islands in Scotland.

The Sally Line
81 Piccadilly
London, W1V 9HF
Tel. 01-409 0536 and
409 2240   or

The Sally Line
The Argyle Centre
York Street
Ramsgate, Kent CT11 9DS
Tel. (0843) 595 522

Service across the English Channel from Ramsgate to Dunkirk, France.

Sealink U.K. Ltd.
Liverpool Street Station or Victoria Station (in person)
P.O. Box 29 (mail only)
London SW1V 1JX
Tel. (01) 828 4142

or
Sealink U.K. Ltd.
Sea Container House
20 Upper Ground
London SE1 9PF
Tel. (01) 928 5550

Reservations only tel. (0233) 47047, Prestel *545040#
Service from Dover to Calais, France (including Hovercraft service); from Folkestone to Boulogne, France; between Weymouth and Portsmouth to Cherbourg, France; between Harwich and Den Haag, Netherlands; between Holyhead and Dun Laoghaire near Dublin, Ireland; between Fishguard and Rosslare, Ireland; and between Stranraer (Scotland) and Larne, Northern Ireland.

Sealink Dieppe Ferries
Newhaven Harbour
Newhaven, East Sussex BN9 6BQ
Tel. (0273) 512 266
Service between Newhaven and Dieppe, France.

Swansea-Cork Ferries
P.O. Box 340
Poole, Dorset BH14 4DD
Tel. (0202) 681 818
Service between Swansea, Wales and Cork, Ireland.

Rail and Ferry Combinations

Every travel agency and British Rail station can sell tickets which combine rail travel with train travel.

Flying to Europe

Almost every international airline flies from Britain to the Continent. In addition, a number of British lines also fly to some Continental destinations.

There are varying types of flights at varying prices.

Full Fare on the Scheduled Airlines

The most expensive way to fly to Europe is to pay full fare on the scheduled airlines. Any travel agent or airline ticket office will sell you a full-fare ticket. Full fare tickets are refundable if you change your plans.

Reduced-Fare Alternatives

Charter Flights

During the summer, some of the cheapest holidays include flights, hotels, and sometimes other amenities, mainly to Spain, Portugal, and Greece. The flights may be on foreign airlines, and are sometimes at inconvenient hours or not at main airports. Many packages are required to offer accommodations in addition to the flight. Some of these packages may include only the most basic accommodation, with little expectation that many people will actually use them.

Travel agencies often can offer multitudes of choices in this area. In addition, newspapers and magazines are full of all kinds of offers of this type.

Charter packages are usually not fully refundable if you change your plans.

Bucket Shops

There are sometimes more seats on regularly scheduled airlines than purchasers at the full fare. They sell excess tickets in bulk to "bucket shops", who then sell directly to the public. You can never get bucket-shop prices from the airline directly.

Availability of flights to any particular place is often sporadic.

Bucket shops are legally permitted to sell you these tickets; the only restriction on their operation seems to be that they cannot mention the airline in printed advertising, which often appears in newspapers and magazines such as "Time Out" and "What's On".

Occasionally one sells questionable tickets: for this reason it is best to actually purchase your ticket in person, and not to spend money until you see the ticket.

London is probably the world centre for bucket-shop tickets.

Bucket-shop tickets are not usually refundable.

Airlines and Telephone Numbers

The main British-owned airlines providing service to the Continent are:

Air Europe
Europe House
East Park
Crawley, Sussex
Tel. (0345) 444737

British Air Ferries
Southend Airport, Southend, Essex SS2 6YL
Tel. 01-379 6055

British Airways
Heathrow Airport, TW6 2JA
Reservations tel. 01-897 4000

British Midland Airways Ltd.
Donington Hall
Castle Donington DE7
Reservations tel. 01-589 5599

Dan Air
Newman House, Horley, Surrey
Reservations tel. 01-680 1011 or Crawley 31299

Virgin Atlantic
3 Woodstock Street
London W1R
Tel. (01) 493 5998

In addition, there are dozens of foreign carriers flying to almost every large city or resort in Europe. Addresses and telephone numbers are found in telephone directories (particularly London Central), listed in the Yellow Pages under "Airlines".

Complaints

If you believe that the airplane is being operated in an unsafe manner, you can contact:

Civil Aviation Authority
Airworthiness Division
Heathrow Airport
Building 209, Epsom Square
London
Tel. 01-759 0205

For all other complaints, contact:
Civil Aviation Authority
CAA House
45 Kingsway
London WC2
Telephone 01-379 7311

Travelling Light

The Baggage Squeeze

Decades ago, when ships and trains were the only way to travel around Europe, baggage allowances were very generous, with lots of space for huge steamer trunks and boxes. There was little or no extra charge if you went over that nebulous limit. Today's jets don't work the same way: you trade weight and bulk for speed.

If you're a light traveller, there's no problem: everything should fit into a single under-the-seat suitcase, duffle bag, or soft pack. But there are almost always additions most people want to include in their luggage. Many flights within Europe strictly enforce a 44-pound (20-kilogramme or -kg) limit for checked-in luggage on economy and a 66-pound (30-kilogramme) first class, and within Yugoslavia, only a 33-pound (15-kilogramme) limit.

Check with the airline in advance of your flight to determine the rules.

Odd Baggage Allowances

Golf Clubs and Skis

Golf clubs must be checked-in and count as one regular piece of baggage. For the preservation of your complete set, you should arrange to have a cover of some sort for the clubs to prevent them from falling out of the bag. (Golf bags can hold a lot of clothes, too.)

Skis also count as a regular piece of luggage. You should be sure the skis are securely fastened together and each ski clearly labeled with your name and address.

Bicycles

A bicycle usually counts as one piece of checked-in luggage. While some airlines have bags or boxes available on a limited basis at check-in, you are wiser to pack the bicycle yourself in a cardboard bicycle box, obtainable from a bicycle shop. There are several advantages to this. First, bicycles, even more than most luggage, can be fragile if dropped in the wrong way. If you pack and protect it yourself, you have a far better chance of having it arrive in condition to ride away quickly from the airport. The more cushioned the box, the better the chances of its safe arrival. Newspapers wadded up are adequate. Plastic bubble packing is better. Styrofoam peanuts or shells provide excellent cushioning but are a mess upon arrival. Perhaps the best padding consists of other soft items such as sleeping bags, panniers, and clothes. Be sure to bring a number of plastic bags to cover greasy parts such as the chain and derailleurs.

When you pack your bicycle, you will need a few tools to reassemble it on arrival. Your pedals must be removed and taped to the frame. The handlebars must be turned sideways. The wheels should be removed.

If you have a very expensive racing or touring bicycle, be sure to buy excess-value insurance when you check in. To prove the value of your bicycle, have and show to the ticket agent your bill of sale or a recent appraisal from a bicycle shop. Otherwise, the airline (or its insurance company) may refuse to pay a damage claim in full.

Firearms

Warning: Due to various countries' firearms restrictions, and the threat of terrorism, do not carry guns without proper authorization! Firearms permits must be obtained from the destination country before boarding. Contact the airline, and pack the firearms in accordance with their instructions. Otherwise, if firearms are found in your luggage, you may be detained and miss your flight, and have your gun confiscated (or worse).

How to Get Extra Baggage on Board

Some travelers using airlines with very small baggage allowances, and some shoppers who can't resist heavy and bulky copper cookware, new skis, or antique bronze sculpture may run over baggage allowances.

Here are a few ways to try to squeeze a little more on the plane . . . most of them free, some requiring a bit of luck, chance, persistence, or fortitude. Some even require a bit of subterfuge at times.

Some possible solutions are:

1. Pay the excess baggage fee (see above, and check with the airline).

2. Look for a light traveller checking in for the same flight. Ask him or her to help you by checking some of yours in as baggage . . . and be sure to get the claim receipt back.

In these days of fear of terrorists, obliging passengers are scarce.

3. Arrive at the check-in counter with your allowed luggage after leaving your (heavy) hand luggage at a coin-operated locker. After check in, retrieve the extra piece from the locker and proceed to the boarding area.

4. Plastic shopping bags from duty-free shops or major European department stores aren't usual-

ly counted as carry-ons. Fill a bag with light- to medium-weight items. The heavy items should be checked-in in your baggage, since the bags aren't always very sturdy.

Using these methods may increase your chances of transporting excess baggage free.

Remember, however, that seats in the front of any cabin just behind the bulkhead have no seats in front of them to store your baggage under. You then have to ask flight attendants to store it somewhere. The somewhere is sometimes inconvenient, especially in crowded planes.

Clothes
Did you really need to take them all?

Comfortable and appropriate clothes can make a large difference in the enjoyment and success of your trip. While there will be seasonal variations in your wardrobe, it is quite reasonable for all your clothes to fit in an under-the-seat carry-on. This small wardrobe can include a few carefully planned accessories. It will serve whether you're going for two weeks or two months, whether hiking your way across the Alps or being chauffeured in a limousine.

Travelling light has obvious benefits: there's less weight to lug around and guard, you have space in your baggage for delectable acquisitions to bring home, and if you don't need to check-in luggage you'll be first through customs and out of the airport. You also reduce the time spent deciding what to wear each day.

Keep three thoughts in mind as you pack (especially if you are inclined to prepare for everything):

Thought 1: You meet different people every day. They don't know today's outfit is similar to yesterday's.

Thought 2: You can use accessories to transform your clothes.

Thought 3: You can "layer" your clothes, creating varying effects.

More on Thought 1

Most travellers wander from city to city like butterflies searching among flowers, alighting for only a limited time in each. Several of these cities have millions of people, most of whom you won't see even once. Those you do see regularly, such as hotel staff, probably won't even note that the clothes are familiar. If by off chance they do, they'll be far too polite to mention it. Travellers are assumed to have limited wardrobes, anyway.

More on Thought 2

Lightweight, compact accessories such as scarves, belts, ties, stockings, jewellery, and caps can transform the basic, sturdy, and multipurpose clothes in your wardrobe. You may want to buy some along the way. A mathematical figuring of two outfits and seven or eight accessories will give you an idea of the variety with which you can spice your clothes.

More on Thought 3

Europe's climates are varied all year round. Coastal southern Italy in winter will usually be pleasant, rather like a cool Alpine summer day. Northern Europe and mountain areas in winter will be cold and snowy. Most of the rest of Europe in winter will be rainy. Southern Spain, Greece, and Italy in summer will wilt the most energetic traveller (small children excepted).

You'll be best prepared for all climates if you have numerous layers of light clothes. The space between each layer will trap air, the most effective insulation and warmth retainer. By the same token, a thin layer of garments will keep you cooler in summer. By coordinating the colours of your layers, you create different looks by using a basic wardrobe and accessories (see Thought 1 again).

Special note: the Arctic areas and high Alps in winter are exceptions, calling for specially designed wardrobes. Down-filled clothing may be best as the top layer to combat severe cold.

Care: The Most Important Factor

Stay-press polyester blends should be the rule for everything except underwear, socks, and dry-clean-only coats. You'll never know exactly how your clothes will be treated by laundries and cleaners, but you should plan on taking care of them yourself (see the chapter about Laundry.)

Men's Clothes

The guiding precepts for men's travelling wardrobes should be simplicity, comfort, and easy care. Above all, take clothes you enjoy wearing, rather than things you think you should wear. Your choices should emphasize quality rather than quantity. You will be able to minimize the quantity by planning your wardrobe around a basic daily "uniform". One or two such uniforms will carry you along for months.

Men's Underwear

Blends with a high cotton content will be by far the most satisfactory; 100% cotton is also good but will take longer to dry after washing in humid climates where it is most comfortable. Coloured T-shirts are recommended and can be worn alone on hot days.

Men's Shirts

Cotton blends are the most durable and resist wrinkles and rigours of travel. Crease-resistant will stay reasonably crisp even when washed in a hotel sink, submitted to a laundry, or dried in a too-hot launderette dryer. White or light blue are the most versatile colors for more formal as well as more casual wear.

Men's Trousers

There are two main kinds of trousers that most travellers should have: those that can be used for more formal events as well as street wear, and those that are for more casual wear. Grey cotton/polyester crease-resistant trousers will serve well for both street and formal wear. You can team them with a blazer for dinner, concert, or theatre, or wear them every day without feeling overdressed. Avoid trousers that must be dry cleaned, since rapid dry cleaning is virtually unknown except for self-service establishments in France and Italy, and is expensive.

Casual wear can be blue jeans. Jeans have many pluses: they don't show dirt when worn day after day, they are comfortable, and they are very durable. (In Eastern Europe, you may be asked to sell the very jeans you're wearing, especially if they're original Levi's. The price offered may be high. Sell at your own risk, since the transaction is illegal.)

Shorts aren't widely worn in cities, except by children. Shorts seem to be more acceptable in resort areas, either mountain or beach, and by bicyclists. Solid colours will make you less conspicuous than patterns.

Blazer

The classic blue blazer is never out of style, doesn't readily show dirt, and with grey trousers lets you go anywhere short of a diplomatic reception. You'll be welcome at the finest restaurants, hotels, and symphony halls. Its fabric composition should be a natural/synthetic blend that is wrinkle-resistant. Otherwise your jacket may resemble a wrinkled prune. It should be the only dry-clean item you have.

A tie will complete your formal ensemble.

Sweaters

You should have at least one middleweight sweater. Much of Europe is cool, even in summer, especially at night. Your sweater should be of conservative style and colour to make it more versatile.

Rain Wear

Rain (and snow) are a fact of life in most of Europe, so plan ahead. A lightweight water-shedding windcheater will serve in most instances. A hood will keep your head dry and avoid the necessity of carrying an umbrella.

A plastic raincoat that comes folded in its own pouch is very handy and easy to pack. Heavy rain gear is usually necessary only in winter, since summer rains are usually light and intermittent.

Men's Shoes

Buy your shoes and break them in before you go! Torment and numerous blisters await those who disregard this warning. While you can get by with one pair, an extra pair is almost a necessity. First, if one pair gets wet, you can change them. Simple classic shoes like loafers or Oxfords will be formal enough to wear anywhere. The other pair should have shock absorbing soles. Note that some soles can be very slick on smooth, wet surfaces. Running shoes are a good choice if they give enough support. You may wish to take hiking boots, which can be heavy, or cycling shoes if you're cycling.

Men's Clothes Checklist

___ Socks (4 pairs)

___ Undershorts (3)

___ T-Shirts (3)

___ Dress shirts (2)

___ Dress trousers (1)

___ Blue jeans (1)

___ Blazer (1)

___ Tie (1 or 2)

___ Swimwear

___ Shoes (dress) (1 pair)

___ Shoes (running, hiking, cycling) (1 pair)

___ Sweater (1)

___ Windcheater, preferably with hood (1)

___ Rain wear

___ Topcoat (optional)

Women's Clothes

The guiding precepts for women's travelling wardrobes should be simplicity, comfort, and easy care. Above all, take clothes you enjoy wearing, rather than things you think you should wear.

Your choices should emphasize quality rather than quantity. You will be able to minimize the quantity by planning your wardrobe around a basic daily "uniform". One or two such uniforms will carry you along for months. They are most practical when they are medium dark colours such as navy or grey that don't show dirt.

Note: in most churches in Italy, Spain, and Portugal, women are supposed to cover their heads and their arms. A light shawl usually suffices.

Lingerie

Your lingerie should above all be comfortable. Generally panties are best when synthetic with a cotton crotch. The bras and slips you wear at home should serve well on the road. Though delicate, you needn't take more than 4 sets, and plan to do laundry fairly frequently.

Dresses

The dress you take should be as all-purpose as possible. It should be durable enough for frequent wear, stylish enough for formal wear with the proper accessories, and comfortable enough for long periods of travel. Avoid colours that show dirt or fluff. Material should be a crease-resistant synthetic or cotton blend that will wear well. It should not require dry cleaning, since dry cleaning is often slow and always expensive.

Skirts and Blouses

Skirts and blouses should be basic colours that won't show dirt, are crease-resistant, and are a synthetic or synthetic-and-cotton blend. While your outfits should have variety, they should be coordinated to harmonize well in any combination. Generally, two skirts and two blouses should be sufficient.

Women's Trousers

Jeans are widely worn, but are considered casual wear. A pair of cotton trousers will suffice for more formal occasions, as well as being cooler than denim. In winter opt for corduroy.

Sweaters

You should have at least one middleweight sweater. Much of Europe is cool, even in summer, especially at night. Your sweater should be of conservative style and colour to make it more versatile.

Rain Wear

Rain in Europe is almost a certainty throughout the year. Lightweight, easy-care rain-shedding jackets offer the best protection from the elements. If you don't have an adequate raincoat, you can purchase one anywhere in Europe. If your jacket or coat has a hood, you can eliminate taking an umbrella.

Women's Shoes

Women should take two pairs of comfortable shoes. Buy shoes well in advance of departure, and break them in. Torment and blisters await those who disregard this warning.

Each pair of shoes should match the basic colour scheme of your wardrobe. Your everyday walking and sightseeing shoes should be low or flats. In part this is because they are better for your feet when walking long distances, and in part because European cities are full of cobblestone or uneven sidewalks and streets. Some women have been very pleased wearing running shoes.

For more formal wear, you should have a pair of medium heels. These should serve in all occasions, and can also be worn during the day to give your other pair of shoes a rest.

While high heels may be "in style", they are poor choices for travelling in Europe. A multitude of holes and cracks await the unwary. In addition, many countries' museums and churches prohibit pointed heels on marble and wood floors.

Accessories

Accessories are lightweight and compact, and add variety and individuality to your wardrobe. Each accessory, whether belt, hat, pins, or other jewellery, should complement your basic wardrobe. You probably shouldn't take your heirloom jewellery as part of your accessory kit.

Makeup

Most women take a small makeup kit with them. If you need to add to your kit while on your travels, makeup is widely available, except in parts of Eastern Europe.

Handbags

If you carry a handbag with you every day, you probably will on holiday, too. However, travelling provides some special considerations which may render the ones you now have unsuitable. Your travel bag should combine durability and safety with style. Make sure it will do what you need. Think through very carefully what you'll be taking in your bag, and where in the bag it will be.

The best travel bag is a hard leather shoulder bag in a colour matching your wardrobe. Plastic will do, but it's liable to wear at the corners during the rough use common while travelling. It should be slightly large, but not a suitcase.

Security is important. The shoulder strap should be firmly fastened to the bag. Avoid flimsy, thin straps and fragile rings holding the strap onto the bag. A shoulder strap will help protect your bag because it is harder to pull it away from you. The main compartment should be closed by a zip, as a deterrent to pickpockets. An additional zippered compartment inside the central compartment is useful for keeping valuables such as passports and money. Because you will undoubtedly acquire small additional items in your travels, your central bag compartment should expand like an accordion. Rigid bags may burden you with extra small parcels that are easy to misplace and lose.

Outside compartments are also invaluable for items of small value and great utility, such as paper and pens, and small change (especially for pay toilets and telephones). You will therefore avoid exposing the real valuables contained in the main compartment, and still obtain daily necessities.

Women's Clothing Checklist

- [ ] Stockings (4 pairs)
- [ ] Panties (4 pairs)
- [ ] Bras (3)
- [ ] Dress (1)
- [ ] Skirt (1 or 2)
- [ ] Blouse (1 or 2)
- [ ] Trousers (1 pair)
- [ ] Sweater (1 or 2)
- [ ] Rain wear: water resistant raincoat
- [ ] Shoes (2 pairs)
- [ ] Swimsuit
- [ ] Accessories: belts, scarves, pins, jewellery, hats.
- [ ] Handbag (1)
- [ ] Makeup kit

Camera and Film

A lasting part of your trip will probably be the photos you take. While there is a variety of cameras, a 35mm camera may be your best choice. Single-lens reflex cameras with interchangeable lenses and zoom lenses are the most versatile but are bulkier than the new, more compact autofocus 35mm cameras. A small fixed-focus 110mm camera is also a possibility: it is easier to use, but less flexible than a 35mm, and the prints are of lower quality than from 35mm cameras. These choices are recommended because you can usually find film for them. Instant-image cameras (such as a Polaroid) provide quick prints, but you need to take a lot of film with you (which can be bulkier than film in rolls or cassettes).

More important than the type of camera is the amount of camera gear you take. Keep it to the minimum you know you'll need. Remember: cameras are relatively bulky, valuable, and present great temptation to thieves. Label the camera with your name and address. Some careful photographers keep a label on, and write the name and telephone of their hotel on it. Some authorities have stated that many cameras are lost and are not returnable because they carry no identification.

Take Plenty of Pictures!

Never hesitate to take a picture! Film is relatively cheap, and pictures are easy to take when you're there. When you get home, it will seem as if you took fewer pictures than you thought, and you may think, "If only I'd taken that picture".

Buying Film

Film is readily available in Western Europe, but harder to find in the Eastern Bloc. If you buy film in Eastern Europe, including the Soviet Union, it can be processed only there (which takes a lot of time) or, alternatively, using the Agfa processing system. Other processing systems, including Kodak, will ruin it. Kodak film can occasionally be bought in hard-currency stores in Eastern Europe, but is very expensive, and may be past its expiration.

Film and Security Checks

Your protection from hijackers and terrorists includes inspection of baggage and persons. Film can fog after exposure to X-rays of sufficient amounts and strength during security checks. Checked-in baggage is often subjected to X-ray inspection, often at much higher intensity than you and your hand luggage. Therefore, try to avoid putting undeveloped film into your checked-in luggage.

Many people have little trouble with film damage as the result of security inspection. Most X-ray equipment will not harm undeveloped film for up to about five passes, according to many authorities. After that number, however, fogging may begin to occur, depending on the length and strength of the exposure. In Eastern Europe, however, X-rays are reported to be much stronger than elsewhere.

If you use fast film (400 ASA or higher), try harder to prevent exposure to X-rays, since it is very liable to fog. Film of less than 400 ASA will not be as severely affected by X-rays.

To reduce potential fogging, you can buy lead-lined film bags at photo supply stores. These bags cut down harmful fogging effects. They come in two types: for slow film and for fast film.

At security checks, you can always request hand inspection of your film and camera to avoid potential fogging by the X-ray equipment. Allow extra time for inspection if you decide to request hand inspection. However, your request may not be honoured, and your film may be exposed to the X-rays anyway. If you carry the film with you rather than subjecting it to the conveyor belt X-rays, you will reduce the exposure. Hand inspection of film is not allowed in France, Belgium, Denmark, Netherlands, Italy, and Spain. Hand inspection is possible in Switzerland, West Germany, and Scandinavia (except Denmark). These policies are subject to change at any time, and the whim of the inspector.

If you take your film out of the canisters it comes in, you'll make hand inspection easier and quicker. You can also see more readily which film you have used. However, the canisters protect the film and can keep it from excessive battering.

A Modest Note About Photo Composition

Your photos will be more interesting if you include people. They also provide a size scale. If you're not photographing a crowd or a group, ask individuals if you can take their picture. Many will be happy to pose and you'll avoid offending those who don't want their picture taken.

In the Eastern Bloc, do not photograph border crossings, military bases, airports, train stations, or bridges. If you do, it could be considered spying! (As you pass military bases, a circular sign slash bar over a camera will sometimes warn you not to take pictures.)

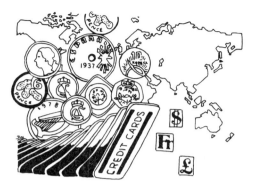

Money
What and How Much to Take?

Traveller's cheques, cash, and credit cards are the easiest forms of money to take with you. Less useful are personal cheques and lines of credit. Money can be wired via telegraph or through a correspondent bank, but is often difficult to arrange. The more money or convenient credit you have at hand, the easier it will be to pay your expenses.

How Much Money to Take?

European travel can be as cheap or expensive as at home. Much depends on the style to which you are (or become) accustomed. The best advice is to take the money you expect to spend plus 50% more. Bear in mind that simple things, such as getting more money, become extraordinarily complicated and difficult when distance is a factor.

Take more money than you think you'll need. It will give you peace of mind, and be invaluable in emergencies.

Bear in mind that large price levels in cities are one-and-one-half to two times higher than the countryside.

Exchange Rates

When changing money, whether traveller's cheques or cash, you will usually receive 2% to 3%

less than the published international London exchange rates because your transaction is considered retail rather than wholesale.

When changing a significant amount of money, you may want to shop around first. Exchange rates between banks often vary widely—as much as 5% to 10% in banks next door to each other. The current rates are often displayed in bank windows facing the street or on boards near the foreign exchange window inside. Over an entire journey, the few minutes spent comparing rates may well pay an extra day of expenses, or at least a good dinner.

Banks at airports and railway stations give less acceptable rates than those in large city centres where large banks cluster.

In some countries, particularly Britain (especially London) but also in the Netherlands and Switzerland, exchange booths called "Bureaux de Change" offer long hours, but often add large commissions (often 8% to 11%) to an apparently good rate. Some Bureaux de Change even look like banks, but don't have the word "bank" in their names. Be sure you know the net proceeds of your exchange before handing over your cash or signing a traveller's cheque at these places.

Cash

All people and businesses in Europe will accept cash, if it is the *local* currency. After all, if someone offered you Italian lire or Polish zlotys in change at home, you probably wouldn't accept them either.

In Western Europe, cash-only policies extend to the more modestly priced stores, restaurants, and hotels, and most garages (Garages on motorways will sometimes accept credit cards and traveller's cheques.) Surprisingly, some of Europe's most expensive restaurants accept only cash or local cheques: they claim they can't afford the credit card commission of 3% to 7%.

The cash-only attitude is particularly pronounced in Eastern (Socialist) Bloc countries, since most individuals and most businesses have no cheques (except in East Germany), no credit cards, and no extended easy-payment credit plans. Cash substitutes can evoke wonder and incomprehension outside the regular Eastern European tourist hotels, restaurants, and airports. Elsewhere, bystanders will sometimes wonder how you have paid the bill, and whether it will really catch up with you.

Take enough cash to avoid inconvenience; in other words plan to take between 10% and 25% of your money in cash. It is handy for quick changes of currency—no forms to fill out. Sterling £5 notes can be very useful if you will be crossing several borders in a short period of time or paying for visas in Eastern Europe. In some places, the anonymity of cash will make certain transactions quicker and sometimes easier. (If you deal in the black market—illegal in Eastern Europe—you must use cash.)

If you're crossing a border in the evening or on a Sunday, you may want to buy some currency of the nation where you'll land before you leave.

Do not buy money in advance of arrival in the Eastern (Socialist) nations, since the import or export of those currencies is generally forbidden, except that Hungary permits 100 forints and Yugoslavia permits 5,000 dinars (either is worth less than £3).

Traveller's Cheques

Traveller's cheques are available from almost every financial institution and many travel agents. Many banks and building societies offer them free, rather than the customary one per-cent charge, even if you're not a customer!

Traveller's cheques are widely available in £20, £50, and £100 denominations Upon request or at a large bank you can get £500 and £1000 cheques, too. These higher denominations are less bulky and easier to carry. American Express will exchange denominations of their traveller's cheques at no charge (either large to small or small to large).

Traveller's cheques are also available from many cheque issuers in foreign currency. These include French or Swiss francs, and West German Deutsche marks. You will almost always have to pay the 1% commission and will receive a poor exchange rate, too.

When you get the cheques, sign them on the spot. You'll also get receipts which have the serial numbers of the cheques printed on them. Make copies of these receipts for your files; leave one at home or with a friend. Keep another one in your luggage—but not with the cheques themselves. The receipt is the best proof of ownership in case your cheques are lost or stolen. The bank will also keep a copy of this receipt, which is eventually forwarded to the cheque-issuing company.

Traveller's cheques are widely used throughout Europe, so you should have no trouble cashing them at any bank or exchange office, or even your hotel. Many Western European hotels and some businesses will accept sterling traveller's cheques, but will give you 5% to 20% less local currency than a bank.

In Eastern (Socialist) nations, however, you'll usually get the same rate at hotels, stores, banks, and the official tourist agency. You should get the "tourist" rate in these countries, which is about 50% better than the "official" rate.

Cashing Traveller's Cheques

Traveller's cheques receive a slightly better exchange rate than cash in most of Western Europe, but you almost always pay a commission not charged on the exchange of cash. According to one European bank manager, there is a rate differential because traveller's cheques are risk-free to the bank, while cash potentially could be counterfeit. It is harder for banks to care for cash, since it must be counted, tallied, and guarded. Paid and endorsed traveller's cheques can be easily routed in the bank's paper stream of cancelled cheques. On the other hand, many countries charge taxes for handling traveller's cheques.

Cash is worth more than traveller's cheques in countries with rapidly depreciating money such as Yugoslavia and Turkey. In those countries, merchants and exchange offices sometimes offer a better rate for cash than banks and a better rate for cash than traveller's cheques, particularly if you've just made a purchase.

In Yugoslavia, when you exchange money, you can get "Dinarcheque" scrip instead of dinars. This scrip has 10% more value at many government-owned stores or businesses than you otherwise would get. This is an anti-black-market scheme. However, you can't reconvert unused Dinarcheques into Western currency.

To cash a traveller's cheque, you'll have to show your passport as identification. Forms will be filled out, though usually not by you. In many countries, you sign the cheque, give the signed cheque and sometimes your passport to the clerk, receive back a numbered slip or copy of the exchange form, and wait at the cashier's window until your name or number is called. You'll get a receipt for the transaction as well. In some places, the whole affair is treated more casually, and everything will be taken care of at one desk or window and you won't have to wait as long.

In some countries there are per-cheque fees for cashing traveller's cheques, while in others, such as Belgium, there is a per-transaction fee. In addition, there may be a commission.

Replacing Lost or Stolen Traveller's Cheques

Each traveller's cheque issuer will give you, upon request, a pamphlet about what to do and where to call if your cheques are lost or stolen. Be familiar with the contents: you may even want to take it with you, since specific replacement procedures vary by country.

If lost or stolen, traveller's cheques can be replaced reasonably promptly if you have copies of the serial-numbered receipts you received with the cheques. While there are minor variations in procedures and speed of replacement between companies, you should be able to get them replaced within one or two days by any company.

Replacing traveller's cheques in the Eastern (Socialist) countries will have to be done in the capital of the country. It will almost always take more time than it would in Western Europe.

Credit Cards

Almost every European country has establishments that welcome credit cards. VISA and Access are the most common. Establishments catering to traveller's and affluent locals are likely to take American Express as well. Diners Club and Carte Blanche are not as widely accepted.

When you use a card in Europe, you'll be presented with a familiar-looking sales voucher (or sometimes just a cash register receipt) with the money given in local currency. Be sure that the total amount has been filled in before you sign. Keep a copy as you would at home, especially since your card statement may be very vague about exactly where and when the transaction took place. For example, folk art purchased at the Handicrafts Shop in Budapest, Hungary, might be listed as "no transaction date, Shop in Hungary, posting date, sterling amount £31.56".

American Express or Diners Club statements will usually include paper copies of your charges with the payment coupon.

(Certain rental car agencies and airlines will provide a substitute, however.)

You can also get local currency cash advances at banks in Europe with these cards, although a small fee may be charged for the service.

Credit card companies usually change foreign currency to sterling at the wholesale exchange rate plus a small commission, usually about one per cent. Depending on the rate on the day your bill clears the card's currency exchange department, you could end up paying more or less than you expected.

Charges can take between two weeks and three months to post.

Personal Cheques

Cashing British personal cheques in Europe is difficult, but take some with you anyway. They may be useful in a pinch or for large purchases. Surprisingly, some stores will take personal cheques for purchases, if you have adequate identification. You don't lose anything by asking.

Before you leave home, ask your bank for the names of its "correspondent banks" in Europe. Even small local banks will have them. These banks have relations with yours and will be slightly more disposed to help. If you do write a personal cheque in Europe, be sure that it is written in sterling. Otherwise your bank will usually refuse to process and honor it.

Holders of some charge cards, such as the American Express Gold and Platinum cards can cash personal cheques at the company's offices.

European Bank Accounts

If you plan an extensive and long journey, you may want to consider opening an account at a European bank. This is quite legal and relatively easy to do. With some banks in some countries (such as Switzerland), it can even be accomplished by post.

While Swiss banks' stability and Swiss secrecy laws are well known, other nations' banks will welcome your money and provide good service, too. A major bank in the nation where you'll spend the most time probably will be more accommodating than small, exclusive merchant banks, unless you bring substantial amounts of money with you. A letter of introduction from your local bank will be helpful.

Eurocheques

Many British and European banks will allow cheques to be written in various different currencies and will take care of the money exchanging. (Ask at the bank about "Eurocheques", which are special cheques backed by a bank guarantee card. Eurocheques can be written in any Western currency; however, the guarantee is limited to a maximum amount for each cheque in each country. Sometimes you may only pay with two or more Eurocheques, each written for less than the maximum guarantee amount. Many establishments, including hotels and restaurants in Western Europe that don't accept credit cards will accept cheques in the local currency with adequate identification.

Getting Money in a Pinch

If you're out of money, you can call home to get more—reverse charges if needed. Money can be wired to you by telegraph; unless you designate otherwise it will be sent to the local telegraph office and paid to you in local currency. These transfers often take a day or two. Money can also be sent by American Express to that company's offices.

Banks will be reluctant to undertake this type of operation unless prearranged, and may suggest picking up the money at their European branches or correspondent banks. Find out from your local bank which European banks are correspondents. This will make it much easier to collect money, cash cheques, and undertake other banking transactions.

Avoid sending money into Eastern (Socialist) Europe, since you will most likely be given non-convertible local currency at the "official" and less desirable rate, unless the wire contains clear instructions to pay the amount in the currency in which it is sent or another "convertible" currency.

If you're without money in a major city, and the above methods haven't yielded any, your embassy can make reverse charge calls to try to find you aid. They will not lend you money. Be thankful when you get help.

Embassies have very small amounts of money to manage as "repatriation loans". Basically, your way could be paid home. Your passport will be restricted to the one-way trip until the loan is repaid. Generally these loans aren't available to the improvident; rather they are used for suddenly destitute, disabled, or mentally disturbed individuals. The embassy staff has full discretion in the matter.

Leftover Foreign Coins and Notes

When you near a border, you should think about the coming change of currency. Try to estimate how much money you'll need in the country you're leaving, since it probably won't be accepted in everyday commerce once you cross the border. Every time you change money, you're charged a commission.

Coins

Coins are of adjoining countries are exchangeable only at some main border crossings in Western Europe, and only during the hours of heavy travel. Otherwise, you have bought yourself a pocketful of souvenirs. Change all of your coins into paper money (see below) or spend them on inexpensive trinkets or snacks at the border.

The money exchange at Amsterdam's Central (rail) Station will take coins of most European nations.

Paper Money

Paper money from Western European countries is exchangeable at banks and exchange offices in any other European country. If you have some left over, you can save it and change it later when you need that amount of local currency. If you bring it home, you can change it for sterling at airport exchange counters and banks. Commissions at banks at home are high and the rate of exchange is much less favourable.

You can also keep the money until your next trip.

Guarding Your Health
Health Care and Insurance

In most European countries U.K. residents can receive free or reduced-cost emergency health care. Coverage varies from country to country. You'll usually receive the same care under the same conditions as local residents. In a few there is no provision for free or reduced-price emergency health care (also see below).

Each country has its own health care system for emergencies, each of which differs from those in the U.K. To receive care, you must comply with all the rules and requirements of the country where you need help. Details of the procedures you must follow to receive free or reduced-cost care in each country are listed later in this chapter.

Even in the most serious emergencies, you cannot receive free transportation home to Britain under the National Health Service (NHS) or the health insurance schemes of European nations. Neither the NHS nor European health insurance schemes pay for transport of corpses back to Britain.

Will You Have to Pay for Emergency Health Care?

Depending on the country where emergency care is needed, you may have to pay none, some, or all of the costs. Each country falls into one of 3 classes to determine the terms of treatment and payment: European Community (EC) nations, nations with reciprocal health care agreements, and nations with no provision for free or reduced-price health care for British residents.

Non-emergency care is not provided in any country without prior approval of the U.K. Department of Health and Human Services (DHHS).

In some countries, you are not covered if you are injured in a driving accident. Private insurance can cover this eventuality (and is included in Green Card insurance policies), and is available from insurance brokers, or from the AA or RAC.

European Community (EC) Nations

The EC countries are: Belgium, Denmark (except the Faroe Islands), France, West Germany (FRG), Greece, Gibraltar, the Irish Republic, Italy, Luxembourg, the Netherlands, Portugal, and Spain (including the Canary Islands).

If you have proper documentation (usually Form E111—see country listings below), you can receive exactly the same emergency medical coverage as any local citizen if you need it. Procedures will probably be different than that which you receive at home. The scope and type of care are determined by the local government—not by the NHS.

If you use private health services, and private service is not covered by that country's national health plan, you will not be reimbursed for any expenses.

If you plan to move permanently to an EC country, contact:
DHHS Overseas Branch
Newcastle-upon-Tyne NE98 1YX

Reciprocal Agreement Countries

Reciprocal agreement countries are: Austria, Czechoslovakia, Finland, East Germany (GDR),

Hungary, Malta, Norway, Sweden, the Soviet Union, and Yugoslavia.

These countries have entered into special "Reciprocal" agreements to provide various types of emergency health care to British residents. Each agreement has its own special limitations and exclusions. Usually your British passport is considered acceptable proof of eligibility.

No-Coverage Countries

No-coverage countries are: Andorra, Cyprus, the Faroe Islands, Liechtenstein, Monaco, San Marino, Switzerland, and Turkey.

These countries make no provision for free or reduced-cost emergency health care for travellers: you must pay for all services rendered. Hospitals often will not admit anyone without a cash deposit or release patients until all charges have been paid. Also, there is no British reimbursement for any health services received in these countries.

Special traveller's health insurance policies are advisable, and are available in the U.K. from travel agents, auto clubs, and insurance agents.

Procedures

Form E111 for EC Countries

In most EC countries, Form E111 guarantees medical coverage. The form is valid from the date of issuance until there is a change in your family composition, residence, or name.

To obtain Form E111, contact the nearest DHHS office and request an application, called Form CM1. Send this form, which asks for name, address, telephone number, and national insurance (NHS or pension) plus answers to a few simple questions. If you need this form quickly, you can obtain it at your local DHHS office in a short time.

Make several photocopies of Form E111, because you need to attach a copy to reimbursement forms if you file a claim in several countries, including Belgium, France, West Germany, Italy, and the Netherlands.

Alternatives to Form E111

In some EC countries, you may use other types of identification to receive free or reduced-price medical care. A British passport is all you need in Denmark, Gibraltar, and Portugal. In the Republic of Ireland no identification is needed.

Documents for Reciprocal Agreement Countries

Your British passport is the evidence of entitlement for service in most reciprocal agreement countries.

Non-citizen residents of Britain (who don't have British passports) are often not covered by reciprocal agreements, but sometimes a NHS card will suffice.

Some countries have different or additional requirements: Bulgaria requires a U.K. passport *and* your NHS card. The Channel Islands will accept any proof of U.K. residence, such as a passport, driving license, or NHS medical card. Poland requires only your NHS medical card. Romania requires your U.K. passport *plus* either your NHS card or driving license.

If You Can't Get a Refund Abroad

In a few circumstances, you can make a claim to DHHS to be reimbursed for services you received in EC countries, but which you paid for at the time and were not reimbursed before you left that country. In these cases, complete documentation is essential.

Send DHHS a written statement about why you couldn't obtain health coverage while you were abroad, along with your Form E111, and all of the bills for service, prescriptions, and anything else related to your medical care. Keep copies of *everything* you send.

If you live in England, Scotland, or Wales, send your claim to:

Guarding Your Health 73

DHHS Overseas Branch (MED)
Newcastle-upon-Tyne NE98 1YX
If you live in Northern Ireland, send your claim to:
DHSS Medicines & Food Control Branch,
   Annex A
Dundonald House
Belfast BT4 3TL

Definitions of Services

- Ambulance: Emergency transportation by ambulance.

- Dental: Dental services including X-rays, extractions, and fillings.

- Inpatient: Admission and treatment at a hospital on an overnight basis. Includes all needed hospital procedures.

- Outpatient: Treatment at a hospital, clinic, or doctor's office, on a nonresident basis.

- Prescribed Medicine: Medicine prescribed by a doctor or other health professional, not available over the counter.

- X ray and Laboratory: Various medical procedures.

Range of Coverage and Claim Procedure

Each country has different services available and different ways to pay for it. Information for each country in Europe follows.

Austria

You can receive free inpatient medical treatment in public wards of public hospitals, but must pay for all prescriptions, outpatient services, ambulance travel, and any treatment by private providers. There is no coverage for dental treatment.

After showing your passport, there is no paperwork or reimbursement procedure that you need to follow.

Belgium

You can receive reduced-cost medical, dental, and hospital treatment, but you must have your E111 form, and a photocopy of your E111 to attach to the paperwork. In general, you are reimbursed for about 75% of the costs by the provincial insurance office, called the Auxiliary Fund for Sickness and Invalidity Insurance ("Caisse auxiliare d'assurance maladie invalidité" in the French provinces and "Hulpkaas voor Ziekte -en Invaliditeitsverzekering") in the Flemish provinces, or the local insurance offices ("Mutualités" in the French provinces, or "Ziekenfonds" in the Flemish provinces). However, there is no reimbursement for ambulance transport.

At a doctor's or dentist's office, or chemist's (for prescribed medicine), show your E111 and pay the fee. You must request an official receipt, called the "Attestation de soins donnés/ Getnigschrift voor verstrekte hulp". At the hospital, show your E111 and ask them to obtain the part-payment certificate, or (if you can) first go to the provincial insurance office for a shared-cost certificate.

To request reimbursement, take your original E111 and a photocopy and official receipts to the insurance office and request payment. Reimbursement must be requested before leaving Belgium. These offices are either the Mutualités/Ziekenfonds or the provincial insurance office.

Bulgaria

You can receive all hospital, clinic, and dental treatment at no charge, and there is no paperwork after showing your passport and NHS card. You must pay for prescribed medicine.

Cyprus

No free or reduced-price health care. Private insurance is recommended.

Czechoslovakia

You can receive all hospital, clinic, and other medical services at no charge, and there is no paperwork after showing your U.K. passport. You must pay for prescribed medicine.

Denmark

All emergency hospital treatment, and most outpatient medical and dental treatment is free. Show your British passport or E111 form to the doctor, dentist, or hospital admissions officer. Prescribed medicine from a chemist is available at reduced cost if you show your E111.

If for some reason you're charged, you can request reimbursement from the local council Social and Health Department ("Kommunsens social- og-sundhedsforvaltning"). Refund or reimbursement requests must be made before leaving Denmark.

Finland

You can receive outpatient consultations at health centres at no charge after showing your U.K. passport.

You must pay for all dental work, inpatient hospital treatment, ambulance travel, and medicine.

France

The French health care system is complex and requires patience to negotiate. You can receive a refund of about 75% of the cost of medical and dental fees, and a refund or payment of up to 80% for hospital treatment, and 40% to 70% of the cost of prescribed medicines.

When you obtain medical out-patient or dental services, be sure to obtain the signed statement of treatment ("feuille de soins") and pay the full amount for the services.

Doctors and dentists can charge as much as they want. However, those who agree to charge no more than the amount approved by the French health insurance agency and participate in the national health insurance health scheme are called "conventionné". In any case, you must pay for all charges over the approved reimbursement amount.

When you buy prescribed medicine, the chemist will return the prescription form after filling it. Attach it to the statement of treatment, along with the small seal to be found on the prescription container.

When making your claim, take the Form E111 and a photocopy of it to the nearest office of the French health insurance agency ("Caisse Primaire d'Assurance-Maladie").

When admitted to a hospital on an inpatient basis, show the Form E111 and you will recieve a certificate of admission ("Attestation"). Usually, the hospital will directly obtain 80% of charges from the French health insurance office. You must pay the balance—20% of charges plus the per-diem hospital charge ("forfait hospitalier").

If the hospital doesn't bill the French health insurance office, you must get the Notice of Admission and Acceptance of Responsibility form ("Avis d'admission—Prise en charge") when discharged, and send or take it, with a copy of the Form E111 to the nearest health insurance office.

Before leaving France, you must send all paperwork to the French insurance office in the region where the treatment occurred.

If you pay all charges, an itemized statement of charges will be sent to your home; afterward, the amount of refund will be sent to your home by money order. This process can take from 3 to 6 months.

East Germany (GDR)

You receive all medical and dental care free upon presentation of your U.K. passport, except for driving accidents, for which the government makes a claim against the vehicle insurer.

West Germany (FRG)

Medical and dental treatment in offices is usually free. Before obtaining treatment, go to the sickness insurance offices ("Allgemeine Ortskrankenkassen" or "AOK") with your E111 form and a photocopy. There, you will receive an Entitlement Certificate ("Krankenschein"). The AOK has a list of approved providers that accept the Entitlement Certificate as payment in full. (There are also private providers that do not accept the Entitlement Certificate, and charge you for all treatments. Avoid them if you want reimbursement.)

When you are treated and give the Entitlement Certificate, you don't have to pay anything.

If you don't have time to obtain the Entitlement Certificate before requesting treatment, ask to be sure that the doctor will accept payment from the AOK. Pay the doctor or dentist when service is given, then go the the AOK, get the Entitlement Certificate, and, if you return within 10 days, your entire payment will be refunded.

You must pay a small price for each prescription.

Inpatient hospital treatment is free in public wards with a certificate from a doctor or the AOK. To obtain the certificate, see a doctor, who will complete the hospital treatment form ("Verordnung von Krankenhauspfleg"). Take it to the AOK, where it will be exchanged for the Free Treatment Certificate ("Kostenübernahmeschein"). Your only costs are the fixed daily room charge for the first 14 days; after that, there are no costs.

In an emergency, if you cannot get the forms from the AOK, show your Form E111 and ask the hospital to obtain the certificate. Otherwise you will have to pay the full cost, and there will not be a refund.

Gibraltar

You are entitled to free outpatient treatment at the Casemates Health Centre and free emergency hospital treatment at St Bernard's Hospital in a public ward. Show either your U.K. passport or Form E111. There is a small charge for each prescription.

Dental care is not included, but inexpensive dental services are available during normal working hours at the Casemates Health Centre.

Greece

You are entitled to free consultation, medical, and dental services from providers who participate in the Social Insurance Foundation (IKA). Take your E111 form and passport to the nearest IKA office, where you'll receive a Health Services Book. Go to the suggested outpatient clinic, doctor, or dentist. The service and call is free, but you will have to pay for X-ray and laboratory tests.

Hospital care is also free up to a certain limit per type of care, but first you must get a hospital voucher from IKA. If there's no time to get a hospital voucher, if you recieve treatment from a private (non-IKA) provider, you must pay, and within 3 days take the receipts to IKA. You'll be reimbursed up to the IKA-allowed amount (usually much less than the amount you paid).

Prescribed medicine is charged at a fixed prescription fee plus 20% of the cost of the medicine.

There are no IKA hospitals and providers in remote areas. If you aren't able to get to an IKA approved provider, you must pay all fees and try to collect a refund when you return home. Be sure to have a copy of every piece of paper you recieve.

Note: The DHHS and others have stated that IKA standards of service are below those in other EC countries and have recommended private health insurance, which provides treatment at private clinics and hospitals, where there is better equipment and more rapid treatment.

Hungary

All medical treatment is free at hospitals and clinics upon presenting your U.K. passport. You must pay for medicines. There is no coverage for eye or dental treatment.

Ireland (Irish Republic)

All medical treatment is free. For medical and dental treatment, contact the local Health Board (found in all county towns). Request treatment under the EC Social Security agreement. If needed, doctors will arrange admission and treatment at hospitals.

If, in an emergency, you go directly to hospital, request treatment under the EC Social Security agreement.

Italy

Note: Because of the complex nature of the Italian health care system, be sure to follow procedures exactly, or you may not be able to obtain refunds to which you are otherwise entitled.

The first step in obtaining medical care is to take your E111 form and a photocopy of it to the Local Health Unit ("Unità Sanitoria Locale" or "U.S.L."). You'll receive a certificate of entitlement and a list of approved doctors and dentists. With this entitlement all medical treatment is free.

If the doctor believes you need inpatient hospital treatment, you will be given a certificate ("proposta de ricovero"), which you must take back to the U.S.L. to obtain authorization for free treatment.

In emergencies, if you are taken to a hospital, show your Form E111 and request free treatment, and ask them to contact the U.S.L. for authorization.

Prescribed medicine is charged for at a fixed fee per prescription plus a percentage of cost (varying on the class of drug prescribed).

Luxembourg

All medical and dental treatment is usually free if you first obtain a Certificate of Entitlement from the National Sickness Insurance Fund for Workers ("Caisse national d'assurance maladie des ouvriers") at either 10 rue de Strasbourg, Luxembourg, or offices in other large towns.

Inpatient hospital treatment requires a certificate of treatment from a doctor, and is free except for the non-refundable daily payment fee.

Prescribed medicine is also free.

If you can't get the Certificate of Entitlement before receiving treatment, pay the amount, obtain receipts for everything, and make a claim for refund at the nearest National Sickness Insurance Fund for Workers office. If you need emergency hospital treatment and do not have a doctor's certificate, show your E111 form to the hospital staff and request them to contact the National Sickness Insurance Fund for Workers.

Malta

You recieve all emergency treatment in government hospitals for free after presenting your U.K. passport or your tourist permit (for noncitizen nonresidents).

There is no coverage for treatment in private hospitals and medicine.

Netherlands

You can receive free outpatient medical treatment from most doctors in the national insurance scheme. Give a copy of your E111 form at the office. Dental treatment is obtained at a reduced charge by giving a copy of your E111.

To receive inpatient hospital treatment, you must obtain authorization from the Netherlands General Sickness Insurance Fund ("Algemeen Nederlands Onderling Ziekenfonds", also known as A.N.O.Z.).

Prescribed medicine is available from chemists, who make a fixed, non-refundable charge for each prescription. You must also provide the chemist with a copy of your E111.

In an emergency, if you are taken to the hospital, ask the hospital to contact A.N.O.Z., and give them a copy of your E111.

Norway

You can receive free hospital inpatient treatment and ambulance service if you present your U.K. passport. There is no further paperwork.

There is no coverage for outpatient surgery, dental treatment (except emergency tooth extractions), and medicine.

Poland

You can receive free emergency treatment at hospitals, clinics, and dental offices. You must present your NHS medical card to receive treatment, but there is no additional paperwork. You must pay for 30% of the cost of medicine.

Portugal

You can receive reduced-price medical treatment at a regional Health Centre (Centro de Saúde). Show your British Passport or E111 form.

Dental treatment under the insurance scheme is very limited.

If you need inpatient hospital treatment, show your passport or E111 to the hospital admission staff. Most treatment at state hospitals (but not private hospitals) is free, but you will have to pay for X rays and laboratory tests, and some other charges.

Most prescribed medicine may be provided at a discount of 45% to 80% from full price. Other medicines must be paid for in full.

Romania

You receive all hospital treatment, outpatient visits to clinics, and some dental care for free.

You need to provide your U.K. passport and either NHS card or driving license, and there is no additional paperwork. You must pay for all medicine.

Soviet Union (U.S.S.R.)

You can receive all inpatient hospital treatment, outpatient treatment at clinics, and some dental treatment for free upon presentation of your U.K. passport. You must pay for all medicine.

Spain

You can only obtain free medical and hospital treatment at National Social Security Institute ("Instituto Nacional de Seguridad Social" or I.N.S.S.) hospitals and approved doctors. There is no free dental care.

As soon as you arrive in Spain (and before any illness begins), take your E111 form to the nearest I.N.S.S. office ("Agencias") or provincial offices ("Dirección Provincial") and request a book of vouchers. It will include a list of doctors and clinics (called "Ambulatorios") participating in the scheme.

Give the doctor a voucher from your voucher book. If hospital treatment is needed, the doctor will arrange admission.

Medicine prescribed at an I.N.S.S. doctor can be bought at any chemist ("farmacía") at less than 40% of the full price, except that pensioners receive free medicine.

In an emergency, if you do not have a voucher book, be sure to go to an I.N.S.S. hospital ("Hospital"). Private hospitals, which you must pay for, are usually called clinics ("Clinicas"). Show your E111 form immediately when you are admitted.

Sweden

All hospital inpatient treatment (including medicines and tests) is free, and dental care for children (only) is free. You must pay for ambulance travel, hospital outpatient and clinic treatment, and medicine.

Switzerland

You must pay for all medical care—and there is no reimbursement. Private insurance is recommended.

Turkey

You must pay for all medical care—and there is no reimbursement. Private insurance is recommended.

Yugoslavia

All hospital treatment, clinic treatment, and some dental treatment is free upon presentation of your U.K. passport without additional paperwork. You must pay for all prescribed medicine.

Finding a Chemist

Chemists are found in villages as well a cities throughout Europe. All sell prescription medicines, and non-prescription medicine and health aids as well.

Often, a chemist in a town must remain open all night; every chemist's door will list the timetable of open chemists.

Chemists go by many names, related to the words "pharmacy" or "apothecary". The terms to look for include "Apotek" in Danish, Norwegian, and Swedish, "Apteekke" in Finnish, "Apotheke" in German, "Apotheek" in Dutch, "Pharmicie" in French, "Farmécia" in Portuguese, "Farmacia" in Italian and Spanish, and "Παρμακειον" (say "Farmakio") in Greek.

The symbol for a chemist's shop in many countries is a green cross, or in Mediterranean countries, sometimes a red cross.

Did You Forget Anything?

Stop just a minute!

In the bustle of getting ready to start your journey, it's easy to leave something essential at home, such as your ticket, your good luck charm, or your prescription medicine.

Knowing each item is in your luggage gives you peace of mind and prevents frustrating experiences, too. This checklist will eliminate lots of worry and doubt. You may even want to tape a copy of this list to your baggage, and check off items as you pack them in.

Use the list to eliminate excess items—the stuff you'd otherwise lug around, unused.

The Before-You-Leave Checklist

___ Handbag

___ Neck pouch

___ Passport

___ Tickets

___ Traveller's cheques

___ Credit cards (Visa, Access)

___ Charge cards (American Express, Diners Club)

___ Cash

___ Personal cheques

___ Reservation slips

___ Prescriptions: medicine and eye

___ Health insurance claim forms or Form E111

___ International driving licence

- [ ] Pen and paper
- [ ] Small notebook for travel and photo log
- [ ] Torch (pocket size)

Carry on luggage (what you'll need as a minimum if the rest of your luggage is lost)

- [ ] Non-electric razor
- [ ] Toothbrush and toothpaste
- [ ] Comb
- [ ] Airsickness medicine (if needed)
- [ ] Shampoo
- [ ] Soap
- [ ] Needle and thread
- [ ] Makeup kit
- [ ] Shower cap (for women)
- [ ] Earplugs (if you're easily disturbed while sleeping)
- [ ] Small towel
- [ ] Facecloth
- [ ] Medicines: prescription or non-prescription
- [ ] Spare glasses
- [ ] Spare contact lenses and kit
- [ ] Rubber bands, paper clips, and safety pins
- [ ] Knife (Swiss army or Opinel folding)
- [ ] Roll of fibreglass tape (for emergency repairs sealing those boxes of purchases you'll pack along the way)

___ Pocket calculator (to determine prices)

___ Book to read

___ Jewellery

___ One change of clothes

___ Film

___ Address list or pre-addressed labels

___ Extra clothes to wear on the plane—heavy and bulky coats

___ Camera(s) (wear around neck)

Checked-in luggage (suitcase, duffel bag, or backpack)

___ Clothes not packed elsewhere

___ Clothes washing kit (see chapter on "Laundry")

___ Guidebooks

___ Presents to friends or relatives overseas

___ Other special items: skis, golf clubs, bicycle

___ Other items you need:

___ Other item:

___ *Did You Remember Your Wallet?*

Crossing the Language Barrier

"Will they understand me?"

Put your fears to rest—if you are polite and can pay your way, most of your worst fears will not come to pass.

English is still the international language. Most students in Western Europe are required to study English in school. In the Eastern Bloc, English is an elective that many students take in addition to the required Russian. Therefore you're likelier to be understood by a school-aged teenager or college student than an older person. Because you speak what seems to be perfect English, some people will consider you as a teacher or adviser and try their English out on you.

If you speak the language of the country you're in, you obviously have a great advantage. If you can say even a few words, you'll often break through the language barrier and may find the person you're talking to willing to experiment with his or her knowledge of English and gesture.

Many Europeans are bilingual or multilingual. Therefore, if you don't speak the language of the area and they don't speak English, try another language if you know even a few words of it.

In Eastern Europe, German is the more commonly known than French or English, particularly by people over 40. In the Soviet Union, most people speak only Russian.

The short Language Key following will give you at least a few words. Words and phrases are found in other sections, such as the Menu Key in "Food and Drink", the Laundry Key in "Laundry", etc.

In addition, a good phrase book will help greatly. There are many pocket-sized books on the market, so look them over carefully for ease of finding phrases, detail, and pronunciation guides. Also, check the binding for one that will stand up under heavy daily use.

Language Key

English | *French*

English	French
Good . . . day	Bon . . . jour
evening	soir
night	nuit
Goodbye	Au revoir
Please	S'il vous plaît
Thank you	Merci
I'm sorry	Je regrette
I don't speak (language).	Je ne parle pas l'français.
Do you speak English?	Parlez-vous anglais?
Where is . . . a hotel	Où est . . . un hôtel?
a restaurant?	un restaurant?
the train station?	la gare?
the airport?	l'aéroport?
a telephone?	une téléphone?
a bathroom?	une salle de bain?
a toilet?	une toilette (W.C.)?
I would like . . .	Je voudrais . . .
some (drinking) water.	de l'eau (potable).
a room.	une chambre.
with bath (shower).	avec bain (douche).
a table for (number).	une table pour (___).
How much is . . .	Combien est-ce(tte) . . .
this?	Combien est-ce(tte)?
a ticket to (place)?	un billet à (___)?
Open	Ouvert
Closed	Fermé
0	zéro
1	un(e)
2	deux
3	trois
4	quatre
5	cinq
6	six
7	sept
8	huit
9	neuf
10	dix
20	vingt
30	trente
50	cinquante
100	cent
500	cinq cents
1000	mille
I am sick!	Je suis malade!

Language Key

German	Italian
Guten Tag	Buon giorno
Guten Abend	Buona sera
Gute Nacht	Buona notte
Auf Wiedersehen	Arrivaderci
Bitte	Per favore
Danke	Grazie
Es tut mir leid	Me dispiace
Ich kann nicht Deutsch.	Non parlo l'italiano.
Können Sie Englisch?	Parla l'inglese?
Wo ist . . . ein Hotel?	Dov'è . . . un albergo?
ein Restaurant?	un ristorante?
der Bahnhof?	la stazione?
den Flughafen?	l'aeroporto?
ein Telefon?	un telefono?
ein Badezimmer?	una stanza da bagno?
die Toilette?	un gabinetto?
Ich Möchte . . .	Vorrei . . .
Trinkwasser.	dell'acqua.
ein Zimmer.	una camera.
mit Bad (Dusche).	con bagno (doccia).
ein Tafel für (___)?	una tavola per (___)?
Wieviel ist . . .	Quanto costa . . .
diese?	questo(a)?
ein Fahrkarte nach (___)?	un biglietto per (___)?
Offen	Aperto
Geschlossen	Chiuso
null	zero
eins	uno(a)
zwei	due
drei	tre
vier	quattro
fünf	cinque
sechs	sei
seiben	sette
acht	otto
neun	nove
zehn	dieci
zwanzig	venti
dreizig	trenta
fünfzig	cinquenta
hundert	cento
fünf hundert	cinquecento
ein tausend	mille
Ich bin Krank!	Sono ammalato!

Transport in Europe

Public transport is generally highly developed in Europe. A few trains can whisk you along at 160 miles (260 kilometres) per hour, through tile-roofed villages with steepled churches nestling in forested hills and across carefully tended plains, arriving in stations that are palatial expanses of marble and glass or huge skylighted Victorian crystal palaces.

You take clean to spotless undergrounds that have trains less than two minutes apart during rush hour.

Some intercity buses, with plush velvet recliner seats and thick pile carpeting, have the stereo playing restful Baroque concerti as you glide through the countryside.

Taxis can range from gleaming Mercedes-Benz diesels to battered, pint-size Fiats.

Not all public transport in Europe is perfect. City buses can be crowded, and finding your way around can be difficult, even with a good map.

Trains, particularly in southern Europe, can be packed with far more people than seats. Again, mainly in southern Europe but occasionally in Scandinavia, the on-time performance may vary wildly from the precision of the printed schedule. In partial compensation, however, fares in southern Europe run from the low to the ridiculously cheap.

Air Travel

Air fares on scheduled flights within Europe are high: the market is controlled and there is little price competition between airlines, with only a few exceptions. Deregulation of the air is starting to change this, however; a few inexpensive scheduled airlines fly between London and the Netherlands, and some discount fares with restrictions are starting to be offered. There will be additional deregulation by 1992.

Baggage limitations on many flights are 44 pounds (20 kilograms) for most travellers and 66 pounds (30 kilograms) for first-class travellers. In Yugoslavia, domestic flights limit travelers to 33 pounds of baggage (15 kilograms).

Excess baggage costs are high, often 1% of the full-fare first-class ticket per kilogram.

Exceptions to the high-fare limited service rule are found mainly on the north-south European vacation routes. Britain is the best place to find these holidays, though other places in northern Europe offer low fare possibilities, too.

Finding Discount Fares Within Europe

Specific flight offers can often be found by scanning the flight ads in the Personals column in the classified sections of The Times, the Telegraph, and other daily British papers, as well as The Evening Standard, and Time Out and What's On. A number of free newspapers (distributed in London) mainly directed at Australians and New Zealanders, such as TNT and LAM, carry all types of discount flight offers. If you see an ad whose offer meets your needs, don't hesitate to call!

London is by far the best place in Europe to look for discount air fares, though some bargains can also be found in Amsterdam.

Bucket Shops

Many flights leave Britain with empty seats to many destinations in Europe, Africa, Asia, and

Australia. To try to fill these empties at the last minute, discounted last-minute tickets are offered through legal but unlicensed travel agencies known as "bucket shops".

Bucket shops operate quite openly, advertising not only in the street, but also in the newspapers, and some magazines such as Time Out. Bucket shop tickets are sold first-come, first-served at whatever price the agents believe someone will pay. Therefore it is wise to find out the full-fare cost from a regular travel agent or airline, and then to call several bucket shops for comparisons.

Often just before (the day before or morning of) the flight, you can negotiate with the bucket shop for a lower price.

Be sure to get your ticket at the time you pay for it. These tickets are usually not refundable, so be sure it's what you want.

Trains in Europe

The European train systems are probably the best in the world, equalled only in Japan. Partly through their excellence and partly through clever promotion, many travellers use trains almost exclusively. Many possibilities exist to take advantage of these trains, including the well known InterRail pass. Trains are one of the best ways to meet people, since the close quarters invite conversation.

Train travel has a few hazards for the unwary traveller. For example, the train may be split during the journey, with some cars going in one direction and the rest in quite another. If you don't watch carefully, you can find yourself hundreds of miles from where you thought you were going. Stops at stations along the route can be for only a minute or two, which requires you to be vigilant and prepared.

If travelling in Eastern Europe, you may not be able to cross borders by train unless you have already obtained a visa in advance. You'll be unceremoniously left at the border crossing station as the train pulls away.

Transport in Europe

Tickets and Reservations

You'll need a ticket unless you have a rail pass. Reservations are required for some (usually first-class) trains. In some areas, a reserved first- or second-class seat can avoid hours of standing in aisles.

For long-distance journeys, both ticket and reservation are best obtained before you arrive at the station. An authorized travel agent either in Britain or on the Continent can sell you a ticket and make you a reservation at the same time and for the same price as if you stood in queue at the station. You can recognize these agents by the logo of the national rail company in their windows.

Reservations are required for most EuroCity and IC (InterCity) trains, and for certain special trains in East Germany (Express), France (TGV) and Spain (Talgo). Reservations can be made far in advance and as little as a couple hours before departure.

Be sure to specify a smoking or non-smoking seat. In an emergency (such as you're late and didn't buy a ticket, or the ticket sellers are on strike for the day), just get on the train and be prepared to pay cash for the ticket plus a penalty or surcharge. In some countries the penalty can be stiff.

The Rail Station—Highly Organized Chaos

A big city railway station anywhere appears chaotic, with trains arriving only to depart minutes later amid garbled announcements in an unrecognizable language, engine noises, whistles, echoing armies of footsteps. But with a bit of knowledge, finding your carriage is much easier than you fear—simple, in fact.

Departure Information: Finding the Train

When purchasing your ticket, especially from a travel agent, ask which station the train leaves from, since many European cities have more than one.

You'll also need the exact departure time and the platform number. Write it down; this information won't always be on your ticket.

As soon as you get to the station, check the poster schedules near the ticket windows. Yellow paper posters are usually departures, white paper posters are usually arrivals. Red print is used for expresses and black print for locals that stop almost everywhere. Or look for the departure board—usually a large scoreboard-like affair on the concourse. It will have the destination (in the local language), departure time (using a 24-hour clock), and platform number. Find the right platform and go there.

The lobby will also usually have complete 24-hour schedules posted in large displays. Usually departures are shown in red ink and arrivals in black.

Finding Your Carriage

European trains are often split during a journey. For example, a train from Paris could be split in the north of France, with one part going to meet the ferry at Calais to Britain, the other part to Belgium.

To avoid arriving somewhere you didn't want to be, look for the right carriage. At the beginning of the platform in the station, look for a signboard marked with the class and destination of each car. Others will be little better than words scratched on a blackboard. This sign may not actually exist at all. In either case, walk along the train. Each carriage will have a sign (usually white with black lettering) on it near each end of the carriage, with the starting city, possibly an intermediate stop in smaller letters, and a destination. Example of a car going from Paris to Geneva:

PARIS
Lyon
GENÈVE

The class of each carriage (or portion of thereof) will be marked at each door: 1 or 2. In addition, first-class compartments' outside window mouldings are often edged in yellow or gold. Second-class carriages often have a green stripe above the windows.

If you have a reservation, check your carriage to be sure its destination is also yours. At your seat, you'll usually find your name inscribed on paper slipped into a holder at the compartment door or aisle end, or onto the seat itself.

If you don't have a reservation, get in the first carriage of the correct class going your way and look for an unoccupied seat that isn't reserved. Be sure it's smoking or non-smoking to reflect your preference.

When you find your seat, sit down and relax.

Intermediate Stops

If you're getting on or off a train on an intermediate stop (neither the beginning nor end of the route), you'll have to be ready to move quickly when the train gets to the station. Stops can be as short as two or three minutes, and European trains generally adhere to very tight timetables.

Baggage on Trains

All European trains allow you to carry your normal luggage on the train with you at no extra cost. In addition, if you wish, you can check-in luggage, though sometimes you'll have to pay extra for the service. Sometimes, checked-in luggage (especially odd-shaped items such as bicycles, golf clubs, and skis, or those checked-in less than an hour before departure) may not travel on the same train but on a later one, often the next day. Bear this in mind if you plan to leave soon after your arrival at your destination. Otherwise your checked luggage-in may never catch up with you.

If you have a bicycle with you, you sometimes have to check it in as luggage. On some trains, you can take it with you, and hang it on bicycle racks right at the end of some carriages. This arrangement is especially common in Belgium, the Netherlands, and Switzerland. The British system of travelling with your bicycle in the guard's van is not to be relied on abroad.

Is a Rail Pass Right for You?

Many train travellers wonder if a rail pass of some type is a worthwhile purchase.

Normal rail fares vary by country, and are charged per kilometre. West Germany's charges are almost twice those of Italy. Second-class fares are generally about two-thirds of the first-class fare. In general, the northern countries have much higher fares than southern countries such as Greece, Italy, Portugal, and Spain. A national rail pass or other discount fare or possibly individually bought second-class tickets could have much the same benefits at a much lower cost.

Before running out and buying any pass, think carefully, and ask several questions.

1. Will you make trains your prime long-distance travel method? Europe has so many ways to get around, including planes, buses cars, bicycles, balloons, and canal boats.

2. Will you be in the high-fare northern countries or the less expensive southern countries?

3. Will you take a large number of long-distance trips? If you take many long trips or use night trains as hotels, the pass may be a big money saver.

4. How many of you will travel together? For two or more, car rental may be more economical.

5. How much do you want to be bound by rail schedules? Not every town and village has frequent service.

Railpasses

European passes can often save you money when compared to individually-purchased tickets. Many can be bought on the spot in Europe with little or no formality. If bought in Europe, you will often have to present identification such as a passport for name, and, in some cases, proof of age. There are several categories of these passes:

Europe-wide, regional, those limited to a single country, and other reduced-fare programs.

Europe-wide Passes

InterRail Junior

InterRail Junior is a one-month, second-class-only card available to persons under 26. It includes all Western Europe plus Hungary, Romania, Yugoslavia, and Morocco.

It can be purchased for £145 from main rail station ticket offices and most European travel agents. If you get and use one, you must pay half fare in Britain, but ride free on other countries' rail systems.

Senior Rail Discount

Seniors can receive a one-third to one-half discount from the standard fares by showing the British Rail Senior Golden Card when purchasing your tickets.

Regional Rail Passes

Some nations participate in multi-country regional rail pass offers. The Benelux Tourrail, which includes Belgium, the Netherlands, and Luxembourg, can be bought at railway stations in those countries. The other main regional pass is the Nordic Tourist Ticket, which covers all of Scandinavia. Details are provided in the Key below. Both are available for either first- or second-class travel.

National Rail Passes

Many European nations offer single-country rail passes, which are (but not always) sold within the country. They are also usually available from national rail offices in Britain. Costs are reasonable, and all of the national passes are available for either first- or second-class travel. See the Key below.

Other Discount Rail Fares

In addition to the rail passes of whatever type, there are dozens of other discount fares. These include the kilometre tickets in a number of countries, family discounts, cheap same-day (almost free return) tickets, and holiday fares. Details of some are given below.

Regional Railpasses

Benelux Tourrail. This pass provides 5 days unlimited first- or second-class train travel, during any 17-day period, anywhere in Belgium, Luxembourg, and the Netherlands, plus bus travel in Luxembourg. Buy it at any rail station in Belgium, Luxembourg, or the Netherlands. Children receive discounts.

Nord Tourist (Scanrail). This pass provides 21 days unlimited first-class (2075 Swedish Kroner or local equivalent) or second-class (1375 Swedish Kroner or local equivalent) travel in any Scandinavian country (Denmark, Finland, Norway, and Sweden), all DSB (Danish) ferries and some other ferries, such as those between Stockholm and Turku (Finland). Buy the pass at any railway station in Scandinavia, or from Scan-Tours Ltd., 8 Spring Gardens, London SW1A, telephone 01-839 2927, telex 919008.

National Railpasses and Discount Fares Key

The name of the pass or card is listed in italics in the foreign language. The English name is either in the parentheses just after the foreign name or at the beginning of the description in regular type.

Austria

Bundesnetzkarte (Federal Network Card). This 9- or 16-day or one-month first- or second-class pass provides unlimited passage on all Austrian trains. Buy at all Austrian railway stations, and central railway stations in Frankfurt, Munich, and Zurich. (Price example for 1989: 9 days: 2200 Schillings first class and 1460 Schillings second class.)

Senioren-Ausweis (Senior Citizens' Discount Card). This card, available to men over 65 and women over 60, provides half-price passage on all rail travel, post buses, and lake steamers in Austria for a year from the date of issuance. Buy it at any Austrian railway station, some main post offices, and main railway stations in Frankfurt, Munich, and Zurich. Requires 1 passport photo and proof of age. The price is 240 Schillings.

Belgium

B-Tourrail. This first- or second-class pass provides unlimited passage on 8 out of a 17-day period on all trains in Belgium. Buy it at any railway station in Belgium. Sold only from two weeks before Easter to September 30. Prices are: 2400 Belgian Francs first class and 1600 Belgian Francs second class (children half-price).

Half-price Card. A discount card providing a 50% reduction in first- or second-class fares during a one-month period. Buy it at any railway station in Belgium.

Cheap round-trip fares on weekends cost just a small amount more than a one-way ticket. Leave after Friday at 5 p.m., return by Monday morning.

Note: Information is available in Britain from Belgian National Railways, 22 Sackville St., London W1X, telephone 01-734 1491.

Denmark

Gruppe Billet (Group ticket). This ticket provides discounts for three or more persons travelling together on DSB trains and ferries during off-peak (non-commuter) hours. Buy these tickets at all railway stations.

Senioren Billet (Senior citizens ticket). This free card, available only to men and women over 67, provides a 50% discount on round trips taken during off peak hours. Obtain it at any railway station in Denmark by showing proof of age.

Finland

Finnrailpass. This first- or second-class pass provides unlimited rail passage for 8, 15, or 22 days. Buy it at any railway station in Finland. Prices for 1988 (increase expected in 1989) are: 8 days first class 600 Finnish Markka (Fmk), second class Fmk400; 15 days first class Fmk900, second class Fmk600; 22 days first class Fmk1125, second class Fmk750.

Group Rail Tickets. When three or more persons travel together, they can receive a 20% or larger discount, depending on the number of persons. The journey must be at least 75 km (48 miles) in each direction to qualify for this discount.

Senior Citizen Discount. This card, available to any person 65 years of age or more, provides a 50% discount on all journeys of at least 75 km (48 miles) each direction. This card is not valid from Friday noon to Saturday noon or Sunday noon to Monday noon. Buy the card at all railway stations in Finland for Fmk50.

France

France Vacances. This first- or second-class pass provides unlimited passage on the French Railways (SNCF) for 4 days in any 15-day period, (first class £90, second class £64), or nine days in any 30-day period (first class £160, second class £108). Night train travel starting after than 7.30 p.m. is included the next day's travel, in effect counting one-and-a-half day's travel as one. Children 4 to 12 receive a 40% discount. In addition, this card provides free transfers from Paris Charles de Gaulle or Orly airports, a free Paris Metro pass (one day with the 4-day card or two days with the 9-day card), and various discounts on sightseeing. Also provides discounts on car hire, the Paris Seine river boats, museums, some hotels and restaurants, and a 50% discount on the Hoverspeed across the Channel.

Available from travel agents or British Rail offices. Not sold in France.

Germany, West

Touristkarte (Tourist Card). This first- or second-class card provides unlimited passage for 4, 9 or 16 days on all German Rail (DB) trains, all Europabus buses, including the Romantische Strasse, and free passage on KD Line Rhine and Moselle riverboats (mid-April to mid-October only), and passage to West Berlin. Buy it at German Rail offices in Europe, or at any international airport or large railway station in Germany. A reduced-cost "Junior Touristkarte" is available for 9 and 16 days to travellers less than 26 years of age.

Bundes Netzkarte (National Network Card). This first- or second-class card provides unlimited passage for one month on all DB trains. Buy it at all large railway stations in Germany. Not sold outside of the country.

Gebeits Netzkarte (Area Network Card). This first- or second-class card provides unlimited passage for one month on all DB trains in a single region. Buy it at all main railway stations in Germany. Not sold outside of the country.

Great Britain

England, Scotland, and Wales

Rail Rover. This pass provides unlimited travel for 7 consecutive days (first class £200, second class £120) or 14 consecutive days (first class £300, second class £190) on all British Rail lines.

Includes ferries to the Isle of Wight and the Firth of Clyde boats. Sold in at main railway stations in large towns and cities. Children 5 to 16 travel at half price.

Day Return. This is a regular discount available on all round-trip tickets when you return the same day. The round-trip fare is just a bit more than one-way fares.

Weekend Return. Identical to the day return except you must leave on a Friday, Saturday, or Sunday, and return on a Saturday, Sunday, or Monday.

Network Card. Regional divisions (Southeast, Southwest, etc.) have special weekly, monthly, and annual network cards. These offer fixed-price access to the system within certain limits. Prices vary with the region and the routes selected.

Young Persons Railcard. Provides a 1/3 discount on most second class (Economy) train fares: cheap and standard same-day returns, special SaverFares, rail rover tickets, and half-price regional Network Cards. Valid one year from date of issuance, costs £12, requires two passport-type photos, and proof of age or student status. Available only to people under 23 or full-time students. The card must be shown when purchasing tickets to receive the discount.

Family Railcard. This card provides half-price or one-third discounts for all adults named on the card, and up to three not named on the card, and up to four children up to 16 years old travel for £1 each (may increase slightly in 1989). Minimum "family" is one adult named on the card plus one child. Requires passport sized photo of adults listed on the card, costs £15. Obtain it at major British Rail stations or travel agents. Temporary card is given immediately, but permanent card will be posted in about three weeks to your address.

Senior Golden Card. Two types provide slightly different disounts, each valid 12 months from the day of issuance. The £7 card offers half-price cheap day returns for journeys up to about 50 miles, and 1/3 off of Rail Rover tickets. The £12 ticket offers the benefits of the £7 card,plus 1/3 off Saver Tickets on journeys of over 50 miles. half-price Standard Day Returns, 1/3 of

Standard tickets for either first or second (Economy) class. The £7 card can be upgraded for an additional £5 to a £12 card. Available to anyone over 60 (British residence not required), sold only in Britain at major British Rail stations, or through travel agents. Requires proof of age (DHSS pension book, passport, or birth certificate).

Disabled Persons Railcard. This card provides at least 1/3 discounts to the blind or partially sighted, deaf, or disabled on a number of already discounted and full-price tickets. Generally limited to British residents, since you must provide proof from the Social Services Department (or in Scotland, the Social Work Department) that you are registered as disabled. For further information, contact British Rail, Department XX, P.O. Box 28, York YO1 1FB.

Britainshrinkers, economical escorted train tours to famous tourist attractions. Obtain information from BritRail or your travel agent.

Isle of Man

Rail Rover Ticket. This provides unlimited train travel during any 3 days within 7 (from May through October) on all Isle of Man trains: between Douglas and Port Erin by steam train, between Douglas and Ramsey by electric tram, and one round trip on the Snaefell Mountain Railway, price £7.70, children £3.85, families £19.25. Available only on the Isle of Man at some hotels or in person or by mail from:
  Isle of Man Passenger Transport Board
  Terminus Buildings
  Strathallan
  Douglas, Isle of Man
  Telephone (0624) 73307

Northern Ireland

Irish Overlander. This pass provides unlimited train and bus travel in Northern Ireland and also in the Republic of Ireland for 7 or 15 days. Buy it at CIE (Irish Transportation Company) offices in main cities in Northern Ireland and the Republic of Ireland.

Rail Runabout. This pass provides unlimited rail passage in Northern Ireland for 7 days. Buy the pass at rail stations in Northern Ireland. Senior citizens (over 60) receive a 50% discount on this card.

Scotland

Scottish Highlands and Islands Travelpass. 7 days or 14 days, discount of 30% from October through May, unlimited second- class (Economy) train travel, plus unlimited bus and ferry travel. Includes travel between Edinburgh and Glasgow, and all transport to the north and west. Available March 1 through October 30.

Freedom of Scotland Ticket, 7 days (second class only) £38 and 14 days £55 includes all trains in Scotland, plus connections to Carlisle or Berwick-upon-Tweed, and passage on Firth of Clyde boats. Purchase at any British Rail station or authorized travel agent in Scotland.

Local Rovers. Available for regional unlimited second-class travel for one or two weeks between Easter and October 1. Sold at all main British Rail stations.

Reiver Rover, for unlimited travel in the Border country. Sold in Britain at the British Travel Centre in London, Scottish Travel Centre in Edinburgh, or in the region.

Note: British Rail offers additional but frequently-changing discount tickets and schemes. Information is available at main British Rail stations.

Greece

Πασο (Pronounced "Paso") (Touring Card). This pass provides unlimited second-class rail travel for 10, 20, or 30 days. There are reductions for groups of two or more travelling together. Buy it at main Greek railway stations. This pass is not sold outside of Greece.

Ireland

Note: Ireland has only one class on its trains and buses.

Rambler Ticket. This pass provides unlimited passage on all CIE (Irish Transportation Company) buses and trains in the Irish Republic for 8 days out of 15, or 15 days out of 30. You can also buy passes valid on only trains *or* buses for the same periods. Children under 15 pay half of the adult price. Dublin city buses and DART trains are not included in these passes. Sold at all CIE train and bus stations in Ireland and by CIE Tours International, 150 New Bond Street, London W1Y, telephone 01-493 3243.

Youth Rambler Pass. This pass is the same as the Rambler Ticket except that it is limited to people 14 to 26 years old, and is sold for the same periods. (15% discount if bought before arrival in Ireland.) Bicycle passage can be added to this ticket for a supplement.

Overlander Pass. This pass provides 15 days of unlimited train and bus passage in Ireland and in Northern Ireland. Buy it at CIE ticket offices in Ireland.

Italy

Biglietto Turistico di Libera Circolazione (Unlimited Travel Tourist Ticket). This pass provides unlimited first- or second-class train travel in Italy for 8, 15, 21, or 30 days. Reduced price for children under 12. Buy it at Italian State Railways offices in Europe, and through travel agents. Not sold in Italy, but when in Italy, you can pay more to extend the time period of all but the 8-day pass at main railway stations.

Biglietto Chilometrico (Kilometric Ticket). This ticket provides first- or second-class train travel on the State Railways (FS) for up to five people (related or not) for up to 20 trips with a maximum combined distance of 3000 km. Buy it from Italian State Railways offices in Europe, or at train stations and travel agents throughout

Italy. Supplements must be paid for passage on EuroCity and Rapido trains.

Cart ad'Argento (Senior Citizens Silver Card). This card, valid for one year from the day of purchase, provides 30% discount on any rail fare for men over 65 and women over 60. It is not valid from Friday to Sunday in July and August, or from December 18 to 28. Buy it for 5,000 Lire at any railway station or travel agency in Italy.

Luxembourg

Carte d'Abonnement (Subscription Card). This card provides unlimited second-class train travel and bus travel for one day (217 Francs), 5 days (658 Francs), or one calendar month (1748 Francs). Buy it at any train station in Luxembourg. Some of these tickets are not valid for trips to a border crossing.

Senior Citizens Discount. Any person over 65 receives a 50% discount by showing proof of age (such as a passport).

Netherlands

All discount cards and fares are available at main railway stations throughout the Netherlands.

Dagkaart (One-Day Network Pass). This pass provides unlimited first-class train travel (78.75 Gulden) or second-class train travel (52.50 Gulden) for one day. A pass for local transportation (Stadstreekabonnement) can be purchased for 5.25 Gulden in addition to the Dagkaart.

3-Dagsenetkaart (Three-Day Rover). This pass provides unlimited train travel for 3 days in first class (118.50 Gulden) or second class (79.50 Gulden). A pass for local transport can be added for 10.00 Gulden.

Weeknetkaart (Seven-Day Rover). This pass provides unlimited train travel for 7 days in first class (161.50 Gulden) or second class (113 Gulden). Local transport can be added for 17.75 Gulden. A passport photo or passport number is required.

Maandnetkaarten (Month Network Pass). This pass provides one month's unlimited first-class train travel (595 Gulden) or second-class train travel (400 Gulden).

Dagretour (Same-Day Return). When you buy a first- or second-class round-trip ticket and return the same day after 6 p.m., the return fare is only a few Gulden more than the one-way fare.

NS-Jaarkaart (Annual Rail Card). This card, which can be purchased for 267.50 Gulden per month (less per person for groups travelling together), provides unlimited use of the Dutch rail network. For further information, and to obtain this card, contact: N.V. Nederlandse Spoorwegen, Bureau Jaarkaarten, Postbus 2368, 3500 GJ Utrecht.

Weekendretour (Weekend Return). When you buy a first- or second-class round-trip ticket and leave on Saturday and return on Sunday, the return fare is only 2.50 Gulden more than a Same-Day Return. Available at any railway station.

60+ Seniorenkaart (Senior Card). This card provides a 40% discount on all other fares for 70 Gulden, but there are restrictions on weekend travel. It is available from any main railway station in the Netherlands. A passport or other proof of age and a photograph are required.

Note: Some of the above rail passes are sold in Britain by: Netherlands Railways, Eggington House, 25-28 Buckingham Gate, London SW1E, telephone 01-630 1735.

Norway

Bargain Rail Pass. This pass is valid for 7 days of actual train travel, with unlimited stopovers not counting. For a slightly lesser fare, you can travel 800 kilometres in one direction only. Buy these passes at all Norwegian rail stations. Second class only, 310 Norwegian Kronor. These passes are not sold outside of Norway, and are not valid on Fridays.

Senior citizen rail discount. Persons at least 67 years old (and spouses of any age!) receive a 50% discount on all first and second class rail journeys. Show proof of age when buying a ticket.

Poland

PolRailPass. This card is for unlimited first- or second-class travel for 7, 14, 21 days, or one month. Buy the card at any Orbis Travel Bureau in Poland and from Orbis' offices outside of Poland.

Portugal

Bilhete Turístico (Tourist Ticket). This card provides unlimited train travel in first- *and* second-class train travel for 7 days (7,225 Escudos), 14 days (11,530 Escudos), and 21 days (16,470 Escudos). Buy it at railway stations in Portugal.
Bilhete Redução a Velhos (Senior Citizen Rail Discount). Senior citizens over 65 are given 50% discount on all railway fares. Proof of age (such as a passport) is required.

Spain

Tarjeta Turistica (Tourist Card). This card provides unlimited first- or second-class rail travel. Eight days cost 13,000 Pesetas (Pta) first class and 9,000 Pta second class; 15 days cost 21,000 Pta first class and 15,000 Pta second class; 22 days cost 25,000 Pta first class and 19,000 Pta second class. Available at all RENFE (Spanish Railway Network) ticket offices, stations, and travel agencies in Spain, and the RENFE office in Paris, France.
Chequetren (Train Check). This card provides about a 15% reduction on first- and second-class fares on all (RENFE) trains for up to six persons travelling together. All the travellers' names must be entered on the Chequetren card at time of purchase. Use for fares, sleeping cars, supplements, or reservation fees. No time or distance limits. Buy this card in Spain at train stations, then spend it like money to buy tickets, sleepers, etc.

Días Azules (Blue Days). You can get a 25% discount for a same-day round trip of at least 200 km on 305 days of the year. (The other 60 days are national holidays, etc.) There are larger discounts for groups and families travelling together.

Tarjeta Dorado (Gold Card). This card provides a 50% discount on all train fares on trips of more than 100 km on all Blue Days (see paragraph just above) and same-day discounts on trips of less than 100 km each way. Men over 65 and women over 60 can buy the card for 105 pesetas at any RENFE railway station.

Sweden

All second-class fares Monday to Thursday and on Saturday receive a 25% discount from full fare. Full fare is charged only on Friday and Sunday.

Group fares. When two to five persons travel together, if the first pays the full fare, all others receive a 30% discount. This discount is available only in second class, and the discount is calculated from the fare in effect on the day of travel.

Family fares. Parents pay full fare, children 16-25 pay half fare, and children under 16 are free.

Children's discount. Children under six travel free; from six to 16 pay half fare.

Senior citizen reduction. Any person over 65 receives a 45% discount on all rail travel in Sweden. Proof of age (such as a passport) is required when you buy tickets.

Switzerland

Swiss Pass This card provides unlimited first- or second-class post bus and Swiss Federal Railways (CFF- SBB) train travel. Four days cost £85 first class and £56 second class; eight days cost £100 first class and £66 second class; 15 days cost £120 first class and £80 second class; one month costs £155 first class and £102 second class, and includes local tram and bus transport in 22 cities and towns. It also provides 50% discounts on most of the private mountain railways. Children under 16 pay half price for the card. Buy the card at Swiss Federal Railways offices and travel agents outside of Switzerland, since the card is not sold in Switzerland.

Environment Ticket (Half-fare Card). Provides 50% discount on all rail, bus, and lake boats in either first or second class. The card costs about £22 for one month and £35 for one year. It can be purchased from travel agents, or at any Swiss train station.

Swiss Pass. Provides a single round-trip ticket from Geneva or Zurich Airport or any border crossing to a single point, plus 50% discount on all other rail travel during one month, first-class about £45, second class £25.

Long-Distance Buses

Europe has a long-distance bus network, providing both national and international services. The widest network is called "Europabus" on the Continent and "Supabus" in Britain. It is affiliated with the national railroads of most (but not all) European nations. Buses not only offer some long- distance services, but also supplement national train services, allowing access to some of the towns and villages inaccessible by trains.

Long-distance buses in a few countries, such as Greece, Spain, Turkey, and Yugoslavia, are often faster and sometimes cheaper than the railways.

Some regions of Europe, such the Highlands of Scotland or Andorra (wedged between France and Spain), do not have railways. But these often have adequate bus service.

Austria and Switzerland have extensive postal bus networks. These deliver mail as well as passengers at least once a day (except Sundays) to even the most remote villages. Schedules are coordinated with train schedules, so that you can leave the train, and a few minutes later be moving away from the station on the bus.

In Britain, the coach fares between major cities (such as London and Birmingham) are cheaper than rail fares.

Bus Stations and Stops

Most large European cities have long-distance bus terminals. Some are adjacent to or near train stations, but most are in other parts of cities or adjacent to access routes.

City maps usually locate bus stations. Tourist information offices can almost always tell you where the terminals are.

Rural bus stops in countries are marked in various ways. When you start a journey, watch for a small sign at the first stop. It may be the symbol of a bus, the word for bus stop, or logo of the bus company.

Public Transport

The underground is the fastest transport method in most major European cities. Buses and trams are usually slower but far more scenic. Some cities also have extensive light rail systems on separate rights of way going to the suburbs, or, in West Germany and Vienna, linking entire regions.

On business days, underground and light rail are the quickest ways to get around: faster than taxis, buses, or foot. Your speed will be about 15 to 30 miles per hour including the walk from your starting point to the underground station, the ride, and the walk from the underground station to your destination. Only bicycle riders can equal the point-to-point speed, and then only by riding in traffic and threading their way through traffic jams.

In general, transport systems are reasonably straightforward, though each city's system has its own aura and eccentricities. Ticket practices vary; some systems charge by distance travelled, others by the ride, and still others by time elapsed. Most, but not all, offer reductions for quantity ticket purchases, or for weekly or monthly or even yearly passes. Still others have special tourist-oriented cards, which often include admission to museums and other attractions, and even shopping discounts. However, the tourist tickets are not usually the most economical.

Many transport systems, particularly in Germany, Scandinavia, Switzerland, and the Eastern European nations, use the honour system. No one will check your ticket as you enter or get on the train or bus. However, these systems may include roving ticket inspectors—often plain-clothes—who will impose hefty fines on the spot for unticketed passengers.

Details about mass transport for many major cities in Europe follow. The first listed transport type in each city is roughly an indication of speed, convenience, and coverage. Therefore, undergrounds are frequently listed first.

In the ticket section, the type of ticket is listed first, then the name of the ticket is given in parentheses.

Public Transport Key

Amsterdam

Main types of transport: Tram, buses, and Metro.
Operating company name: GVB, or Gemeentevervoerbedrijf (108-114 Prins Henrikkade, Postbos 2131, 1000 CC Amsterdam, tel. 27 27 27, 7 a.m.—4:30 p.m. telex 12708; (note: suburban lines are operated by other companies, though all accept the same tickets.)
Hours of operation: 5 a.m. to 1 a.m., plus night buses on a limited route network and schedule.
Tickets: Fares are charged by distance and time. The same ticket is valid on all forms of transport. Tickets are not collected at the end of the journey. Any journey takes one fare zone to get on plus one additional strip per zone.
How and where to buy tickets:
- Individual tickets *(Uurnetkaart)* are sold only on the bus and Metro, 2.60 Gulden, and 2.50 Gulden at night.
- Strip tickets *(Nationale Strippenkaart)* of 10 strips (8.65 Gulden) on buses and trams, and at the GVB office on Prins Henrikkade and post offices, both of which also sell tickets of 15 strips (8.65 Gulden) and 45 strips (25.35 Gulden).

- Rover passes *(Dagkaarten)* for one day (8.65 Guilden) to nine days (8.65 Gulden for the first day plus 2.70 Gulden per extra day) at GBV office at Central Station or GBV office on Prins Henrikkade.
- Monthly passes *(Netabonnement)* at GBV offices. Photograph is required and laminated to the card. Cost depends on number of zones purchased. (All of central Amsterdam is in one zone.) Also requires a photo ID card (Stamkaart), available free from GBV offices, bring a photo.

How to find your way around:
Get free maps from VVV or GBV offices; complete route map of entire area is 1.50 Gulden. Ask at the VVV office if you need detailed directions.

Special information: Night bus routes are shown in the map at the beginning of the Yellow Pages of the phone directory, or in the GBV pamphlet "Nachtbussen." For transport information call 27 27 27 (7 a.m.—11 p.m. Strip tickets are valid on buses, trams, and undergrounds in

"Nationale Strippenkaart" (reduced)

all other cities in the Netherlands. Fine for travelling without a valid ticket: 26 Gulden. All ticket inspectors are uniformed officers.

Exits are marked "Uitgang".

Taxis: Expensive and hard to find. Because of crowded, narrow one-way streets, taxis are sometimes slower than walking, especially in the central city. Call 77 77 77 for taxis. Tip is included in the fare.

How to get to and from Schiphol airport: Trains directly between airport (station in front of the terminal) and Central Station every 15 minutes during the day and hourly between 1 and 6 a.m., costs 4.40 Gulden. Buses from Schiphol to Royal Sonesta Hotel in the city centre, costs 12.50 Gulden.

Berlin (West)

Main types of transport: Underground (U-Bahn), light rail (S-Bahn), and buses.

Operating company name: BVG, or Berliner Verkehrs-Betriebe (Potsdamer Strasse 188, postal district 30, tel. 25 61, fax (030) 216 41 86, telex 302020 BVG).

Symbols: U-Bahn: white U in blue circle. S-Bahn: white S in green square.

Hours of operation: 4:30 a.m. to midnight.

Tickets: Tickets are valid for a trip in any one direction in West Berlin for a maximum of 120 minutes (including round trips), from the minute you time-stamp your ticket. The same kind of ticket is used on all public transport. Transfers (including between bus, U-Bahn, and S-Bahn) are free and no new ticket is needed.

How and where to buy tickets
- Individual tickets *(Einzel-Fahrschein),* Deutsche Marks (DM) 2.70, at any BVG ticket office, U-Bahn, or S-Bahn station, or buses, provides unlimited use of bus, U-Bahn, and S-Bahn, including unlimited transfers.
- Individual short-distance tickets *(Kurzstreckentarif)* For less than 6 bus stops or 3 U-Bahn or S-Bahn stations, DM1.70.

- Five-Ride cards *(Sammelkarte)*, for DM11.50 (a large discount from single-ticket prices). Buy them at BVG offices.
- Rover passes *(Berlin Ticket)*, for 24 hours, DM9 at BVG office at Kleistpark U-Bahn station, at BVG office at the Zoo Station, and most U-Bahn and S-Bahn stations. Unlimited use of the West Berlin transport network, including riverboats.
- Weekday rover ticket *(6-Tage-Karte-Jedermann)*, DM 26 for entire network except riverboats, or for DM19 for a single fare zone. Valid Monday to Saturday only. Requires a photograph.
- Weekly group tickets *(Wochenkarte)*, for 7 days. Buy at BVG offices. Groups must number at least 6, but a member can travel individually on the West Berlin network.
- Monthly pass *(Monatswertmarken)*, at BVG offices. Photograph is required and will be attached to the card. Valid for a calendar month, costs DM89 for entire BVG network ("Superticket)", or DM 70 for a single zone ("Kleinticket).

How to find your way around: Transport maps are sold at all underground ticket windows, DM2; schedule book DM2.50.

Special information and pitfalls: West Berlin transport tickets aren't used in East Berlin. Fine for riding without a valid ticket is DM40.

Exits are marked "Ausgang".

Taxis: Fares are high, with an extra charge for each piece of luggage. Most taxis are immaculate Mercedes-Benz diesels. Taxis are at stands on the street or call for taxis at 69 02, 26 10 26, 21 60 60, or 24 02 02. Tip 10%.

How to get to and from airports:

Tegel (West Berlin) airport: Frequent city buses (Line A9) arrive and depart from Tegel airport. Any regular West Berlin transport ticket can be used.

If you land in East Berlin's Schönefeld airport (which is outside East Berlin city limits), buses will take you to East or West Berlin. You will have to get an East German transit visa, available at the airport upon arrival (no charge).

Note on transport in East Berlin: You can get a day rover pass for all public transport in East

Berlin for 2 Marks (M), or S-bahn for M 1 at any S-bahn station or from the tourist office at Alexanderplatz 5. Transport maps are sold (but are rarely in stock). However, you can also buy tickets on buses and S-Bahn stations for M 0.20—0.30. Remember to validate ticket in the stamping machines before you enter (push very hard!).

Brussels

Main types of transport: Underground (Metro), trams and light rail (called Pre-Metro), and buses.
Operating company name: STIB, or Société des Transports Intercommunaux de Bruxelles (French) and Maatschappij voor het Intercommunaal Vervoer te Brussel (Flemish) (head office at avenue de la Toison d'Or 15, 1060 Bruxelles, tel. for information 515 30 64 Monday to Friday 8:30 a.m.—4:30 p.m.
Symbol: Metro: stylized white M in blue rectangle.
Hours of operation: 5 a.m. to midnight or 1 a.m., plus limited night bus service.
Tickets: Fares are charged per entry and the same tickets are used on all systems (bus, Pre-Metro, Metro) except suburban (orange) buses. Tickets are valid for a one-hour trip in any direction, plus two transfers in the second hour. Passes can also include suburban trains. Tickets are not collected at the end of the journey.
  How and where to buy tickets:
- Individual tickets *(Billet Direct)*, 35 Francs (F) at Metro ticket booths, from bus drivers and on light rail.
- 5-ride tickets (140 F), sold on buses, light rail, and Pre-metro and Metro stations.
- Rover passes *(Carte 24-Heures)*, 140 F for 1 day, at airport tourist information, all underground stations, STIB offices at Rogier and Porte de Namur Pre-Metro stations. (Note: also valid in 25 cities and towns the same day throughout Belgium.)

- Monthly passes *(Abonnement Mensuel)*, 880 F at S.T.I.B. offices, requires a photograph for ID card.
- Annual Passes *(Abonnement Annuel)*, 8800F at S.T.I.B. offices, requires a photograph for ID card.

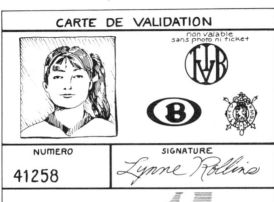

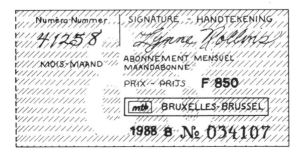

Photo Identification Card and Monthly Coupon (actual size)

How to find your way around: Get free transport maps from all Metro, Pre-Metro, and S.T.I.B. offices in Brussels. Free tourist office map shows some Metro and Pre-Metro routes, but is not as detailed as the S.T.I.B. map.

Special Information: Exits are marked by an arrow pointing out of a box; if in words, "Sortie" (French) and "Uitgang" (Flemish). Fine for attempting to ride without a valid ticket: 1,000 F plus cost of a ticket (first offence) to 10,000 F.

Taxis: Expensive, charging by distance and time. Night taxi fares are double the daytime fare. Hail taxis at taxi stands, train stations, or other busy areas, or call 511 22 44. Tip is included in the fare.

How to get to and from Zaventem (Nationale) airport: Trains between airport basement and Nord and Central (Midi) stations approximately every 20 to 30 minutes from 6 a.m. to 11:30 p.m.

Copenhagen

Main types of transport: Electric light-rail trains (S-tog) and buses.

Operating company names: HT, or Hovedstadsområdats Trafikselskab (Toftegårds Plads, Gammel Køge Landevej 3, 2500 Valby, tel. 01-44 01 44, fax 01-44 01 19,) and DSB, or Danske Statsbaner.

Hours of operation: 5:30 a.m. (6 a.m. Sundays) to 12:30 a.m., plus a few bus routes until 2:30 a.m.

Tickets: Tickets are valid for one hour within each transport zone. When you go more than one zone, you must have one ticket per zone. Transfers within zone are free. Tickets are valid on both buses and S-tog. Tickets are not collected at the end of the journey.

How and where to buy tickets:
- Individual tickets *(Grundbillet)* 8 Danish kroner (Dkr) for two zones, from bus drivers and at S-tog stations.
- 10-ticket books for Dkr 70 at train stations and from bus drivers.

- Rover passes *(1-Day Rover)*, Dkr 80 for 24 hours at railway stations and some large hotels. Two types: Greater Copenhagen includes the city; Metropolitan Area includes suburbs and costs twice as much.
- Area rover passes *(Around the Sound)* Dkr 140 for unlimited travel for 2 days, including travel to Elsinore and Malmö, Sweden.
- Tourist passes *(Copenhagen Card)*, Dkr 80 for 1 day, Dkr 140 for 2 days, Dkr 180, sold for 3 days at airport, railway stations, tourist information offices. Benefits in addition to transport include free admission to almost all museums, Tivoli Gardens, 25% or 50% discount (depending on time) on hydrofoils to Malmö, Sweden.
- Monthly passes *(Maanedsbillet)*, Dkr 240 at Hovedbanegården (main railway station). Good within 3 fare zones nearest to city centre; you need one photograph for free ID card.
- All tickets are half price for children from 5 to 11 years old.

How to find your way around: Get free maps from all tourist information offices.

Special information and pitfalls: Stamp your ticket at the yellow time-stamp machines on train platforms. Part of the ticket is removed, the remainder is time-stamped. Fine for failure to have a valid ticket is Dkr 150 on buses and Dkr 250 on the S- tog.

Taxis: Plentiful but expensive. Do not tip! No additional night charge. Call 01-35 35 35 for taxis.

How to get to or from Kastrup airport: SAS (Scandinavian Airlines) buses between airport and bus terminal across street from Vesterport railway station every 15 minutes from 6 a.m. to 10 p.m. Also, HT bus from City Hall Square. Pay the bus driver, or take a taxi.

Frankfurt

Main types of transport: Underground (U-Bahn), light rail (S-Bahn), buses, and trams.
Operating company name: FVV, or Frankfurter Verkehrs-und-Tarif-Verbund (for all tickets) (Mannheimer Strasse 15-19, Postfach 16349, 6000 Frankfurt 16, tel. (069) 2 69 40, 9 a.m—3:30 p.m.), Stadtwerke Frankfurt am Main (Underground, trams, buses), Deutsche Bundesbahn (DB) for S-bahn, suburban buses.
Symbols: U-Bahn: White U in blue square; S-Bahn: White S in green circle. Bus or tram stop: green H in yellow circle.
Hours of operation: 5 a.m. to between 10 p.m. and 1 a.m. depending on line.
Tickets: Single tickets are valid for one ride, on any and all forms of transport within a fare zone. (All of central Frankfurt is in the same fare zone.) This system extends as far as Hanau to the east and Wiesbaden and Mainz to the west. Maps at all stations and most tram stops show zone boundaries.
How and where to buy tickets:

- Individual short-distance tickets *(Kurzstrecke Fahrschein)* for 1.20 Deutsche Marks (DM), if journey is not over 2 km during peak hours, sold at blue ticket machines at underground stations and tram stops.

Individual tickets *(Fahrschein)* DM1.70) at blue ticket machines at underground stations, tram stops, and in buses from the driver. Not sold on U-bahn or S-bahn trains.

- Rover passes *(24-Stunden-Ticket)* for 24 hours day in the city for DM8 at blue ticket machines at stops and stations, and from bus drivers.

"24-Stunden-Ticket"

- Weekly passes *(FVV Wochenkarte)* from Monday through Friday or Monday to Sunday at FVV ticket counters at the Hauptbahnhof (main railway station) and the Hauptwache in the city centre. Price varies by number of fare zones purchased. A photograph is required for free ID card.
- Monthly passes *(FVV Monatskarte)* for a calendar month at FVV ticket counters at the Hauptbahnhof and the Hauptwache. Price varies with the number of fare zones purchased, maximum DM170. A photograph is required for free ID card.
- Yearly passes *(Pluskarte)* for 12 months from the first of the month following date of purchase DM760, only at FVV ticket counters.

How to find your way around: Get free maps from tourist information offices. While trams do not have route maps, clear and distinct recorded announcements are made before each stop. Since stops can be short, know the name of your stop to avoid passing it.

Special information and pitfalls: Tickets are sold by zones; while the central city is in one zone, outlying areas and the airport are two to four zones away.

Most tram stops and all underground stations have blue ticket-vending machines, which have signs reading "Fahrscheine." Tickets are time-stamped by the machine or bus driver. You must have a ticket before you enter the underground, trams or S-Bahn. Fine for failure to have a valid ticket is DM40.

Exits are marked "Ausgang".

Taxis: Expensive, mostly Mercedes-Benz diesels and a few large Japanese cars. Tip 10%. Call 23 00 01 for taxis, or find them at taxi stands. Some take credit cards (and will have appropriate stickers).

How to get to or from the Flughafen Frankfurt airport: S-Bahn between basement level of Terminal B to the Frankfurt central station (Hauptbahnhof) every 10 minutes, takes 11 minutes, lines 14 and 15.

London

Main types of transport: Underground (or Tube), Docklands light rail, buses (including express "Hoppa" minibuses), and suburban British Rail trains.

Operating company name: London Transport (55 Broadway, SW1H 0BD). Information offices at Victoria and Euston railway stations, Piccadilly Circus, King's Cross, and Oxford Circus, and both Heathrow Underground stations, or tel. 222-1234 24 hours a day.

Symbol: Circle with horizontal line through it; arrow will point into building or underground.

Hours of operation: Underground, 6 a.m. (Sundays 7:30 a.m.) to midnight. Timetables for buses are found at bus stops. No transport service on Christmas Day except Airbus A1, and limited service on December 26.

Tickets: Underground and bus tickets are charged by zone, and are not interchangeable. No transfers between bus and rail. Underground single-journey tickets are collected at the end of the journey. Bus tickets are not collected after issuance, but should be retained until the end of the journey in case an inspector boards.

All tickets and a multitude of passes are sold at all underground station ticket windows.

How and where to buy tickets:

The London region is divided into five fare zones: the Central Zone (1) includes all of the area inside the Circle Line, and a little further in some directions. Zones 1, 2, and 3 are within the boundaries of Greater London.

- Individual tickets: at underground station ticket booths, and ticket machines at main underground stations, from bus conductors (who may take a minute or two to get to you after you've boarded the bus). Minimum cost is 50p (60p in the Central Zone), up to £1.90 for five zones.
- Daily, weekly, monthly, or annual passes *(Travelcard)*, valid on buses, British Rail, Docklands light rail, and the underground. Sold by zones, and valid only in the boundaries of Greater London. The *CapitalCard* passes include suburban areas reached by

British Rail in addition to London Underground and buses.

The Central Zone (Zone 1) includes all of central London; the Inner Zone (Zone 2) includes the rest of London, and the Outer Zones (Zone 3, 4, and 5) include the suburbs to about 15 miles from London.

- *One-Day Travelcard*, valid for Zones 1 and 2, and the parts of 3 within the Greater London boundaries, sold at every London Transport Travel Information Centre, underground station, and bus garage. Cannot be used before 9:30 a.m., costs £2.30. No photo required, except by children aged 14 and 15.
- *Weekly Travelcard*, bought any day and valid for seven consecutive days; £6.40 for the Central Zone, up to £17.70 for five zones within the Greater London boundaries. Requires photo (photo booth and passport pictures OK), which is placed onto a free identification card.
- *Monthly Travelcard*, bought any day and valid for 30 days; £24.60 for the Central Zone, up to £68.00 for all five zones within the Greater London boundaries. Requires

Weekly Travelcard and Identification Card (reduced)

photo, which is placed onto free identification card.
- *Annual Travelcard*, bought any day and valid for one year; £256 for the Central Zone, up to £708 for five zones in the Greater London boundaries. Requires photo, which is placed onto a free identification card.
- *Bus Pass*, valid only on buses and sold by zone, but not sold for the Central zone.
- *One Day Bus Pass*, valid all day (including morning rush hour). Not sold for Central zone; ranges from 90p for one zone to £1.70 for four zones. Can be bought ahead of time with scratch-off dates. No photo required.
- *7 Day Bus Pass*, valid for seven consecutive days, sold by zones, £ for the local area, 2.80, to four zones £6.50, but not available for the Central Zone.
- *Monthly Bus Pass*, valid for one month, sold by zones, £10.80 for the local area, to £25.00 for four zones, but not available for Central Zone.
- *Annual Bus Pass*, valid for one year, sold by zones, £148 for one zone, to £260 for four zones, but not available for Central Zone.
- *Capitalcard*, which includes all Underground and red buses plus British Rail commuter trains outside the Greater London boundaries (all 5 zones and beyond). Price depends on exact areas included. Requires photo, which is placed onto a free identification card.

How to find your way around: Get free maps at all London Transport ticket booths. Each underground line has its own colour and name, which is consistently used in all maps, signs, and stations.

Special information and pitfalls: Sunday underground service is infrequent on some lines and some stations are closed. Underground system is colour coded, easy to understand and follow, and the sign design is virtually unchanged since developed by calligrapher Edward Johnston in 1907.

If you have a Travelcard or Capitalcard and travel outside your zone, you can use it and pay only an "excess fare" for travel outside the permitted zone.

One-Day passes are not valid on night bus services (line numbers preceded by an N, usually after 11 p.m.). Minimum night bus fare is £1.

Exits are marked "Way Out".

Taxis: Not cheap but set an unexcelled standard of comfort, roominess, and courtesy. Hail taxis on the street when "For Hire" sign is lit. Tip 10 to 15%.

How to get to and from airports:

- Heathrow—underground (Piccadilly line) goes directly to Heathrow (all terminals) every five to ten minutes; buses from Heathrow to the London bus terminal at Victoria Station near the Coach Station (Bus A1) every 20 minutes from 6:35 a.m. to 9:40 p.m. Bus A3 goes from Euston station every 20 or 30 minutes. Night bus N97 goes from Heathrow to Trafalgar Square and Liverpool Street Station, and makes stops upon request. From the southwest, British Rail to Woking station (main line), then Railair Link Heathrow-Woking bus every 20 minutes, takes one up to hour (depending on terminal), 7 a.m. to 9:15 p.m.
- Gatwick—Gatwick express train every 15 minutes to and from east end of air terminal to Victoria Station, journey takes 30 minutes, £5 second class, £7.50 first class. You can't take luggage trolley to railway platforms at Gatwick. Green Line buses leave every hour from Victoria Coach Station, just up the road from Victoria Station, takes about one hour and a half, and Wandsworth Arendale, takes about one hour, £3.50. Luggage trolleys are plentiful at Gatwick's bus stop. For Greenline information, tel. 01-668 7261.
- London City—London Transport bus line 173 directly to airport, or by British Rail to London City Airport (Silvertown) station, or by riverbus (ferry) from Charing Cross Pier at 10 minutes past the hour, takes 35 minutes, £5, and from Swan Lane at London Bridge at 30 minutes past the hour, takes 30 minutes, costs £4, from 7 a.m. to 6:00 p.m.

Madrid

Main types of transport: Underground (Metro) and buses.

Operating company name: EMT, or Empresa Municipal de Transportes (Alcántara 24, 28006 Madrid, tel. 401-9900).

Hours of operation: Metro: 6 a.m. to 1 a.m.; bus: 5:30 a.m. to 11 p.m. or to 2 a.m. depending on line.

Tickets: Fares are charged per ride. Tickets are not collected at the end of the journey.

How and where to buy tickets:

- Individual tickets *Boleto*, bus, 60 pesetas (pta) from bus drivers, Metro: 60 pta, except the Colón-Aeropuerto is 200 pta, from Metro ticket offices.
- Ticket books 10 bus rides *(Bono-bus)*, 370 pta, or 10 metro rides *(Taco)*, at ETM kiosks or ETM headquarters.
- Weekly pass *(Abono Transporte)*, valid on bus and metro, zone A (all of the central city), 3000 pta, to all zones, 4500 pta.

How to find your way around: Get free maps from EMT offices (Plaza Cibeles, Plaza Callao, and Puerta del Sol) and tourist information offices.

Special Information: Microbuses (70 pta) run along main routes and are more comfortable and much faster than regular city buses.

Exits are marked "Salida".

Taxis: Hail taxis on the street (sign "Libre", or green dome light at night), or from taxi stands (with sign with large white T on a blue background). Extra charge on Sundays (50 pta), holidays (50 pta), when leaving a bus or rail station (50 pta), and for each piece of luggage. Night surcharge after 11 p.m. (50 pta) Tip 10%. Be sure meter has been started after you get in.

How to get to and from Barajas airport: Buses leave every 15 minutes between airport and City Air Terminal underground at Plaza Colón, 6 a.m. to 11 p.m., fare 200 pta, or take a taxi.

Milan

Main types of transport: Underground (Metro), trams, and buses.
Symbol: Metro: MM (Metropolitana Milanese).
Operating company name: ATM, or Azienda Trasporti Municipali (Foro Buonaparte 61, 20121 Milano, information tel. 669 7081 and 669 7047, telex 330564 ATMSA).
Hours of operation: 6:20 a.m. to 12:30 a.m.
Tickets: The same tickets are used on all public transport. Time-stamp your ticket when you first get on a bus or tram, or enter the Metro station. Transfers are free, and you need only keep your original ticket. Tickets are not collected at the end of the journey.
How and where to buy tickets:
- Individual tickets *(Biglietto Ordinario)*, 800 Lire, at tobacco stands (Tabacchi) with ATM logo, all Metro station stands, and ticket machines. Tickets are valid for 75 minutes unlimited use of the system.
- Carnet *(Carnet di Biglietti Urbani)*, a book of 13 tickets, 10,000 Lire, at most Metro stops and all ATM ticket offices.
- Tourist ticket *(Tesserino Turistico Giornaliero)* valid for 1 day, 3,200 Lire, at Ente Provinciale di Turismo office in the Piazza Duomo and Centrale railway station, all Metro stations, and ATM information offices. Proof of non-residence (such as a passport) is required.
- Weekly passes *Abbonamento Settimanale a Vista*, valid from Monday to the following Sunday night, 8,400 Lire. Allows unlimited

Biglietto Ordinario

travel on urban Metro, tram, and bus lines. Requires a photograph, and can be obtained at main Metro stations.
- Annual passes *(Abbonamento Annuale di Libera Circolazione)*, valid for a calendar year, 330,000 Lire, requires a photograph. Obtainable only at ATM headquarters at via Ricasoli 2 entrance.

How to find your way around: Get free map at main Metro ticket offices and ATM headquarters (even has a street index!); a less-accurate but usable map free from tourist offices.

Special information and pitfalls: You must stamp your ticket when you enter Metro station, bus or tram. The air on Line 1 of Metro is very stuffy most of the year. Supplemental fares will be charged for suburban travel.

Exits are marked "Uscita".

Fine for failure to have a valid ticket: in city limits 20,000 Lire, outside city limits 10,000 Lire, plus the cost of a single ticket.

Taxis: Numerous, mostly occupied. Tip 5%. Find at taxi stands at train stations and in the central district, or call 8585 or 6767 for taxis.

How to get to and from the airports:
- Linate: Buses every 20 minutes between airport and city air terminal at Piazza Luigi di Savoia (Metro: Centrale) or take Metro Line 1 to San Babila, then Bus 73 to Linate.
- Malpensa: Buses between airport and city air terminal meet each flight. Malpensa is very far from Milan: take the bus at least 2-1/2 hours before departure. Buses may not serve charter flights. Taxi fares can be up to £18.

Note: For flight arrival and departure information at both airports, call 74 85 2200.

Munich

Main types of transport: Underground (U-Bahn), light rail (S-Bahn), buses, and trams.

Symbols: U-Bahn: White U in blue square; S-Bahn: White S in green circle; Tram stop: "Haltestelle" sign on pole.

Operating company name: MVV, or Münchener Verkehrs- und Tarif-Verbund (Thierschstrasse 2, postal district 22, Postfach 260154, 8000 München 26, S-Bahn information tel. 55 75 75, U-bahn, bus, and tram information 21 91 1).

Hours of operation: 5 a.m. to 1:30 a.m.

Tickets: Munich is divided into fare zones. On transport maps, the inner zone is blue, and outer zones are various shades of green. Single-ride and strip tickets are valid for two hours in any one direction of travel. If crossing fare zones, you need an extra ticket or strip for each additional fare zone. The same tickets and passes can be used on any public transportation without a separate transfer.

How and where to buy tickets:
- Single tickets *(Fahrschein)* at Einzelfahrkarten machines at U-Bahn and S-Bahn stations, and at tram and bus stops; not available on board. Minimum cost is 2.40 Deutsche Marks (DM), more for extra zones.
- Strip tickets at Mehrfahrkarten machines at all underground and S-Bahn ticket booths. Tickets of 10 strips *(Kleine Streifenkarte)* are blue and cost DM9.50 (DM); tickets of 16 strips (*Grosse Streifenkarte*) are green and cost DM15.
- Rover Passes *(24-Stunden-Ticket—Innenraum)* for 24 hours' unlimited travel in the inner zone costs DM7.50. Purchase at all Mehrfahrkarten machines, and underground and S-Bahn ticket booths.
- Rover Passes *(24-Stunden-Ticket—Gesamttarifgebeit)* for 24 hours' unlimited travel on any central city and suburban transport costs DM15.
- Monthly Passes *(Monatskarte)* for DM40—DM160 depending on fare zones included. Valid for a calendar month, and requires a photograph. Obtain it from MVV offices.

How to find your way around: Free city maps available from tourist information offices and at Hauptbahnhof (main railway station). MVV has a detailed explanation of transport in the multilanguage publication, "Verbundfahren in München", available from tourist information offices or MVV.

Special information and pitfalls: Two strips are required for a journey within the city; more strips are required on the S-Bahn to suburbs. Time-stamp your ticket in the Entwerterautomaten machine (blue boxy machine with a big yellow E) before you get on a bus or tram or enter the underground or S-Bahn. Fine DM40 for failure to have a valid ticket (or enough validated strips) payable on the spot.

Exits are marked "Ausgang".

Taxis: Expensive; mainly immaculate Mercedes-Benz diesels and now a few equally immaculate large Japanese cars. Tip 10%. Find taxis at stands at railway stations, the city centre, or call 21611 for taxis.

How to get to or from Riem airport: Buses between airport and Arnulfstrasse on the north side of the Hauptbahnhof (main railway station) every 20 minutes from 5:40 a.m. to 8:40 p.m. Fare is DM7.

Paris

Main types of transport: Metro, RER, (Réseau Express Régional) to suburbs, and buses.
Subway symbol: Letter M inside circle (infrequently used), or word Metro, or sometimes Metropolitain on the 1900's Art Nouveau entrances. RER—look for letters RER inside circle.
Operating company name: RATP, or Régie Autonome des Transports Parisiens (53ter, quai

"Coupon Jaune:" (Use with identification card)

des Grands Augustins, 75006, 75271 Paris Cedex 06, tel. 43.46.14.14).

Hours of operation: Metro and RER: 5:30 a.m. to midnight. Bus: Full service 5:30 a.m. to 8:30 p.m., reduced service 3:30 p.m. to 1:30 a.m., skeleton night bus schedule hourly from 1:30 to 5:30 a.m. RER: 5:15 a.m. to 1 a.m.

Tickets: Tickets on the underground are valid for one entry. Short bus trips take one ticket, longer trips take two or more. The same type of ticket is used buses and Metro. Tickets are validated when you go through the turnstiles, or when you enter the bus. Use Metro tickets on RER inside Paris, RER tickets when travelling beyond the city (otherwise you will not be able to get out of the suburban RER station). Tickets are not collected at the end of the journey, except on

Photo Identification Card

RER lines. In any case, keep your ticket until you pass the "limite de validité de billets" at the exit.

How and where to buy tickets:

- Individual tickets *(Ticket à l'Uniteé)* at all Metro stations, on buses. Buy RER tickets at all RER stations from coin-operated ticket machines (change given) or ticket booths.
- Discounted group of 10 tickets *(Carnet)* at all Metro station ticket booths, 27.50 F., little more than half price of ten single tickets.
- Rover pass *(Paris Sesame)*, good for two, four, or seven days of first-class travel on all Metro, buses, and all RER trains. Buy at most Metro stations, Paris tourist offices, at SCNF window at Charles de Gaulle 1 airport, and French Railways offices in other countries.

(In spring 1989, this pass will be changed to 1, 3, or 5 days, and will be valid on all Metro, RATP buses, and SNCF suburban trains.)

- Weekly passes *(Coupon Jaune)* for Metro and (if desired) RER zones, valid from Monday to Sunday, at all Metro station ticket booths, or RATP head office. Photo required for the free identification card *(Carte Orange)* needed to buy pass.
- Monthly pass *(Coupon Orange)* for Metro and (if desired) RER, valid for a calendar month, sold by zones (two zones cover all of the city, Zones 3, 4, and 5 are in the suburbs), at Paris Metro ticket offices, or RATP head office. Photo required for free identification card *(Carte Orange)*; then buy the pass.

Coupon Orange (Use with Photo Identification Card)

How to find your way around: Get free maps at all Metro ticket booths, Paris tourism offices, and most French Government Tourist Offices in other countries.

Special information and pitfalls: The Paris underground has first- and second-class cars. First-class cars are in the centre of trains, often painted blue and marked with a "1" next to each door. Only first-class ticket holders can use first-class cars between 9 a.m. and 5 p.m.

To find your way in the Metro, you need to know the station at the end of the line in the direction you're going. System is not colour-coded, and sometimes signs aren't well located. All Metro signs on every line are either blue on white or white on dark blue.

Exits are marked "Sortie".

Taxis: Expensive and full of hidden charges: each piece of luggage costs extra. The maximum number of passengers in a taxi is three. Fares more than double from 10 p.m. to 6:30 a.m. Find taxis at the head of taxi stands (Arrêt Taxis, Tête de Station), or by telephone (look in classified under "Taxi"). If you call, you pay for time and distance the taxi uses until it arrives. Tip 15%.

How to get to and from airports:
- Charles de Gaulle: Frequent buses between airport and Gare du Nord and Gare Montparnasse railway stations. Also, RER line B3 ("Roissy-Rail") goes near the airport, includes free shuttle bus, costs 23 F. In addition, Air France buses from Arc de Triomphe and Porte Maillot (Palais de Congrès) every 12 minutes, costs 35 F. RATP bus lines 350 from Gare de l'Est and 351 from Place de la Nation, costs less (varies with destination). Air France bus to Orly every 20 minutes from 6 a.m. to midnight from Gates A3 or B10.
- Orly: Frequent buses between airport and Gare Montparnasse and the air terminal near Les Invalides: trip takes one hour, more during rush hour. Quicker bus service with the "Orlybus" between Orly and Place Denfert-Rochereau Metro station (leaving every 15-20 minutes): trip takes 35 minutes, costs 18 francs or 6 yellow Metro tickets or a Coupon Jaune valid for zones 1-4.

Rome

Main types of transport: Buses, underground (Metro), and trams.

Operating company name: ATAC, or Azienda Tramvie e Autobuse del Comune di Roma (65 via Volturno, central tel. 46 95, telex 610091 ATAC).

Hours of operation: Bus: 5:30 a.m. to midnight with skeleton night "Notturno" service on main lines 24 hours. Metro: 5:30 a.m. to 10:30 p.m.

Tickets: One per ride, not collected at the end of the journey, or a pass.

How and where to buy tickets:

- Individual tickets *(Biglietto),* different kinds for bus and metro, 700 Lire at ATAC offices, ticket machines, tobacco shops, and newsstands. Not available on buses.
- Group of 10 tickets *(Blocchetto da 10 Biglietti di Corsa Semplice)*, provides 10 individual tickets for 6,000 Lire, at ATAC offices, ticket machines, and some tobacco shops and newsstands.
- Half-day rover pass *(Biglietto Orario)*, provides unlimited use from either 5 a.m. to 2 p.m. (rose), or from 2 p.m. until midnight (celeste), costs 1000 Lire, at ATAC offices, ticket machines, and some tobacco shops and newsstands. Must be time-stamped when starting the first journey.
- Day rover pass *(Biglietto Integrato Giornaliero or B.I.G.)*, provides unlimited use of the Rome bus and metro system, 2,800 Lire at at ATAC offices, ticket machines, and some tobacco shops, and newsstands.
- Tourist rover passes *(Carte Settimanale per Turisti):* 7 days, 10,000 Lire, at ATAC office in front of Stazione Termini or main ATAC office. Also gives free admission to municipal museums.
- Monthly passes *(Tessera di Abbonamento Mensile—Intere Rete Urbana)*, 22,000 Lire at ATAC kiosk in front of Stazione Termini, or main ATAC office. These passes are used on buses and trams but not the Metro. For the same price, a pass can be bought for the

Metro and one bus line *(Una Linea ATAC e Linee A e B della Metroplitana).*
How to find your way around: Buy maps at ATAC offices. "Tuttocittá" section of the phone book has a transport map.
Special information and pitfalls: Metro Line B is dingy and slow; Metro Line A is newer, cleaner, much faster. Some stations have long underground corridors. Buses often get stuck in traffic jams.

Exits are marked "Uscita".

Taxis: Get taxis at taxi stands or by telephone. Be sure the meter starts after you get in. Extra charges made after 10 p.m., Sundays, holidays, and for each piece of luggage. Tip 10%. Call 3570, 3875, 4994, or 8433. Avoid unlicensed gypsy cabs.

How to get and from airports:
- Fiumicino (Leonardo da Vinci) airport: Acotral buses between airport and air terminal on Via Giolitti near Stazione Termini.
- Ciampino airport: Metro Line A to Subaugusta station. From there, then Acotral bus to the airport. (This airport is sometimes used for charter flights.)

Stockholm

Main types of transport: Underground (Tunnelbanan or T-bana), buses, ferries, and local trains.
Operating company name: SL, or Storstockholms Lokaltrafik (Tegnérgatan 2A, Box 6301, S-113 81 Stockholm, information tel. 23 60 10 (7 a.m.—midnight, head office tel. 786 10 00, telex 19159 SL TRANS S).
Tickets: Tickets for buses, underground and local trains are interchangeable and are valid for one hour unlimited travel including unlimited transfers within the city limits. Each zone crossed requires validation of an additional coupon (maximum 8 coupons). Central Stokholm is all in one zone. Stamp your ticket when you begin to use it. Tickets are not collected at the end of the journey. (Note: fare increases expected in early 1989.)

Stockholm   Public Transport   137

How and where to buy them:
- Individual tickets *(Biljetter)*, 7 Kronor, at T-bana ticket offices, and from bus drivers (actually consists of two 3.50 Kronor coupons).
- 18-strip tickets, *(Rabattkuponger)*, 45 Kronor, at T-bana ticket offices and Pressbyrå shops.
- Tourist tickets, *Turistkort;* for 1 day 22 Kronor within Stockholm city limits, or entire Stockholm region for 40 Kronor, or 3 days 76 derground stations and T-bana ticket offices; full use of local transport system and the Djurgård ferry; also allows free admission to Skansen, Kaknästornet, and Gräna Lund, and the Transport Museum.
- Tourist passes *(Stockholmskortet)* for 1, 2, or 3 days, at tourist information office, in Centralstation, and Sweden House. Unlimited transport in Stockholm and suburbs on underground, bus, and train. Includes free admission to 70 museums, sightseeing tours. Priced from 70 to 240 Kronor.
- Monthly passes *(Månadskort)* for a calendar month for 200 Kronor, at T-bana ticket offices or Pressbyrå shops. Requires photograph for free ID card, plus purchase of monthly ticket.

How to find your way around: Get free maps from tourist information offices, or buy Transport maps *SL Kartor)* at SL offices or Pressbyrå shops.

How to get to and from Arlanda airport: Frequent buses between airport (front of international terminal building), the Vasa Terminal on Vasagatan, with direct access from the T-bana Central station and the Central Railway Station. Buses leave every 5 minutes during peak periods (alternately to international and domestic terminals), and 15 minutes during non-peak periods (all buses serve both terminals). Allow 40 minutes to get to airport check-in from Vasa Terminal, costs 30 Kronor.

Taxis: Expensive. Call 15 00 00 for taxis. Tip is 10%.

Venice

Main types of transport: Boats (vaporetti, literally little steamers), privately owned water taxis, and gondolas, and buses in suburban Mestre.

Operating company name: ACTV, or Azienda Consorzio Trasporti Veneziani (Sant' Angelo Corte dell' Albero 3880, Casella Postale 688, tel. (041) 528 7886, fax (041) 5207135, telex 223487 ACTVVE I

Hours of operation: 24 hours, though vaporetti offer minimal service at night, and none to La Giudecca after about 10 p.m.

Tickets are valid for one trip (cost depends on distance), not collected at the end of the journey.

How and where to buy tickets:
- Individual tickets *(Biglietto)* at the ticket booth at the landing before you get on the boat. Minimum price 1500 Lire, to 2500 Lire for longer trips.
- Ticket book *(Carnet di Biglietti),* a group of prepaid tickets in various denominations from 100 Lire to 2000 Lire. They can be used as ordinary tickets. Buy them at the ACTV office, or at some tobacco shops. These tickets must be date-stamped before boarding.

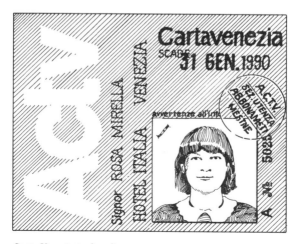

Carta Venezia (reduced)

- Rover pass *(Biglietto Turistico)* for 24 hours. 8000 Lire at ticket booths at vaporetto stops.
- Discount card *(Carta Venezia),* provides three years of vaporetto service at a two-thirds discount, costs 8,000 Lire. Buy at ticket booths at vaporetto stops, and ACTV offices. Photo required.
- Monthly pass *(Abbonamento)* at ACTV offices. The identification card costs 8000 Lire, and a photo is required. After purchasing the card, you can buy a monthly ticket for unlimited travel for 25,000 Lire. A monthly pass card can be used as a *Carta Venezia* if the month's coupon has not been bought.

How to find your way around: Get free maps from Venice tourist offices at Piazzale Roma, Santa Lucia railway station, and Piazza San Marco.

Special information and pitfalls: Vaporetti come in three speeds: motoscafi (express), diretto (semi-express), and accellerato (stops at every landing). Also, large pieces of luggage over 50 cm in any dimension cost one ticket per piece.

Gondola prices are unregulated and expensive (50,000 Lire and up). Be sure you agree on length of ride as well as the route before you get in. Singing by the gondolier usually costs extra. Gondola crossings of the Grand Canal cost 300 Lire and take only a few minutes.

Exits are marked "Uscita".

Smoking is prohibited in vaporetto cabins; fine for smoking inside is 5,000 to 15,000 Lire, payable on the spot.

Water taxis and gondolas are found at landings or along quays. Agree to a firm price before you get in. Call 32326 or 22303 for water taxis.

How to get to and from Marco Polo airport: Buses leave every hour from Piazzale Roma at 10 minutes past the hour, with a stop in Mestre, trip takes 20 minutes. Scheduled motorboats also go between the airport and the San Marco vaporetto landing, and meet most flights. Special note: be sure you are on the scheduled boats, since water taxis lie in wait and are exorbitant for this trip.

Vienna

Main types of transport: Underground (Stadtbahn), light rail (Schnellbahn), trams, and buses.

Operating company name: VOR, Verkehrsbund Ost-Region (Postfach 308, Neubaugasse 1, 1010 Wien), telephone 93 95 08-0.

Hours of operation: 5 a.m. to midnight.

Tickets: The system is based on transport zones, using zoned tickets and passes. All of central Vienna is in the kernel zone (Zone 100). Outlying areas are in other zones. When using a ticket, you must stamp it once for each zone boundary on an uninterrupted journey in a single direction using underground, trams, and buses. Stamp the ticket once in the Entwerter machine (insert ticket in yellow slot) for each zone of your journey on the bus or at station entrance. Tickets are not collected at the end of the journey.

How and where to buy tickets:

- Individual tickets *(Fahrschein)* 19 Schillings, at station ticket offices or from bus drivers.
- Strip tickets *(Streifenkarte)* with 4 tickets (52 Schillings) or 8 tickets (100 Schillings) at station ticket offices, tobacco shops (tabak). Children 6 to 15 and dogs pay half price.
- Three-day rover passes *(72-Stun-*

"Streifenkarte" (reduced)

Vienna   Public Transport

den Wien Netzkarte) for three days' travel on all Vienna public transport, sold at Vienna tourist information offices and VOR station ticket offices.
- Eight-Day Pass *(8-Tage Umweltstreifennetzkarte)* 200 Schillings, valid for unlimited passage only in the central kernel zone for eight days
- Monthly passes *(Monatskarte)*, sold at VOR and railway station ticket offices, tobacco shops (tabak). This pass is sold by zone: costs range up to 1,094 Schillings per month. Photo required for identification card, available at VOR station ticket offices.

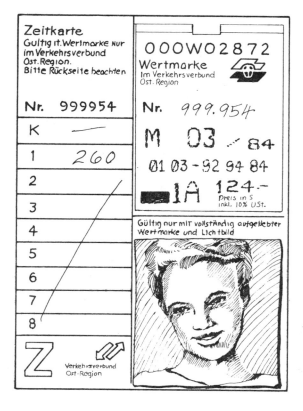

- Yearly passes *(Jahreskarte)*, sold by zone at prices up to 10,940 Schillings, sold at VOR ticket offices. Photo required for identification card.

How to find your way around: Get free maps of Vienna from tourist office, or transport map at nominal cost from any VOR office.

Special information: Colour-coded graphics on the underground and Schnellbahn. Signs show the next stop just before leaving the station. Some stations are modern, others date back to the turn of the century.

Dogs and children ride for half of the adult price.

Exits are marked "Ausgang".

Taxis: Many are Mercedes-Benz diesels. Hail a cab from a taxi stand, most often at railway stations and along the Ring, or call 3130, 4369, 6282, or 9101. Taxis charge extra for each piece of baggage. Add 10% tip to the meter charge.

How to get to and from Schwechat airport: Buses every 20 to 30 minutes from 6 a.m. to 7:20 p.m. between the airport and the City Air Terminal at the Hilton Hotel. There are also buses every 30 minutes to the Westbahnhof and Südbahnhof stations every 30 minutes from 7 a.m. to 7 p.m. Buses will wait for planes arriving later in the evening. Also, you can take the train from the airport to City Air Terminal every hour from 7:30 a.m. to 7 p.m. to the Wien Mitte and Wien Nord stations.

Cars and Driving

When you drive, you are unfettered by schedules that may not convenient. Roads and byways are numerous and pass through almost every village. You can pull over to marvel at a Gothic church or an Alpine peak looming beyond a wildflower-splattered meadow. You can effortlessly cross mountain passes seemingly at the roof of the world, find tranquil picnic spots by the side of the road, and discover cozy, out-of-the-way inns. The charms of the countryside are easy to see at your own pace, since you can stop, even if only to compose a photograph.

You can rent, lease, or purchase cars in Europe, either on the spot or before you leave Britain.

If your car has proper registration or a rental contract and insurance (see below), there is no problem crossing borders in a car.

Almost anyone who drives in Britain can successfully drive in Europe, once you have got used to driving on the right, of course. To be sure, there are those places—mainly city centres—where driving can be challenging or frustrating, depending on your point of view. Traffic can seem very fast or be agonizingly slow—almost gridlock at times—and a parking place can be almost impossible to find. Fortunately, these same city centres have developed public transport to a fine art: efficient, fast, and cheap.

Speed limits and distances everywhere outside Great Britain (and older signs in the Irish Republic) are in kilometres.

Rules of the Road

1. Speed limits are different from country to country. Motorway and main road speeds are usually higher than other speed limits in the same country. In West Germany, there is no speed limit at all on the autobahn. In much of Europe, speed limits don't seem to be strictly enforced.

East German autobahns, however, are frequently patrolled and speeds over 100 km per hour, or often poorly-marked lower speed limits, are carefully measured. In some areas with poor maintenance, speed limits are reduced suddenly, and the police lie in wait. Fines are payable on the spot, in Western currency only. A recent fine was approximately £1400!

Some countries have speed traps on main roads. France is notorious. The fine is imposed and payable on the spot in local currency. No credit cards, traveller's cheques, or foreign currency are accepted. When you see cars flash their head lights as they come toward you during the day, slow down! Speed trap ahead! They're only trying to save you the cost of a fine.

Usually the speed traps are found on main roads and not autoroutes. Police by the roadside radio ahead and you're pulled over at a more convenient place a couple of miles down the road.

2. On a motorway or dual carriageway, flashing headlights from the car behind you mean "move over fast" to a slower outside lane. Most European cars are designed with an easy flash control, which encourages frequent flashing. On the other hand, if you signal, the driver in the other car will give way.

3. Road markings are generally standard. Don't pass on a solid line, don't begin to pass on a short dashed line. All lane lines are white except in work zones, where they are all yellow.

4. Seat belts must be worn in nearly every country. You may have to pay a fine if stopped and you aren't wearing one. In addition, children

under six years of age cannot sit in the front seat in most countries. In some countries, young children must wear seat belts or be in car seats whether in the front or back seats.

5. Parking restrictions are strictly enforced in some cities, seemingly never in others. But don't park near a sign showing a tow truck taking a car. Tickets are frequently given to offenders. Tickets given in the same country may eventually be charged to you by car rental companies if you don't pay them. Tickets given in one country are almost never passed along to another one. Before disregarding a parking ticket, search your conscience and check where the car is registered.

6. Parking meters may or may not be similar to those you've cursed at home. There may also be a single meter for an entire street. You park the car, buy a timed ticket, and put it on your dashboard. In some places, there are individual guards, too. Be careful that the guards are official, though. Sometimes they're just neighbourhood residents lying in wait for some extra coins.

7. Some countries, including Belgium, France, Germany, and Italy, have "blue zones" where parking is limited in time. The car should come with or you should get a time disk, available in Europe at garages, car parts stores, and curio shops. When you park, place the disk on the dashboard showing your arrival time. The disk will automatically show the time you should leave. If you don't have a disk, put a slip of paper with your arrival time on the dashboard. You probably won't have any problem if you return before your time is up.

8. Roundabouts are found all across Europe. In West Germany, as in Britain, do not stop when entering unless there is a dashed line across your lane or a yield sign directed at you. If there is a dashed line across your lane, yield whether entering or already circling. Elsewhere, those entering usually have the right of way.

9. If you are handicapped and have a wheelchair placard, take it with you. In virtually all of Europe, you'll be extended the same courtesies and consideration you would receive at home. The only difference in the placard is

that in some European countries the background for the wheelchair symbol is orange, in others it is blue.

10. You are permitted to drive a right- or left-hand drive car anywhere in Europe.

11. A few countries have special rules or regulations which drivers should know.

In many countries, it is acceptable (and sometimes required) to drive only with parking lights in built-up urban areas with acceptable street lighting.

In Sweden, remember to turn on your headlights night and day. In Finland and Norway, lights must always be on except in cities and towns.

In Switzerland, you have to buy an annual sticker (30 Swiss Francs) to drive on the motoways (defined as any road with green direction signs) and many mountain tunnels. These stickers are sold at every major border crossing by the customs and immigration officers. The fine for driving on a motorway without a sticker is 100 Swiss Francs, plus you have to buy the sticker on the spot.

European Road Signs

European road signs are remarkably standard; most are pictograms. A key to the common ones is below.

Triangles give warning of hazards. They're white with a red outline and black pictorials.

Exception: yellow diamonds are used in the Irish Republic.

Circles give orders, prohibitions, or limits. These signs are white with a red outline. Some have the red diagonal slash and some do not.

Blue circular signs with white arrows give orders, usually permissible turning directions.

Rectangles give information and directions.

Direction and information signs in many countries are colour-coded. Blue signs with white lettering in most countries point to or are on motorways.

Exceptions are Belgium, Italy, Switzerland, and Yugoslavia, where blue is the colour of ordinary signs. There, green is the motorway colour.

In Belgium, green signs with yellow writing direct you to motorways but signs on them are blue. In the Netherlands blue is used for all directional road signs on motorways and surface streets.

Signing shouldn't give you a great deal of difficulty. Signs are particularly well designed and placed in Belgium, Switzerland, and West Germany.

Drunk Driving

Many countries are *very* serious about preventing driving after drinking. Permissible levels of alcohol in the blood vary widely, and in some nations the limit is 0.0%.

Nations especially strict and severe are Norway, Sweden, Finland, Denmark, and the Soviet Union. In these countries, roadblocks are set up, particularly on Friday and Saturday nights. Everyone driving, whether under suspicion or not, may be stopped and subjected to a breath test. Other countries are hardly lenient.

Driving Paperwork

Licence

If you drive in Western Europe, your own driving licence will be accepted (and demanded) when you rent a car or are stopped by traffic police. Some nations (such as Italy) say that you must have a translation of the conditions of your licence. This provision is rarely enforced. Many

European Road Sign Key

Remember that there are national variations!

No right turn

No left turn

Do not enter

Left turn only

No U turn

Right turn only

No vehicles

No passing

Passing zone

No cars

No pedestrians

No bicycles

Speed limit

End speed limit

No stopping

One way street

No parking

Keep right (left)

Cars and Driving

European Road Sign Key

Signs sometimes vary from those shown here.

Curve right

Zig-zag curve

Intersection

Road work

Rough road

Yield

Height limit

Danger ahead

Slippery

Rail crossing

Pedestrians

Traffic circle

Weight limit

Hill

Expressway

Eastern European nations will accept your licence, some subject to a similar condition as Italy.

A few, such as Bulgaria and the Soviet Union, require an International Driving Permit. This permit is available to all licensed drivers at any office of the AA and RAC for £2. You don't need to be a club member. You will need your driving licence and two passport photographs.

Payment must be made in cash if you are not a club member. The permit is issued and signed on the spot. It expires one year from the date it is issued or on the date your regular licence expires, whichever comes first.

Insurance

Insurance is required for all European driving (except in Greece). A policy issued in one European country is valid and honoured throughout Europe, except in the Soviet Union where you will be required to buy Soviet insurance at the border. If travelling to Spain, be sure that the policy includes a Spanish bail bond endorsement; there is usually no extra charge for this.

Insurance papers are pale green; therefore, they are known as "Green Cards". Further information about insurance is included in the sections on car rental, lease, and purchase sections below.

Renting a Car

Car rental agencies are common throughout Europe. While cars can legally be rented to anyone with a valid licence, many rental companies require a minimum age as high as 25. Major companies such as Hertz, Avis, and Europcar are found in many Western European countries.

In the Socialist (Eastern) bloc, rentals are most easily arranged through the national tourist agencies.

Rental rates vary widely by company, by country, and by season.

If you reserve (and usually pay for) the rental in advance, there are large discounts available, especially if you rent for a week or more. Shop around. In general, car rental is least expensive in Spain, Britain, and West Germany. Prices are usually highest in Eastern Europe and Scandinavia.

Cars rented in West Germany, Switzerland, Belgium, and Scandinavia are usually in the best condition.

Basic liability and collision insurance is included in the rental contract. Deductibles range from about £15 to about £1000, depending on the policy. The deductible amount is quoted in local currency. Rental agencies will press optional non-deductible coverage on you. It is very expensive in proportion to the benefits paid. You can waive it. If you waive, carefully check the car for damage before you accept it. Inspect it for scratches and dents in the body and tears and cigarette burns in the upholstery. Make the agency note the flaws on the contract before you leave. Otherwise you risk having to pay for someone else's damage.

The insurance papers will be in the rental packet or the glove compartment. Be sure you have them before you leave the rental site.

When you rent a car, you get only one set of keys. Get a spare set made at a locksmith to avoid being stranded. Locksmiths may be hard to find, but a spare key is worth the effort. The rental agencies for some reason rarely want the spare set back to make it easy on the next renter. It is usually easier to have keys made in the country where you obtain the car; otherwise you may have trouble finding the proper blanks (especially for locking petrol caps).

Most Western European nations charge Value Added Tax on top of the rental charge. The rental rate you are quoted virtually never includes this tax, which must be paid in local currency or included in credit card bills. When picking up a car in one country and dropping it off in another, the nation where you get the car rental determines the tax rate. When you pick up the car, you must usually leave either a sizeable cash deposit or a signed credit card charge slip with the amount left blank. Since these rates vary greatly, carefully consider the country where you rent a car. It can make a great difference in the ultimate price of the rental.

Key to Value Added Tax Rates on Rental Cars

Austria: 21%; if over 21 days, 33.3%
Belgium: 25% (not charged on short-term leases)
Denmark: 22%
Finland: 19.05%
France: 28% (not charged on short-term leases)
Germany (West-FRG): 14%
Great Britain: 15%
Greece: 18%
Ireland: 10%
Italy: 19%
Luxembourg: 12%
Netherlands: 20%
Norway: 20%
Portugal: 16%
Spain: 12%
Sweden: 23.46%
Switzerland: 0 (no tax)
Yugoslavia: 15%

Car Hire Companies in Britain

This list includes only a sampling of the many car hire companies from whom you can rent a car. Absence of a listing for a particular company is no reflection on its services; it is just that it would require a volume the size of a large phone book to include them all. Exact details have to be obtained from each rental agency directly or through your travel agent, since conditions and prices change very frequently.

In addition the central addresses and central reservation numbers below, you can also through local offices throughout Britain.

Avis
Hayes Gate House
Uxbridge Road
Hayes   Greater London
Tel. 01-848 8733

Budget
International House
Great North   Road
Hatfield Herts.
Tel. 01-441 5882 or
(0800) 181181

Europcar
Bushey House
High Street
Bushey Greater London
Tel. 01-950 5050

Hertz
1272 London Road
London SW16
Tel. 01-679 1777

Leasing a Car Tax Free

France and Belgium, with two of the highest Value-Added Tax rates on car rentals, offer an attractive alternative if you plan to use the car for 21 days or more: a short-term lease for three weeks to one year. You must be at least 18 years old to lease a car. For slightly more than the lowest priced rental for the identical car and model, you can lease a new, fully insured (zero deductible) car with full factory warranty. In France, your choice is limited to Peugeot, Renault, and Citroen. In Belgium many more makes are offered, including campers and luxury cars. For more information, contact the manufacturer's British office.

In all leases, full payment must be made in advance.

Allow at least two or three weeks to make and confirm arrangements.

Buying a Used Car

If you plan to stay in Europe for at least a couple of months, a used car, van, or caravanette can save you money. It requires you to be flexible and willing to spend a few days buying and selling your vehicle. You should plan to sell the vehicle in the same country you bought it in to eliminate extra red tape. If you plan to bring the car home, see the end of this section.

You can buy a car at any of the thousands of new and used car dealers in Western Europe. You can also look in classified ads for private parties selling their vehicles. "Exchange & Mart" and "Auto Trader" are weekly classified ad newspapers in London (price 60p). "Paris Hebdo," a classified ad newspaper, issued every week, lists lots of cars for sale. Paris-based International Herald Tribune newspaper also has a classified column of cars for sale, though they tend to be luxury models.

On weekends in Paris near the Malesherbes Metro station, there is an auto flea market with hundreds of cars for sale; there is also a regular auction at Drouot Véhicules, 17 rue de la Montjoie, 93210 La Plaine St-Denis; payment required by certified check. Near Frankfurt, the drive-in movie (Autokino) also is, on occasion, an auto flea market.

There's also a car market on Saturday near the RAI Center, Amsterdam, and in front of American Express' Paris office (11 Rue Scribe, 75009) and sometimes their offices elsewhere.

Buying a Van or Caravanette

You can also buy a van from a departing traveller. For more than 20 years, travellers have bought and sold cars and vans in London. The weekend Jubilee Road market near Waterloo Underground station has been moved. Now it takes place on weekends on Provost Road, just north of the Old Street underground station. This market attracts mostly Australians and New Zealanders selling out after their long holiday or Grand Tour. At some times of the year, there may be dozens of caravanettes (mostly Volkswagen), and a few motorcycles for sale. Many cars and vans have left-hand steering wheels suited for driving on the Continent.

There is also a weekly used van market in Amsterdam; information is available from the VVV in front of Centraal Station.

There are a number of specialized dealers handling sales and rental of caravanettes. In the London area, it is easiest to find them listed in free give-away newspapers aimed at Australians and New Zealanders, such as LAM, and TNT, and Australasian Express. In Amsterdam, the VVV at the Central Station has a complete list. While there are many dealers in Germany, there isn't a centralized list of them.

Things to Know When You Buy a Used Car

1. You'll usually have to pay cash. You'll have to pay the registration fee (road tax) and Value-Added Tax, (unlike in Britain, where used cars are exempt).

2. You will have to insure and register the vehicle promptly. While simple to accomplish, you should remember you're dealing with a

foreign bureaucracy and a different shade of red tape.

3. It is harder to buy low in June and sell high in September, partly because of tourist demand, and partly because of the arrival of the new model year.

4. Most European countries require regular safety checks. The seller should produce a valid certificate before you buy the car, since it is required for registration.

Insuring a Used Car

If you buy a used car from a private party, you must get insurance on your own, since registration may not be issued until proof of coverage is provided. Insurance agencies are common throughout Europe. Organizations such as the AA and RAC in many countries can arrange for insurance. A statement of accident-free driving from your insurance company and a copy of your British driving licence can sometimes lead to a lower insurance rate.

In some countries, including Denmark and Austria, non-residents cannot obtain insurance, and therefore cannot register a car. However, you can often take a vehicle to another country, register it there, and then insure it.

Petrol

Unleaded petrol is now gaining popularity in Western Europe, but because it has recently introduced, is often difficult to find, particularly in southern Europe. It is known as "bleifrei" in German, "sans plombe" in French, "senza piomba" in Italian, and "sin plomba" in Spanish. Unleaded is most likely to be found at stations on superhighways.

In general, with a car that can use leaded gas, high performance cars will take "super", a universally known term. Cars such as Volkswagens, Fiats, and Renaults will take "regular". This may be known as "essence" in French, "benzin" in German, or a similar term.

In Eastern Europe, almost all petrol is sold at the infrequent state oil company stations. Unleaded petrol is very rare in Eastern Europe, and available only at a few stations for tourists. Usually, there's only regular and super. All cars should be filled with super (or unleaded if your vehicle requires it) in these countries.

Diesel fuel is generally available throughout Europe, though it goes under many names: "gazole" in French, "gasoil" in German, and "gazolio" in Italian.

Oil is available at garages. Sometimes it is only available in two-litre containers, and is relatively expensive.

Many service stations throughout Europe are the full-service type, especially in large city centres. Your windows will on occasion be washed, the oil checked, and water added to the radiator. The attendants pump petrol, and even smile sometimes.

Self-service stations are a bit cheaper—but not by much. They are most often found on approach roads to major towns and on some main roads.

At self-service as well as motorway service stations, instructions will usually be shown on the pump, though they all operate in much the same way. Pay at the cashier's counter, usually inside, after you finish pumping.

Garages in Eastern Europe are not as common as in Western Europe, and are found on main routes, but there may be only one in a town. There may be long queues. In some countries (East Germany, Poland, U.S.S.R.) you may have to buy petrol coupons with Western currency at the border or at the official tourist offices in the country. Having foreign number plates may get you quickly to the front of the queue (their orders, not your choice) or, alternatively, into special garages reserved only for foreigners.

Discount Petrol Coupons

Czechoslovakia

Coupons for petrol and diesel are sold by Cedok at its offices abroad and at the borders. The coupons entitle you to about a 20% discount on fuel and are accepted at all garages in Czechoslovakia.

East Germany

Coupons for oil and petrol are sold at all branches of the Reisebüro der DDR and international service stations, only for hard (not local) currency in denominations of M5, M1, and M20. West German Deutsche Marks are accepted at garages on West Berlin access routes.

Italy

Italy offers packets of discount coupons for petrol at some Italian tourist offices in Western Europe, border crossings, and some Automobile Club d'Italia offices inside Italy, to all persons not resident in Italy. The discount is approximately 20%, and the packets include coupons good for free passage on the autostrade (toll motorways). All garages in Italy accept these coupons.

Poland

Motorists can receive an approximately 40% discount on fuel if they buy coupons. They are sold for hard (Western) currency only at border crossings and all Orbis offices inside Poland. Unused coupons can be reconverted to hard currency at the border; you may receive the money in several different foreign currencies.

Romania

Fuel will only be sold to foreign-registered cars in possession of fuel coupons. You have to buy the coupons for hard (Western) currency. They are sold at border crossings, tourist offices, and service desks of hotels catering to Western travellers.

Soviet Union (U.S.S.R.)

Motorists driving foreign-registered cars in the Soviet Union should buy petrol coupons from Intourist service desks and offices. They come in 5-, 10-, and 20-litre values, and must be bought in hard (Western) currency.

Yugoslavia

Coupons usable for petrol or diesel are sold at border crossings. They entitle you to 5% more fuel than you pay for. Coupons must be paid for in hard (Western) currency or traveller's cheques. These coupons are available in various denominations. Fuel can also be bought with Yugoslav dinars.

Car Repairs

If your car needs repairs, garages are plentiful throughout Western Europe. Service is widely available for major European cars. Garages will most likely have parts for cars made in the same country: Fiat in Italy; Peugeot, Renault and Citroen in France; and BMW, Volkswagen, German Ford, and Opel (GM) in Germany. Finding parts for foreign cars will be easiest in major cities.

The Michelin red guides list all factory authorized service locations in the countries and cities they cover. The listing for each city includes the makes serviced, along with the garage name, address, and telephone number. The garages are pinpointed on the city maps found in the guide. If you don't have a Michelin red guide or are in an area for which no guide is issued, the police will know the local garages.

In the Eastern (Socialist) countries, service and parts are much more difficult to find. Garages offering repairs are few and far between. Those that exist are accustomed to working on Eastern European makes such as Skoda (Czech), Lada (Soviet), and Polski Fiat (Polish). Take parts with you if you think you'll need them. Sometimes the only alternative is to make a special quick trip West to buy parts. If you drive into the Soviet Union, you must promise to take your car out with you, even if it becomes a total wreck. Otherwise, *you* may not be permitted to leave either.

Not all garages, whether in Eastern or Western Europe, are full of expensive modern equipment that makes the garage look more like a laboratory. Don't be upset as your car is taken apart and laid out on the plaza. It will most likely run well when the parts are put back together.

When you need a puncture repaired, do not go to a garage except to ask, "Where is the nearest tyre repair shop?" Tyres are repaired at tyre repair shops and tyre stores.

Emergency Road Service

Most nations have breakdown and towing services provided by national motor clubs. Many motorways and main roads have emergency phones every kilometre or so. If you have an emergency, use the phones: a repair car or tow truck will be dispatched. In some countries, members of the AA or RAC receive breakdown service on the same terms as members of the local clubs. Service is sometimes round the clock, though it is more likely to be dawn to dusk. On motorways and certain other main roads, there may be roving patrols to provide service.

If you're on a road with no emergency phones or motor club patrols, the phone numbers and names of some motor club emergency services are given below.

You can often purchase a membership a European motor club from any office in that country.

Phone Numbers for Emergency Road Service

An asterisk (*) indicates that emergency service to AA members is on the same basis as its own members. In some countries, this is free, in others, a charge is made.

Austria*: Tel. 95-40 nationwide, but use emergency call boxes on autobahns. Free breakdown service; charge for towing. (Service provided by ÖAMTC, the Austrian Automobile and Motorcycle Club.)

Belgium: Tel. (Brussels area) (02) 736 59 59 for service by Royal Automobile Club de Belgique (numbers vary in other areas), or (02) 512 78 90 for service by Touring Secours (numbers vary in other areas).

Bulgaria: Tel. 146 in main towns and along main roads. (Service provided by SBA, Bulgarian Auto Club.)

Czechoslovakia: No general breakdown number.

Denmark*: Use emergency phone boxes on motorways, or call FDM at (01) 38 21 12 from 9 a.m.—5 p.m. (Service arranged by FDM, Federation of Danish Motorists, but service provided by contracted garages has a fixed price.)

Finland*: Tel. (90) 694 0496 (Finnish Automobile and Touring Club).

France: You must call local garages, except on some main roads and all autoroutes, which have emergency phones every kilometre.

Germany, West (BRD)*: "Strassenwacht" road service patrols on autobahns by ADAC (German Auto Club), or phone number in most areas (city code) + 19 21 1, or by Avd (Auto Club of Germany) service patrols.

Great Britain*: AA (Automobile Association) and RAC (Royal Automobile Club) road patrols on main roads. Some motorways and main roads have emergency phone boxes. Otherwise check phone book for nearest AA Service Centre.

Greece*: ELPA (Automobile and Touring Club of Greece) road patrols on motorways provide free service, or call tel. 104, 7 a.m.—10 p.m. in main cities and main roads.

Hungary: Budapest: 260-668. Service provided by MAK (Hungarian Auto Club).

Ireland*: AA road patrols on a few main roads. Otherwise check phone book for nearest AA Service Centre.

Italy*: Phone boxes every two kilometres on autostrade, or tel. 116. (Service provided by ACI, Automobile Club d'Italia.) A service fee is charged.

Luxembourg*: Road patrol service 24 hours a day. (Service provided by ACL, the Luxembourg auto club.)

Netherlands*: Road patrols on motorways and main roads. Emergency phones along motorways also summon help. If you are not a motor club member, the charge is 65 Guilders. (Service provided by ANWB, the Dutch auto club.) No motor club service in most cities; private garages charge for service.

Norway*: Road patrols on main roads 10 a.m.—8 p.m. provide free assistance from June to August; at other times it must be paid for. Call (02) 42 94 00 for help 24 hours a day for a contract service, with fixed prices. (Services provided by NAF, the Norwegian Automobile Federation.)

Poland: Call local offices of PZM (Polski Zwiazek Motorway), the Polish Auto Club; Warsaw telephone 29 62 52.

Romania: Call local offices of the ACR (Automobil Clubul Roman) for emergency service. The numbers are on road signs as you cross regional boundaries; record them if you think you'll need them, since there are no phone books.

Switzerland: Telephone 140 or use emergency telephones on motorways to summon help. A reasonable charge is made for each service call.

Yugoslavia: Tel. 987 8 a.m.—8 p.m. (Service provided by AMSJ, the Yugoslav Auto Club.)

Where is that Car From?

European number plates come in many sizes, colours, and shapes. Most plates are rectangular or square, though some temporary West German plates are oval. The name of the country on number plates is found only on those from Monaco and Andorra, and on personal cars of United States and Canadian military personnel. Separate white ovals with letters designating the country of registration are found on the backs of cars. Letter codes are listed below.

Exceptions: military vehicles almost never have number plates: rather the number is painted on near the number plate space. Small national flags may be painted on too, near the numbers. In some countries, tractors and farm machinery are unlicensed—but rarely cross national boundaries.

Country codes for the ovals you're likely to see are listed in the following Key:

Code	Country	Country in foreign language
A	Austria	Österreich
AL	Albania	Shqiperia
AND	Andorra	Andorra
B	Belgium	Belgique (French), België (Flemish)
BG	Bulgaria	(Cyrillic)
CDN	Canada	Canada
CH	Switzerland	Suisse (French), Schweiz (German), Svizzera (Italian). CH stands for Confoederatio Helvetica (Latin)
CS	Czechoslovakia	Ceskolovenskò
CY	Cyprus	Κνπροσ (Greek)
DDR	Germany, East	Deutsche Demokratische Republik
D	Germany, West	Bundesrepublik Deutschland
DK	Denmark	Danmark
DZ	Algeria	(arabic or Algerie)
E	Spain	España
F	France	France
FL	Liechtenstein	Furstentum Liechtenstein
GR	Greece	ΕΛΛΑΣ (Greek)
H	Hungary	Magyarorszag
I	Italy	Italia
IL	Israel	Israel
IRL	Ireland	Éire
L	Luxembourg	Luxembourg
M	Malta	Malta
MA	Morocco	Maroc (French)

MC	Monaco	Monaco
N	Norway	Norge
NL	Netherlands	Nederland
P	Portugal	Portugal
PL	Poland	Polska
R	Romania	Romana
RL	Lebanon	Liban (French)
RSM	San Marino	Repubblica di San Marino
S	Sweden	Sverige
SF	Finland	Suomi/Finland
SU	Soviet Union, U.S.S.R.	CCCP
TN	Tunisia	Tunisie (French)
TR	Turkey	Türkiye
USA	United States	
V	Vatican City	Cittá Vaticano
YU	Yugoslavia	Jugoslavija

In addition, you may also see other ovals, including:

CD	Diplomatic Corps
C	Consular Corps

Letters and Packages

When you're away from home, letters are a pleasure to receive.

You may also bring joy to people by sending letters and postcards, and maybe keep in contact with your business.

Sometimes you'll need or want to send or receive packages.

This chapter gives details on how.

Dealing with post offices and express offices is something most travellers do: it can be an adventure in many places. Sometimes, especially in southern Europe, you can bypass the post office to buy stamps. For packages, however, the post office or express office often can't be avoided.

Sending Mail to Europe

There are several ways to receive post: each one has plusses and minuses. All require a bit of planning on your part so that you and your post eventually meet. A few instructions apply to your correspondents regardless of whether they write to a post office, American Express office, hotel, or in care of a business or personal acquaintance.

How to Address Letters Sent to Europe

Proper addressing will increase the chances that your post—all of it—will reach you.

1. All letters addressed to you should have your last name written in capital letters and preferably underlined. Mail is held for pickup in alphabetical order and, if your last name isn't clear, it may be filed under your first name, or even filed under Mr., Mrs., or Ms. (If you expect some mail and don't receive it, you probably should ask the clerk to check under your first name also.) Typed addresses are preferable, since each nation's handwriting characteristics vary widely. If not typed, addresses should be printed.

2. Addresses should be in the local country's style whenever possible, using its order for addresses. For example, many countries put house numbers after the name of the street, and others put the postal code before the name of the city. In the Soviet Union, the country comes first, then the region, then city, then the street address, and at the bottom, the individual's name. When sending mail to Bulgaria, Greece, the Soviet Union, or parts of Yugoslavia that use other alphabets, you can neatly address it only in Latin letters and it will still be translated and delivered.

3. Post is usually held 30 days from its receipt. If you're not sure you'll be able to claim it in time, it may be held longer if the envelope requests that the mail be held until a specific date before it's returned as unclaimed.

The request is likelier to be honoured if written in the local language. Often, the months are written in Roman numerals. For example, if writing to France and you want the mail held until July 18, 1990, write on the envelope, "SVP Tenir jusqu' à 18 VII 1990". Even better is to write out the name of the month rather than using figures, but in this case the month should be written in French "18 juillet 1990".

4. When sending post inside Western Europe, you can put either the country name on the address or use the one, two, or three letter country designation in front of the post code or city. The designations are the same ones used on cars: see the last pages of Cars and Driving in this book for all the codes. For example, Switzerland's letters are CH: a letter would be properly addressed and correctly delivered from anywhere in Western Europe when addressed:

Roger SMITH
Post Restante
CH-6900 Lugano

Sending to Post Offices

Post sent to post offices can be held for pickup if you have no local address. This service, equivalent to general delivery, is called "Poste Restante" in most of Europe: every post office employee will know this French term even if the local language has another word, such as "Postlagernd" in German, "Fermo Posta" in Italian, and "Lista de Correos" in Spanish.

When writing to Poste Restante, in large cities include the address of post office at which you'll be picking it up. (Large cities may have dozens.) If not sure, post should be sent to the main post office. You can ask at the tourist information office for the location of the main post office.

For example, letters sent to the main post office in Paris, should be addressed:

Susan JONES
Poste Restante
Hôtel des Postes
52 Rue de Louvre
F-75001 Paris
France

It is usually easier to receive Poste Restante post in small towns and villages than in large cities, because there are fewer people calling for post (which reduces the chance of missing a letter that's waiting for you), and also because small town post offices are usually much less crowded.

Since small towns and villages usually only have one post office, letters can simply be addressed:

Roger SMITH
Poste Restante
D-8113 Kochel am See
West Germany

Sending to American Express

American Express offices are located in most major cities of Europe and will hold letters for pickup. Look for their addresses in an American Express pamphlet available at all their travel agency offices or from banks selling American Express travelers cheques. Send mail in care of "Client Mail Service".
Post is held 30 days, unless a specific "hold until" date is placed on outside of the envelope. If you use all numbers for dates, remember to put the day before the month.

Sending to Hotels

You can have letters sent to hotels you plan to stay at. Correspondents should note the estimated date of arrival on the outside of the letter, and address care of the hotel. For example:

Susan JONES
SVP Tenir jusqu' (please hold until) 15 octobre 1989
c/o Hôtel Truffe Noir
22 boulevard Anatole France
F-19100 Brive-la-Gaillarde
France

The easiest way to send letters to East Germany or the Soviet Union is to send them to hotels, since there are only a few hotels open to Western travellers, and they are usually listed in the planned itinerary.

Sending to Businesses or Private Residences

Just write to the individual, care of the business or person whose address you're using, just as if it were a hotel.

Sending Small Packages to Europe

Small packages can be sent to Europe either by air or by surface (parcel post).

Sending by Express Mail or Private Air Express Services

Sending letters and small packages by Swiftaire or air express delivery services (such as DHL, Federal Express, Securicor, and TNT Overnite) is easy though relatively costly. Delivery to major cities in Western Europe is usually within two days, though some services can offer overnight delivery to Paris, Frankfurt, and Milan from a few major metropolitan areas such as London, Birmingham, and Manchester.

Delivery (where available) takes two to four business days to smaller cities, and to those cities in Eastern Europe that are served. (Note: Eastern Europe isn't served by all, but most Eastern European capitals are served by Airborne Express, DHL, and TNT.)

Most express companies serving Europe will provide a service guide upon request, listing their office addresses and rates (which are sometimes called tariffs).

In Eastern Europe, countries, many deliveries are made by airline companies under contract.

Private air express companies cannot deliver to post offices (including Poste Restante), but can usually have items held at their offices or delivered to any street addresses.

You must use a special international air waybill for international shipments. Ask for the proper form.

Packages require a customs declaration, which will be furnished by the post office or the shipping company.

Airline Air Freight

Most airlines will accept unaccompanied baggage or packages as air freight, and hold it for pickup at the airport terminal in Europe. Call the airlines you're considering for detailed information. The minimum charge, which varies by airline, is based on weight, and destination.

Parcel Post

Every post office in Britain can accept parcels for shipment to Europe.

Surface mail may take one week to three weeks to Western Europe, and up to two months to Eastern Europe.

Be sure the packaging is secure, especially for shipments to southern Europe, where post offices can be chaotic behind the counter as well as in front of it.

Receiving Post in Europe

You can pick up post at many places: post offices, American Express offices, and hotels.

Identification Required for Pickup

You must prove your identity to receive letters at any place except a private home or business address.

If you're a British citizen, a passport is the acceptable proof.

If a citizen of any other European country, a national identity card is acceptable.

Other identification (often including driving licences and credit cards) will not be as readily accepted, and many types may not be accepted at all.

Post Offices

Post offices are usually open from Monday to Friday and often on Saturday mornings.

Some post offices in large city centres, main railway stations, and airports have extended hours. In the largest cities such as Paris, Munich, and Vienna, they are open on Sundays; a few are open 24 hours a day year round.

Go to the Poste Restante counter or window, present your passport or identity card, and receive your post.

Delivery Service Charge

Some countries, including France and Italy, charge for the pick up service of mail at Poste Restante windows. The fee is equal to the rate for a first-class letter, regardless of the weight of the letter or whether it has been sent by air or surface mail.

American Express Offices

Postal service at American Express offices is free and to be used by American Express customers. A customer is a holder of an American Express Card or at least one American Express traveller's cheque.

If you're not an American Express customer, some offices will refuse to search and others will charge a stiff fee for looking and giving you any letters they have. (You can always buy some American Express cheques at banks or American Express offices and instantly become a customer.)

American Express offices are usually conveniently located in large city centres in Western Europe, but are not found in some Communist countries. Local telephone books always list their addresses under American Express in the telephone book alphabetical pages. You cannot, however, call to find out if you have letters there—you have to go in person.

Post is usually held for a maximum of 30 days, but if the envelope requests holding it a bit longer, it will usually be held.

Some large city American Express offices (mainly in southern Europe but also sometimes including Paris) can be overcrowded and frustrating places to retrieve post. Others (often in northern Europe) are uncrowded and offer comfortable lounges to read the letters you've just received.

Hotels

To ask for post, go up to the reception desk and ask. If you have a confirmed reservation at a good to luxury hotel, post will often be automatically put in your box.

Hotels are usually accommodating about holding post for longer periods than either post offices or American Express offices.

Receiving Packages

Parcel post or Swiftaire packages can be received at most locations, including Poste Restante windows at post offices.

Air express packages must be held at the express company or airline offices for pick up or delivered to a street address (including hotels).

Sending Mail to Britain

Sending mail home can be either easy or complicated, depending on the country you're in and the type of item you're sending. Packages are usually more difficult to send than letters and post cards.

Postcards and Letters

Postcards and letters are handled in the same way, though the costs may be different.

In most EC countries, mailing a single-sheet letter or postcards to Britain costs the same as within the country. (Check to be sure.) Airmail usually costs more, but is faster.

Postal Services Key *(Continues across)*

English

Air Mail
Letters
Stamps
Packages
General Delivery

French

Par Avion
Lettres
Timbres
Colis/Emballages
Poste restante

Where to Send Mail From

Post Offices

Post offices are found in every city, town, and village in every country of Europe. Rate information is available from counter staff, or occasionally from information provided on posters or reference guides in post office lobbies. A few countries' post offices, including France, and West Germany, have free brochures available that give the rates.

Waiting in queues in Scandinavia, Switzerland, and West Germany is like waiting in Britain. In France, queues form along the counter, to the right side of the window. One queue can cross right through another without losing its identity. In Italy, people just crowd up at each open window. Don't be bashful, and eventually you'll get to the front of the mob.

Most post offices have specialized counters for bill paying and postal savings banks: don't go to them for stamps.

Buying Stamps, Not at Post Offices

A number of other places to buy stamps can be found in many countries, particularly in southern Europe. If you buy stamps at places other than post offices, be sure you already know the postage rates, because most vendors may not know all the rates to Britain.

Other than post offices, tobacco shops are the best places to buy postage stamps. Where tobacco sales are carefully regulated or a state

Postal Services Key *(Continued)*

German	*Italian*
Luftpost	Per via aerea
Brief	Lettere
Briefmarken	Francobolli
Paketen	Pacchi
Postlagernd	Fermo Posta

---

monopoly, such as Spain, Austria, and France, you're likely to be able to buy stamps at cost at tobacco shops.

Most hotels will have stamps to sell or send letters at cost, if you're a hotel guest.

Occasionally souvenir and post card vendors will have stamps, but there is occasionally a mark-up.

Post Boxes

Post boxes are always found near post offices, but post wall slots are often only outside the building. Boxes are also found in main streets and village centres. They come in all sizes and colors, but many countries' boxes have a post horn on them.

In very large city centres, boxes may be scarce, except in front of the post offices or in office building lobbies.

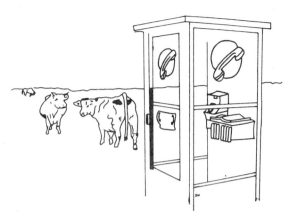

Using European Telephones

We take the telephone for granted, always there when we need it. But each European country's telephone system has its unique variations. Unfamiliarity with the system can cause phone frustration.

Obviously, British coins won't work in European coin phones. Less obviously, in some countries local coins won't work either. You may need to buy a special token or phone card. Operators may be difficult to reach, and calls to them may not be free. In some countries, operators can speak English, in others many cannot.

The telephone service in almost every European country is government-run rather than privately owned. Since most countries have organized the phone service as part of the postal system, post offices are usually excellent places to find phones, particularly for making long-distance and international calls. In major cities, some offices are open for extended hours: a few (such as 52 rue du Louvre in Paris) are open 24 hours.

Some countries, such as Italy, Greece, and Spain, have national phone companies separate from the post office (as in Britain). In those countries, look for the telephone calling offices (see Telephone Keys for names). Many post offices in those countries don't have coin phones.

Most countries in Europe charge telephone calls by units or "pulses", even for local calls. Each pulse gives you a certain amount of time, depending on distance and often the time of day. A pulse on a long-distance call may last only a few seconds, particularly on an international call. The pulse system is used with both pay phones and non-coin phones, for local, long-distance, and international calls placed without the help of an operator.

When your time is almost up at a pay phone, you will usually be warned in some way to put in more money or be cut off.

Local Calls

The minimum rates are shown in the Telephone Key for each country. The rates for local calls from pay phones are often different and a bit higher than from non-coin phones. Note that every year, one or two countries raise the price of a local phone call.

Long-Distance and International Calls

Long-distance calls can be made from telephone offices (whether at the post office or elsewhere), coin and card phones in many but not all countries, and hotels, as well as private homes and businesses. In addition to the phone number you want to reach, you'll need the access code (which gets you into the long-distance or international network). In some countries, after dialling the access code, you must wait for a second dial tone before continuing to dial the country and city or area code. In Sweden, the second dial tone comes after you dial the country code.

The access code for each country and dialling instructions are included in each Telephone Key. Each Key also includes the complete code for dialling Britain.

Where to Call From

Telephone Offices

The usual procedure is to tell the clerk in the office where you want to call. You will be directed into a booth, and in most countries you will actually direct dial the call. As soon as your connection is completed, a meter at the cashier's desk begins counting pulses, much like a remote-controlled self-service petrol pump. At the end of your call you pay the cashier or clerk.

In a few countries, calls must be placed through an operator. In this case, you tell the clerk the country and number you want to call. In other respects the procedure is similar. There will usually be a three-minute minimum charge if an operator dials the number.

Pay Phones

Direct-dial long-distance and international calls can be made from pay phones in many countries. Calls made from phone booths and telephone offices offer the lowest available rates.

In many countries, some pay phones accept only telephone cards. These are for sale at post offices and telephone offices, and often at some tobacco shops or newsstands. Most countries' cards come in various denominations, each one providing a certain number of pulses. In general, you insert the card into the slot on the telephone and then make calls until the pulses on the cards run out.

Cards can only be used in one country's telephones, and you cannot receive pro-rata refunds on partially-used cards.

In a few phones in London, you can use most credit cards in special telephones for calls.

Private Homes

All kinds of calls can be made from private home telephones. In most countries you can direct dial from telephones in private homes, including countries in Eastern Europe, even those where you cannot make long-distance calls from pay telephones.

Offer to pay for the calls when you make them: many people have pulse counters right by the telephone, or you can ask them to have the operator call back with the charges.

Hotels: Watch Out!

European hotels have long considered the telephone a prime profit-producing instrument. Most hotels own their own internal systems and run them as a major profit centre. The method is simple and unsubtle: the hotel adds a surcharge, whether local, long distance, or international, on calls made from all its phones. Surcharges can be "modest" (up to 40%) but can also be 300% more than the normal cost of the call. This practice isn't limited to luxury palaces or run-down pensions, or to particular countries.

Some establishments have agreed to limit their surcharges; in any case, the first rule is to check *before* using any hotel phone to avoid unpleasant and expensive surprises. In some hotels, there are cards near the telephone listing the amount of surcharge. In most, however, there is none—and the hotel operator may not be willing to tell you in advance the amount or percentage of the surcharge.

Look for dialling instructions near the phone in the room or ask the hotel operator to place your call. In some large hotels, you need to dial the numeral "8" or "0" to get an outside line. This starts the time-and-charges counter.

Some hotels even make a charge for reverse-charge or telephone calling card calls. If you must talk from a hotel house phone, either in the lobby or in your room, arrange to be called, or keep the call short and ask to be called back immediately.

If there is a country-wide limit to telephone surcharges, it is shown in the "Hotel Surcharges" section of each Telephone Key. Only Ireland and Portugal currently have a nation-wide maximum surcharge.

Businesses and Government Offices

Many large organizations, including large businesses and government offices, have internal telephone systems. Often, these systems require you to dial an access number, usually "0" (zero), or sometimes "8" or "9", in order to use an outside telephone line. Then wait for another dial tone and dial the number you want to call.

Dialling Your Call

Local Numbers

Local phone numbers in a single city can have from two to seven digits. Phone numbers in Italian cities, for example, can have from four to seven digits. All can be dialled from any phone.

Long Distance: City or Area Codes

Area codes or city codes, which have from one to six numerals, begin with the numeral "0" in many countries. You must dial the "0" when making long-distance calls within a country. In most countries using this system, the "0" is written on all phone numbers on letters, cards, and brochures. In a few countries, such as Finland and Spain, the prefix is a "9" instead of "0".

When calling from another country, do not dial the "0". For example, when making a call to London from elsewhere in Britain, dial 01-XXX XXXX. When calling the same number from another country, dial the access code (which varies), then the country code (44), then the city code (1), and the number (XXX XXXX). Exceptions are Finland and the Soviet Union, where the "0" is a necessary part of some city codes, whether called from inside or outside of the country. If calling Spain or Finland, do not dial the initial "9."

Telephones

Toll-Free Calls Inside a Country

A number of European countries have set up toll-free numbers similar to the (0800) numbers in Britain. Generally, you just dial as any long-distance call. These have various names, such as "Appel Vert" in France. Where such systems exist, they are listed in each country's Telephone Key.

Answering Machines

If a phone customer has an answering machine, in many countries, that person's number in the telephone directory will be noted with a reversed Q symbol (Ø) or in Spain, with an asterisk (*). You will be charged for the call when answered.

Telephone Calling Cards

You can use your telephone calling card (sometimes called a credit card) in all European nations except West Germany and Portugal. Request one from the telephone company. The call is billed to your account at the higher operator-assisted rate rather than the direct-dial rate, with a three-minute minimum charge.

You can only use your telephone calling card to make calls to Britain. You generally cannot, for example, use it to make a call from France to Germany if you live in the Britain.

You can make calling card calls from virtually any pay phone—even most of those from which you usually can make only local calls. In many countries, especially in Eastern Europe, you can use your calling card only through an international operator. Local operators won't even know what a telephone calling card is.

Call Home "Direct"

In a number of Western European countries, you can make a special local or free call, which connects you with an international operator in Britain (or, with the correct code the United

States or Canada). You will be billed to your own calling card or to your telephone number at the operator-assisted rate (higher than the direct-dial rate but lower than a collect call through the foreign operator).

The telephone numbers to call for this service are listed in the "Special Information" section of each country's Telephone Key.

Calls made on these "Direct" program usually will be billed on your regular telephone statement.

"U.K. Direct"

British Telecom introduced this program. Calls can only be made to the U.K. (Not available in the United States or Canada.) There will be an increasing number of countries operating this service as time passes. For information, contact the nearest British Telecom office.

"U.S.A. Direct"

AT&T was the first company to offer this type of service to call home. Calls can only be made to the United States, except not to Alaska or Hawaii. For information, call (800) 874-4000. (Not available in Canada.)

"MCI Call USA"

MCI introduced this service in late 1988. Calls can be made to any number in the United States. (Not available in Canada.) For information, contact:
MCI Communications Corporation
1133 - 19th St. N.W.
Washington, D.C. 20036

or your nearest MCI office (various (800) numbers throughout the United States).

"Canada Direct"

Telecom Canada, a consortium of Canadian telephone companies, introduced this program in late 1988; further expansion is planned in the

near future. Calls can only be made to Canada. (Not available in the United States.) For information, contact:
Canada Direct
Telecom Canada
410 Laurier Ave. West
Box 2410, Station 'D'
Room 950
Ottawa, Ontario K1P 6H5
Tel. (800) 561-8868

Calling Europe

If you call Europe, you can in most areas direct dial from your phone at home or office. To do so, dial the access code (010) + country code (see top right of the each country's Telephone Key) + the area or city code + the subscriber's local number.

If you don't live in an area where direct dialled international calls are possible, call the operator, who will put your call through.

International Directory Assistance

Don't know the telephone number of a hotel, a friend, or the opera house box office? International directory assistance can get it for you at no charge, regardless of where you are. (This no-cost feature is guaranteed by international agreement and is not subject to change.) Dial the international operator (the number is in your code book, usually 155), and give the operator your request. Your operator will be connected with an English-speaking operator in the country you're requesting information from; sometimes you can listen in.

Telephone Tones

When you pick up a telephone receiver, you will hear a variety of sounds that may differ greatly from those you're familiar with at home. Standardization of dial tones in Western Europe by the year 2000 is planned, but progress is glacially slow.

The tones found in each country are shown schematically and described in the country Telephone Keys. The diagrams show the type of signal, its sound (with passing time shown in seconds), and a description of the tones. In some countries there may be more than one tone representing the same result.

In your travels you may find some variations that aren't listed in the charts, as the result of differences in equipment and varying national or local standards.

On international calls, any sounds you hear after you dial the country code (such as ringing, busy, or out of order) will be those of the country you're calling, not the country you're calling from.

Using Computers and Modems European Telephone Systems

Most Western European countries' telephone systems are of adequate quality for data transmission. However, wiring connections to telephone lines vary from country to country. Generally, they are being made compatible with CCITT data transmission standards. However, you'll either need to rewire your modem, use a modem made for that country, or use an acoustic modem, or (carefully) take apart the telephone mouthpiece.

In Eastern Europe, clarity of transmission is not always adequate for data transmission. In addition, modems are virtually unknown. Since these areas are changing rapidly, check with local computer users or (with less hope of success) the data transmission bureau of the telephone system of the country you're in.

In some countries such as France (almost always), when using public (coin or card) telephones, the end of each pulse is noted with an audible tone that make it almost impossible to transmit files by modem. This doesn't seem to occur when calls are made from provate or business non-coin or card phones.

Fax Machines

Fax use is increasing rapidly in Europe. Many businesses have dedicated fax lines. In addition, travelers can find public fax machines in some telephone offices, main post offices, airports, and occasionally other locations. Most fax machines are CCITT Group III compatible, so that transmissions can easily be made.

Telephone Keys

The next pages are country-by-country Keys to using the telephone in each country. They include not only how much money to put in a phone for a local call, they also tell you in what order and also about special tricks you need to know in order to cope successfully with a particular system.

Austria
Country code: 43. Telephone: TELEFON.

Pay Phones are found at post offices, train and underground stations, street booths, and on some special trains. Card phones are found in similar locations (about 3,000 card phones throughout the country).

Phone Directories contain White and Yellow Pages, often in separate volumes. There is no English summary for either local or long-distance calling. Find directories at post offices, phone booths, and hotels.

Using Pay Phones: Use 1 Austrian schilling coin per 2 minutes (3 minutes 6 p.m.-8 a.m.) for local calls. Other coins accepted are 5, 10 schilling.

How to make a call:
1. Pick up receiver, wait for dial tone.
2. Put in money.
3. Dial number.
4. On some phones, push the button on the phone (Zahlknopf) when called party answers.
5. Put in more money when you hear buzz signal or you'll be cut off.

Using Telephone Card Phones: Buy telephone cards "Telefon-Wertkarte" (50 pulses, 48 schillings, 100 pulses, 95 schillings) at post offices and Tabak Austria shops.

How to make a call:
1. Pick up receiver.
2. Put card in slot at bottom; see how many units remain on digital display.
3. Wait for dial tone.
4. Dial number.
5. After call, card is disengaged from phone; don't forget to take it with you!

Operator calls cost 1 schilling; most international operators speak English, local ones may not.

Local information and local directory assistance dial 16.

Long distance information and long-distance directory assistance dial 16. (No operator-assisted calls are made.)

International operator dial 08.

Emergency calls are usually free (no coin required). Police dial 133; Fire dial 122; Ambulance dial 144.

Long-Distance Calls inside Austria, made from post offices and pay phones that take 5- and 10-schilling coins. Dial 0 + city code + subscriber number. (If the city code you have starts with 0, don't dial another zero.)

International Calls from Austria, made from post offices and private phones, and all card phones, and pay phones that take 5- and 10-schilling coins. Dial: for Italy 040 + city code + subscriber number.

For most of the rest of Europe dial 00 + country code + city or area code + subscriber number.

For rest of world: 900 + country code + city or area code + subscriber number.

To call Britain: 900 + 44 + area code + number. In some provincial areas dial 00 + 44 + area code + number.

"Dial Direct" access codes: AT&T "USA Direct" dial 022 903 011.

Hotel Surcharges: No maximum percentage.
Things You Should Know: There is no reduced-rate international calling time. Telephone credit cards are accepted, but not for calls made from coin phones.

Telephone Sounds You May Hear:

Kind	Seconds 0 1 2 3 4 5 6 7 8 9 10	Description
Dial tone	▮ ▮ ▮ ▮ ▮	Short tone and interval, then long tone and interval.
Ringing	▬ ▬	1 sec. ring and 5 sec. intervals.
or	▬ ▬ ▬	1 sec. ring and 3 sec. intervals.
Add money		Watch indicator on phone; add when flashing.
or	▬	Buzz 10 sec. before time is up.
Busy	▮▮▮▮▮▮▮▮▮▮▮▮▮▮▮▮▮▮▮▮▮▮	¼ sec. tone and ¼ sec. interval.
or	▬ ▬ ▬ ▬ ▬	1 sec. tone and 1 second interval.
Out of order	♪ ♪ ♪ ♪ ♪	3 rising tones in 1 sec. and 1 second interval.
or		Recording.

Belgium

Country Code: 32. Telephone: French area: TÉLÉPHONE. Flemish area: TELEFOON.

Pay Phones are found at post offices, transport stations, airports, and on street. Two types of coin phones: Belgium only and international, and telephone card phones.

Phone Directories contain White and Yellow Pages. Yellow pages have an English index of classifications but no summary about making either local or international calls. There is also a Fax directory at RTT offices. Find directories at post offices, hotels, shops, and most phone booths.

Using Pay Phones: Use two 5F coins per 2 minutes 40 sec. 8 a.m.-6 p.m. (5 min. 20 seconds nights and weekends) for local calls. Other coins accepted are 5F and 20F in international coin phones.

How to make a call:
1. Pick up receiver.
2. Deposit coin and wait for dial tone.
3. Dial number
4. Coin will be returned if number is busy or not answered.

Using Telephone Card Phones: Buy "Telecards" (20 Units 200F, 105 Units 1000F) at post offices and telephone calling offices (found in transport centres).

How to make a call:
1. Pick up receiver.
2. Insert card into slot near bottom of phone.
3. When you see number of units left in digital display (may be faint), dial number.
4. Card will be disengaged when you hang up.
5. If you run out of units and have another card, remove old card and insert another card as it uses the last unit.

Operator calls cost 10 F; most local and all international operators speak English, especially at the Flemish-language numbers.

Local information and directory assistance dial 1207 (Flemish); 1307 (French).

Local operator for assistance dial 1280 (Flemish); 1380 (French).

Long-distance information in Belgium dial 1208 (Flemish); 1308 (French).
Long-distance operator for assistance dial 1229 (Flemish); 1329 (French).
International information in Europe, North Africa, and Greenland dial 1204 (Flemish); 1304 (French).
For international telephone country and city codes dial 1224 (Flemish); 1324 (French).
International operator to make calls in Europe, North Africa, and Greenland dial 1224 (Flemish); 1324 (French).
For international information outside Europe, North Africa, and Greenland dial 1222 (Flemish); 1322 (French).
International operator to place calls outside Europe dial 1222 (Flemish); 1322 (French).
Emergency calls are free. Police dial 101; Fire dial 100; Ambulance dial 100.
Tourist information dial 513 30 30 (Brussels tourist office).
Long Distance Calls inside Belgium, made from post offices and all coin phones. Dial 0 + area code + subscriber number.
International Calls from Belgium, made from post offices and phone booths with European flags, and telephones accepting 20F coins, and all telephone card phones. Dial 00 + wait for second dial tone (in some but not all exchanges) + country code + city or area code + subscriber number.
To call Britain: dial 00 + second dial tone + 44 + area code + number.
"Dial Direct" access codes: AT&T USA Direct dial 110010; MCI Call USA dial 110012.
Hotel surcharges: No maximum percentage.

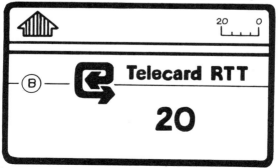

Belgium   *Telephones*   189

Things You Should Know: 1. Reduced-rate direct-dialled international calls can be made between 10 p.m. and 10 a.m. and all day Sunday.
2. Information numbers are Flemish (start with 12) and French (start with 13). Flemish operators are likelier to speak English.
3. Some Telecards are have pictures below the band.
4. Long-distance free calls (like "0800" or local-rate "0900" numbers are called "Numéros Verts/ Groene Nummers". Free calls start with "11", local-rate calls start with "15". These numbers are listed in the phone book just before the alphabetical listings.

Telephone sounds you may hear:

Kind	Seconds 0 1 2 3 4 5 6 7 8 9 10	Description
Dial tone	▄▄▄▄▄▄▄▄▄▄▄	Steady tone.
Ringing	▄ ▄ ▄	1 sec. tone and 3 sec. interval.
Line busy	▪▪▪▪▪▪▪▪▪▪	½ sec. tone and ½ sec. interval.
System overload	‖‖‖‖‖‖‖‖‖‖‖‖‖‖‖‖‖	3 tones and 3 intervals per sec.
Second dial tone	♪♪♪♪♪♪♪♪♪♪	3 short rising tones in 1 sec.
Out of order	♪ ♪ ♪ ♪ ♪	3 short rising tones in 1 sec. and 1 sec. interval.
or		Operator.

Bulgaria
Country Code: 359. Telephone: ТЕЛЕФОН

Pay Phones are found at post offices, restaurants, hotels, phone booths on the street.

Phone Directories have "private" and "public" pages. There is no English summary or instructions. Find directories at some post offices and some hotels.

Using Pay Phones: Use 5-stotinki coin or token (costs 5 stotinki) for untimed local calls. Some special long-distance phones accept 5, and 50 stotinki coins.

How to make a call:
1. Place coin in slot at top of phone.
2. Wait for dial tone.
3. Dial number.
4. On some pay phones you must push a button to be heard.

Operator calls cost 5 stotinki or 1 token; some international operators speak English, local ones almost never do.

Local information dial 145.

Local directory assistance dial 144.

Long distance information and international operator dial 0123.

Emergency calls cost 5 stotinki. Police dial 166; Fire dial 160; Ambulance dial 150.

Tourist Information from BalkanTourist offices—various numbers in different cities (Sofia: 84-131).

Long-Distance Calls inside Bulgaria, made from post offices, hotels, long-distance pay phones (50 stotinki per 2 minutes). Dial city code + subscriber number.

International Calls from Bulgaria, made from post offices, hotels (but not from coin phones). International direct dialling from coin phones is not possible.

To call foreign countries dial Operator at 0123.

Hotel surcharge: maximum surcharge unknown.

Things You Should Know: 1. International calls take up to one hour to be connected.
2. Sometimes lines are crossed during a conversation.

Bulgaria Telephones

3. Main Post Office telephone office (4 Gurko St., Sofia 1000) is open 24 hours a day, includes calling booth for direct-dial international calls to Western Europe and the rest of the world.

Telephone sounds you may hear:

Kind	Seconds	Description
	0 1 2 3 4 5 6 7 8 9 10	
Dial tone	▮■ ▮■ ▮■ ▮■ ▮■	Short tone and interval, then long tone and interval.
Ringing	■	1 second tone and 9 second interval.
Busy	■ ■ ■ ■ ■ ■ ■ ■ ■ ■	½ second tone and ½ second interval.
Out of order		Busy signal or silence.

Czechoslovakia
Country Code: 42. Telephone: TELEFON.

Pay Phones are found on the street (orange or green booths), in hotels and restaurants, and at post offices.

Phone Directories contain White Pages. There is sometimes a short English summary, including international instructions. Find directories at all post offices, most hotels and some phone booths.

Using Pay Phones: Use 1 koruna (Kcs) per untimed local call. No other coins are accepted, except at new long-distance and international booths accepting 1-, 2-, and 5-Kcs coins.

How to make a call:
1. Wait for dial tone.
2. Dial number.
3. When answered, insert coin.
4. Do not put in money until you hear the right person.
5. If you already put coin in, it is returned if you hang up with no answer.

Operator calls cost 1 koruna; few operators speak English.

Local information and local directory assistance dial 120.

International directory assistance dial 0149.

International operator dial 102 or 108.

Emergency calls cost 1 koruna (free from some phones). Police dial 158; Fire dial 150; Ambulance dial 155.

Long-Distance Calls inside Czechoslovakia, made from pay phones, post offices, and hotels. Dial 0 + city code + subscriber number.

International Calls from Czechoslovakia, made from post offices, hotels, private phones, and pay phones accepting 2 and 5 Kcs coins. Dial 00 + country code + area or city code + subscriber number.

To call Britain: dial 00 + 44 + area code + number.

Hotel surcharge: No maximum.

Things You Should Know: Telephone credit card calls can be made only from post offices.

Some old pay phones have no coin return.

Czechoslovakia Telephones

Telephone sounds you may hear:

Kind	Seconds 0 1 2 3 4 5 6 7 8 9 10	Description
Dial tone	▮▮ ▮▮ ▮▮ ▮▮ ▮▮	Short tone and short interval; then long tone and long interval.
Ringing	▮▮ ▮▮	1 second tone and 4 second interval.
Busy	▮▮▮▮▮▮▮▮▮▮▮▮▮▮▮▮	5 tones and 5 intervals per 3 seconds.
Out of order		No sound.

Denmark
Country Code 45. Telephone: TELEFON.

Pay Phones are found at telephone offices, post offices, transport stations, airports, cafes, a few booths in the street.

Phone Directories contain White alphabetical and Classified pages, often in separate volumes. There is an English summary, including international calling information. Find directories in telephone offices, phone booths, hotels, and shops.

Using Pay Phones: Use 2—25 øre coins per 3 minutes local call (per 6 minutes 10 p.m. to 8 a.m.). Other coins accepted are 1 krone, 5 kroner, 10 kroner.

How to make a call:
1. Put in money.
2. Dial number.
3. If no answer, try another call (there is no coin return).
4. Add money when you hear rising tones.

Operator calls cost 50 øre (2 x 25 øre); most operators speak English.

Information dial 0030, local directory assistance dial 0034.

Long-distance operator and directory assistance dial 0038.

International operator dial 0039.

Emergency calls are free and no coin is needed. Police, Fire, and Ambulance dial 000.

Long-Distance Calls inside Denmark, made from telephone offices, all coin phones. Dial 0 + two digit area code + subscriber number.

International Calls from Denmark, made from telephone offices, all pay phones (from pay phones you'll need a lot of coins). Dial 009 + country code + city or area code + subscriber number.

To call Britain: dial 009 + 44 + area code + number.

"Dial Direct" access codes: AT&T USA Direct dial 043-0010; Canada Direct (begins June 1989, code not available at press time); MCI Call USA dial 0430-0022.

Hotel Surcharges: No maximum percentage.

Denmark   *Telephones*   195

Things You Should Know: 1. Pay phones have no coin return—if no answer, try calling another number. Otherwise, you'll lose your money.
2. Some phones have a squeeze button on receiver: if you don't squeeze during the conversation, the other party can't hear you.
3. These letters are at the end of the Danish alphabet: å/aa, ä, æ, ö/ø, and ü.

Telephone sounds you may hear:

Kind	Seconds (0-10)	Description
Dial tone	▬▬▬▬▬▬▬▬▬▬	Steady hum.
Ringing	▬ ▬	1 sec. ring and 7 sec. interval.
Add more money	♪ ♪ ♪ ♪ ♪	3 rising tones in 1 second and 1 sec. interval.
Busy	‖‖‖‖‖‖‖‖‖‖‖‖‖	Rapid buzz and interval (3 per 2 seconds).
Out of order	♪ ♪ ♪ ♪ ♪	3 rising tones in 1 second and 1 sec. interval.
or		Operator.
Phone off hook	‖‖‖‖‖‖‖‖‖‖‖‖‖‖	Short rapid tones and intervals.

Finland
Country code 358. Telephone: PUHELIN.

Pay Phones are found on the street, in official buildings, Teleservice calling offices, and transit stations.

Phone Directories contain White and Yellow Pages. White pages have English summary, including international calling information. Find directories at post offices, telephone offices, phone booths, hotels, and shops.

Using Pay Phones: Use 1 markka coin for timed local calls (except for operator and service calls which cost 50 pennis + time charges). The other coin accepted is 5 markka.

How to make a call:
1. Lift receiver, wait for dial tone,
2. Put in coin.
3. Dial number.
4. Phone will ring or you'll hear busy tone.

Operator calls cost 2 markka; most operators speak English. For information dial 09, for local directory assistance dial 012.

Long-distance operator and long-distance directory assistance dial 020.

International operator dial 92022.

International calling cost, dial information, 92020.

Emergency calls are free; Police, Fire, and Ambulance dial 000.

Tourist Information: English recording: Helsinki dial 058. (50 pennis + time charge), or Helsinki tourist office dial 169-3757 (local call). Daily news in English dial 040. (50 pennis + time charge.)

Long-Distance Calls inside Finland, made from coin phones, post offices, teleservice offices. Dial 9 + area code + subscriber number.

International Calls from Finland, made from coin phones, post offices, teleservice offices. Dial 990 + country code + area or city code + subscriber number.

To call Britain: dial 990 + 44 + area code + number.

"Dial Direct" access codes: AT&T USA Direct dial 9800-10010.

Finland   *Telephones*

Hotel Surcharge: No maximum.
Things You Should Know: 1. Å, Ä, Ö, are listed after Z.
2. Reduced rate international calls from 10 p.m.—8 a.m. weekdays and all day Sunday. (Direct-dialled calls only.)

Telephone sounds you may hear:

Kind	Description (0–10)	Description
Dial tone	▬▬▬▬▬▬	Steady hum.
Ringing	■ ■	1 second tone and 4 second interval, or
or	■	1 sec. tone and 9 second interval.
Busy	■■■■■■■■■■■■■■■■	5 tones and 5 intervals per 3 seconds.
Out of order		Busy, silence, or ringing.

France

includes Andorra & Monaco, Country code 33.
Telephone: TÉLÉPHONE.

Pay Phones are found in street booths, post offices, train stations, airports, and most bars and cafés.

Phone Directories contain White and Yellow Pages, separate volumes in large cities (Paris has 5 volumes). Instructions are at the beginning of the Yellow Pages. There are only short or no English summaries or instructions. Find directories at post offices (all of France!), hotel reception desks, bars and cafes, and a few phone booths (usually binders are there but books are missing).

Using Coin Phones: Use 1-franc coin for local calls of 6 minutes during the day, 12 minutes during the evening, and 20 minutes from 10 p.m. to 7 a.m. Other coins accepted are 1/2 F, 1 F, 5 F, and occasionally 2 F.

How to make a call:
1. Put in coin(s).
2. Wait for dial tone.
3. Dial number.
4. Coins are taken smallest first to larger later.
4. When finished, hang up.
5. Unused coins are returned.

Using Telephone Card Phones (found in most major cities and almost exclusively in Paris): Buy a "Telecarte" (40 units or 120 units) at any post office and some tobacco shops.

How to make a call:
1. Pick up receiver.
2. Put card in slot.
3. Close door over the card.
4. Dial when you see "Numerotez" on digital readout.
5. When completed, hang up and door will open.
6. Remove card (don't forget it).

Operator calls are free from card and some coin phones; at others, pay 3.50 F. Some local and most international operators speak English. Information and directory assistance dial 12.

Long-distance operator dial 10.

International operator dial 19 + dial tone + 3333.

Emergency calls are free—deposit coin, which is returned. Police dial 17; Fire dial 18; Ambulance dial 18; 24-hour English SOS dial (Paris) 47.23.80.80.

Long-Distance Calls inside France, made from post offices and all pay phones:
 1. Within Paris region: dial 8-digit number.
 2. From Paris region to provinces: dial 16, wait for second dial tone, dial 8-digit number.
 3. Provinces to Paris: dial 16, wait for second dial tone, dial 1 then 8-digit number.
 4. Provinces to provinces: dial 8-digit number.

International Calls from France, made from post offices, all coin phones. Dial 19 + wait for second dial tone + country code + city or area code + subscriber number.

To call Britain: dial l9 + wait for second dial tone + 44 + area code + number.

"Dial Direct" access codes: UK Direct dial 19, wait for second dial tone, then dial 0044, AT&T USA Direct dial 19, wait for second dial tone, then dial 0011; Canada Direct (begins February 1989, code not available at press time); MCI Call USA dial 19, wait for second dial tone, then dial 0019.

Hotel Surcharge: No maximum.

Things You Should Know: 1. To extend long-distance calls made from pay phones, watch out for flashing red light at top left of phone about 10 seconds before money runs out.

2. Operators may take several minutes to come on the line—let it ring.

3. Reduced-rate international direct-dial calls (including from pay phones) 10 p.m.—10 a.m. and all day Sunday.

4. Toll-free calls (similar to "0800" calls) are called "appel vert," always begin with "0505."

5. You can receive calls at telephones with a blue sign of a bell and the booth telephone number (see similar illustration in Germany (West) Telephone Key).

 6. Some telecarte cards carry advertising.

Telephone sounds you may hear:

Kind	Seconds (0–10)	Description
Dial tone	▬▬▬▬▬▬▬▬▬▬	Steady tone.
Ringing	▬ ▬	1½ second tone and 3½ second interval.
Add more money	▬	High rapid tone and/or flashing light at top left of box.
Busy	■ ■ ■ ■ ■ ■ ■ ■ ■ ■	½ sec. tone and ½ sec. interval.
Routing tone (call going through)	‖‖‖‖‖‖‖‖‖‖‖‖‖‖‖‖‖‖‖‖	10 short tones and intervals per sec. (May last 40 seconds)
Out of order	♪ ♪ ♪ ♪ ♪	3 rising tones in 1 sec. and 1 sec. interval, then recording

Germany (East)
Country code 37. Telephone: TELEFON.

Pay Phones are found at post offices, on the street, train stations, underground and public transport stations.

Phone Directories are found in post offices, hotels, and shops (but infrequently).

Books have only White Pages with some classifications listed in the book. There is no English summary for either local or international calling.

Using Pay Phones: Use 20 pfennig per 3 minutes for local calls. Some phones also accept 20, 50 pfennig and 1 Mark coins.

How to make a local call:
1. Deposit coin, wait for dial tone or, on phones taking 20-, 50-pfennig and M1 coins, dial while light at coins is red (about 10 seconds).
2. Dial number.
3. When phone is answered, speak.

Operator calls are free; local operators rarely speak English, but international operators often do. Local directory assistance dial 180.

Long-distance operator dial 181 (deposit money, returned).

International operator to U.S. and Canada dial 01-12. For operator to call other countries see page 1 of phone book (numbers vary). For international information and directory assistance dial 183.

Emergency calls are free, no coin needed. Police dial 110; Fire dial 112; Ambulance dial 115,.

Tourist Information call 2150 (Berlin, Reisebüro der DDR).

Long-Distance Calls inside the GDR, made from post offices, hotels, phones accepting 20-, 50-pfennig, and 1-mark coins. Dial city code + subscriber number.

International Calls from the GDR, made from post offices, hotels, private phones, pay phones accepting 1M coins. No direct-dial international calls from pay phones, except to West Berlin and the rest of Europe from East Berlin on phones accepting 1M coins. Dial 06* + country code + city or area code + subscriber number.

*In some areas outside of East Berlin, access code is 000 or 012.

To call Britain: dial 06 + 44 + area code + number. In many areas, can call only through international operator.

Hotel Surcharge: No maximum.

Things You Should Know: Allow 30 seconds for international direct-dial calls to be connected.

Telephone sounds you may hear:

Kind	Seconds 0 1 2 3 4 5 6 7 8 9 10	Description
Dial tone	■ ■■ ■■ ■■ ■■ ■	¾ sec. tone, ¾ sec. interval, ¼ sec. tone and interval.
Ringing	■■ ■■	1 sec. tone and 4 sec. interval,
or	■■ ■■	1 sec. tone and 5 sec. interval,
or	■■	1 sec. tone and 9 sec. interval.
Busy	‖‖‖‖‖‖‖‖‖‖‖‖‖‖‖‖‖‖	0.1 sec. tone and ½ sec. intervals.

Germany (West)
Country code 49. Telephone: TELEFON.

Pay Phones are found in booths on the street, transport stations, airports, autobahn rest stops, and at all post offices.

Phone Directories contain White and Yellow Pages, often in separate volumes. Directories do not have English summary or international calling information. Find directories in phone booths (sometimes, in large cities), at post offices (for entire country), hotels, and shops.

Using Pay Phones: Use 2—10 pfennig coins (30 pfennig) per 8 minutes 8 a.m.—6 p.m. weekdays (12 minutes all other times). Two types of pay phones:

Rotary-dial phones for calls within Germany only; accept 10, 50 pfennig, DM 1 coins. Push-button pay phones (with "Ausland" or "International" sign) can make calls within Germany and direct-dial international calls also; accept 10 pf., DM 1 and DM 5 coins. Some push-button phones also accept 50 pf, and DM 2 coins.

How to make a call:
1. Pick up receiver.
2. Deposit coin(s).
3. Dial number.
4. Add money when "Bitte Zahlen" or arrow at coin slot lights up.
5. If calling long distance, add several coins in advance.
6. Unused coins will be returned. You can add small coins to obtain refund of partially-used high-value coins *before* you replace the receiver.

Using Telephone Card Phones. Buy telephone cards ("Telefon-Karte"), at main post offices. 45 units cost DM 13.50, and 92 units cost DM 27.60. These phones are new, and are found only in a few city centres and airports.

How to make a call:
1. Pick up receiver.
2. Insert card into slot near bottom of phone.
3. When you see number of units left in digital display (may be faint), dial number.
4. Card will be disengaged when you hang up.

5. If you run out of units and have another card, you can insert another card as it uses the last unit.
6. Remove your card—don't forget it!

Operator calls cost 30 pfennig; some local and most international operators speak English.

Local information and local directory assistance dial 1188.

Long-distance operator dial 010.

Long-distance directory assistance dial 01188.

International operator dial 0010.

International information dial 00118.

Emergency calls are free; deposit 20 pfennig, coins returned. Police dial 110; Fire dial 112; Ambulance dial 110. Some booths marked "SOS" have a direct no-coin box with SOS knob for police and fire. Just push the SOS knob to the left (green) for police, to the right (red) for fire. Emergency Numbers vary in some rural areas: check front of phone book for "Notruf".

Long-Distance Calls inside West Germany from all coin phones, at post offices, hotels. Dial city code + subscriber number.

International Calls from West Germany, made from post offices, "Ausland" coin phones, hotels. Dial 00 + country code + subscriber number.

To call Britain: dial 00 + 44 + area code + number.

Germany (West)   Telephones

"Dial Direct" access codes: AT&T USA Direct dial (0130) 0101; not available in Frankfurt.

Hotel Surcharge: No maximum percentage—could be 300%!

Things You Should Know: 1. You can't use telephone credit cards in West Germany.

2. Don't use "0" as part of city code except when calling another West German city.

3. You can be called at any booth with a red sign and white bell with the phone number written in under the bell (see illustration).

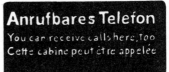

Telephone sounds you may hear:

Kind	Seconds (0–10)	Description
Dial tone	▬▬▬▬▬▬▬▬▬▬	Steady tone.
Ringing	▪ ▪	1 second tone and 4 sec. interval.
Add more money		No tone, but watch for flash at coin slot.
Busy	▪ ▪ ▪ ▪ ▪ ▪ ▪ ▪ ▪ ▪	½ sec. tones and intervals.
Out of order	♪ ♪ ♪ ♪ ♪	3 rising tones in 1 sec. and 1 sec. interval or
or		Recording

Great Britain
Country Code 44. Telephone: TELEPHONE.

Pay Phones are found in red phone booths (call boxes) or in some areas, phones in half-booths on streets (yellow for coin-operated and green for Phonecard phones). Also found in transport stations, airports, British Telecom calling offices, pubs, hotels, and large department stores.

Phone Directories contain White and Yellow Pages, with separate volumes in most areas. Instructions and international calling information are in English. Find directories at phone booths in transport terminals and rural areas, sometimes in city phone booths, and in hotels, shops, and Telecom offices. Business-to-business Yellow Pages are published for London and a few other large cities, but are never found at phone booths.

Using Pay Phones: Use 10 pence coin per 5 minutes (varies with distance and time of day). Different types of phones take different coins.

How to make a call:

"Pay and Answer" rotary-dial phones take only 10, rarely 50, pence coins; found in many hotels, shops, and rural areas.

1. Have money ready.
2. Lift receiver for dial tone.
3. Dial number.
4. When answered, you will hear high pips—push coin(s) in immediately. When money is accepted, pips will stop.
5. If you hear more pips, add more money or you will be cut off.

Note: International calls can be made from this type, but are not recommended, since you can't push money in fast enough.

"Blue Payphone" push-button phones take 2, 10, 50 pence coins in separate slots; if a single slot, takes 5, 10, 20, 50 pence and £1 coins.

1. Put in coins.
2. Watch value of money on digital display (sometimes, credit doesn't register and you have to redeposit money).
3. Dial number.
4. During conversation, digital display shows how much credit is left and flashes when

you need to add more money.
5. Unused coins are refunded.
6. These phones are rare—only in airports, train and underground stations, a few city-centre phone booths.

Using Telephone Card Phones. Buy "Phonecards" (10 units £1, 20 units £2, 40 units £4, 100 units £10, 200 units £20) at main post offices and newsstands, kiosks, and railway station buffets where the green phonecard sticker is found.

How to use a Cardphone:
1. Pick up receiver.
2. Push card into slot in phone.
3. When digital display shows remaining credit, continue as for "Blue Payphone."
4. When you hang up, card will be pushed out of slot.
5. No operator services are available from these phones.

Operator calls are free; all operators speak English.

Local information dial 100. Local directory assistance dial 142 (for London numbers), or 192 (for numbers elsewhere).

Long-distance operator and directory assistance dial 191.

International operator for Europe dial 104 or 105. For directory assistance for Europe dial 102 or 103.

International operator and directory assistance for the U.S. and Canada dial 155.

International operator and directory assistance for the rest of the world dial 108.

Emergency calls are free and require no coins. Police, Fire, and Ambulance dial 999.

Tourist Information call London 246-8041 (recording), Edinburgh: 246-8041 (summer only).

Long-Distance Calls inside Britain, made from any coin phone, Telecom offices, hotels. Dial 0 + city code + subscriber number. City codes are listed in the front of the white pages.

International Calls from Britain, made from coin phones, telephone offices, some post offices. Dial 010 + country code + area code + subscriber number.

"Dial Direct" access codes: AT&T USA Direct dial 0800-89-0011; Canada Direct dial 0800-89-0016; MCI Call USA dial 0800-89-0222.

Hotel Surcharge: No maximum percentage.

Things You Should Know: 1. City codes have two to five digits, including initial 0; numbers have 3 to 7 digits.

2. You may have to wait a long time to be connected to operator. Be patient; let it ring.

3. You'll find some coin phones out of order.

4. Reduced-rate direct-dialled international calls from pay phones and private phones from 8 p.m.—8 a.m. weekdays and all day Saturday and Sunday.

5. When coin boxes are full, you can dial only emergency (999).

Telephone sounds you may hear:

Kind	Seconds (0-10)	Description
Dial tone	▬▬▬▬▬▬▬▬	Low hum.
Ringing	▪▪ ▪▪ ▪▪ ▪▪	2—0.4 sec. tones separated by 0.2 sec. interval, then 2 second interval.
Add more money	‖‖‖‖‖‖‖‖‖‖‖‖‖‖‖‖‖‖	4 rapid pips and 4 intervals per second.
Busy	▪▪▪▪▪▪▪▪▪▪▪▪	⅜ sec. tone and ⅜ sec. interval.
Out of order	▬▬▬▬▬▬▬▬	Steady high tone, or
or		Silence, or
or	♪ ♪ ♪ ♪ ♪	3 rising tones in 1 sec. and recording.

Greece

Country code 30. Telephone: Τηλεφωνο.

Pay phones are found at newsstand kiosks, OTE (Greek telephone company) offices, bus depots, railway stations, airports, and booths.

Phone Directories have White and Yellow Pages, with short Latin alphabetical listings at end of White Pages and short classified listing of the Yellow Pages. There are no English instructions or international calling information in these. There is also an English-language Blue Pages Classified directory, which includes international calling information. Find directories at OTE telephone offices, hotels, and shops.

Using Pay Phones: Use 5 drachma coin plus 2 drachma coin per 5 minutes for local calls. No other coins are accepted.

How to make a call:
   1. Pick up receiver.
   2. Deposit coins for dial tone.
   3. Dial number.

(If phone doesn't have coin slot, you'll have to pay the kiosk attendant; price may be higher.)

Operator calls are free. A few local operators and most international operators speak English.

Local information dial 134.

Local directory assistance dial 131.

Long distance operator dial 151.

Long distance directory assistance dial 132.

International operator dial 161.

Emergency calls are free. Police dial 100 (Athens and Salonika only) or 109 (elsewhere); Fire dial 199; Ambulance dial 150 or 166. In Athens, dial the English-speaking Tourist Police at 171.

Long Distance Calls inside Greece, made from OTE telephone offices, public phones at kiosks with pulse meters. Dial 0 + city code + subscriber number.

International Calls from Greece, made from OTE telephone offices, public phones at kiosks with pulse meters. Dial 00 + country code + city or area code + subscriber number.

To call Britain: dial 00 + 44 + area code + number.

Hotel Surcharge: No maximum percentage.
Things You Should Know: 1. If making a long-distance call from a kiosk without a pulse meter, price could be exorbitant.
2. It is much harder get a long-distance connection from the provinces than from Athens (the calls originating in Athens seem to get priority).

Telephone sounds you may hear:

Kind	Seconds 0 1 2 3 4 5 6 7 8 9 10	Description
Dial tone	▪▪ ▪▪ ▪▪ ▪▪ ▪▪	2 short tones in 1 sec. then 1 sec. interval.
Ringing	▬ ▬	1 sec. tone and 6 sec. interval.
or	▬ ▬	1 sec. tone and 4 sec. interval.
Busy	▪▪▪▪▪▪▪▪▪▪▪▪▪▪▪▪	0.3 second tone and 0.3 second interval.
Out of order	▪ ▪ ▪ ▪ ▪ ▪ ▪ ▪ ▪	½ sec. tone and ½ sec. interval.
or		Silence.

Hungary
Country Code 36. Telephone: TELEFON.

Pay phones are found at post offices, street booths, bars, most pastry shops, railway stations.
Phone Directories have White Pages only and Yellow Pages in separate volumes. There is an English-language summary in the Yellow Pages. Find directories in post offices, hotels, shops, and many phone booths.
Usng Pay Phones: Use 2-forint coin per 3 minutes 7 a.m.-6 p.m. (6 minutes 6 p.m.-7 a.m.) for local calls. No other coins accepted except red pay phones with push-button dialling also take 10- and 20-forint coins.

How to make a call:
1. Lifl receaver for daal tone.
2. Insert coin(s).
3. Dial number.
4. Add money before time is up to extend call—sometimes no warning signal before connection is cut off.

Operator calls cost 2 forints; only a few local and some international operators speak English. Local information dial 01, local directory assistance English in Budapest dial 172-200 (weekdays 7 a.m.—8 p.m.

Long-distance operator and long-distance directory assistance dial 01.

International operator dial 09 (no charge).

Emergency calls are free—deposit coin, which is returned. Police dial 07; Fire dial 05; Ambulance dial 04.

Tourist Information (English) dial 172-800 in Budapest.

Long-Distance Calls inside Hungary, made from post offices, red and yellow coin phones that take 2-, 10-, 20-forint coins. Dial 06 + and wait for second dial tone + area code + subscriber number.

International Calls from Hungary, from post offices, red pay phones accepting 2-, 10-, and 20-forint coins. Dial 00 + wait for second dial tone + country code + subscriber number.

To call Britain: dial 00 + wait for second dial tone + 44 + area code + number.

Hotel Surcharge: Maximum 50%.

Things You Should Know: 1. Sometimes (maybe 5%) you'll get a wrong number even though you dialed correctly. Hang up and try again.

2. When making a long-distance or international call from a red pay phone, you must put in at least 40 forints. Also, second dial tone is high-pitched. After you finish dialing, you will hear a single routing tone; wait while your call is connected.

3. Dial slowly, or you will hear a busy signal.

Telephone sounds you may hear:

Kind	Seconds 0 1 2 3 4 5 6 7 8 9 10	Description
Dial tone	▬▬▬▬▬▬▬▬▬▬▬	Steady hum.
Ringing	▬ ▬	1 sec. tone and 6 sec. interval.
Add money		No warning tone or signal.
Busy	▪▪▪▪▪▪▪▪▪▪▪▪▪▪▪▪	0.3 second tone and 0.3 second interval.
Out of order	♪ ♪ ♪ ♪ ♪	3 rising tones in 1 sec. and 1 sec. intervals.
or		Operator.

Ireland
Country code 353. Telephone: TELEFÓN.

Pay Phones are found at post offices, hotels, restaurants, pubs, and blue and white concrete boxes, and silver, orange, black and and gold aluminum boxes.

Phone Directories contain White and Yellow Pages (entire country: 7 volumes White and Yellow Pages). Instructions and international calling information are in English. Find directories at post offices, hotels, shops, and phone booths (sometimes missing or vandalized).

Using Pay Phones: Use 2 10-pence coins per 4 minutes 45 seconds for local calls. There are several different types of pay phones. Other coins accepted are 5 P on all types and 50 P on new STD (Subscriber Trunk Dialing) phones only.

How to make a call:

Type 1—STD Type:
1. Line up coin(s) on ramp at top of phone (at least 20 P local, 50 P long-distance, £1 international).
2. Listen for dial tone: may take 20 seconds.
3. Dial number.
4. When answered, the first coin(s) will be taken automatically. Additional coins will fall in as needed.
5. 10 seconds before time is up, you will hear a beep. Add money quickly to continue call.
6. No coin return on this kind of phone; but you can make another call to use up credit if you dial within 30 seconds.

Type 2—A and B Button Phones:
1. Listen for dial tone.
2. Insert money.
3. Dial number. (long distance, dial operator.)
4. When answered, press "A" button usually on right side of phone box.
5. If not answered, press "B" button to return coin.

Operator calls are free; except extra 20 P charge to make a connection. All operators speak English.

Local information and directory assistance in entire Republic of Ireland dial 190.

Long-distance operator and directory assistance dial 10.

International directory assistance dial: for U.K. 197, International dial 114.

For international operator-assisted calls dial 10, except in Dublin calling area dial 10 for the U.K. and 114 for the rest of the world.

Emergency calls are free; Police, Fire, and Ambulance dial 999.

Long-Distance Calls inside Ireland, made from post offices, Telecom Eireann calling offices, all coin phones. Dial 0 + city code + subscriber number. (Most written phone numbers include the 0.)

International Calls from Ireland, made from post offices, Telecom Eireann calling offices, and STD pay phones.

Dial: For Great Britain: 03 + city code + number. For all other countries: 16 + country code + city or area code + number.

Hotel surcharges: 25% service charge, or £7 per call, whichever is less.

Things You Should Know: 1. Wait up to 20 seconds after dialing to hear any further sounds for calls inside Ireland; 30 seconds on international calls.

2. In some phones, call can't be extended by adding more money. When cut off, call again.

3. When all long-distance lines are busy, priority service is available from operator at double the normal cost.

4. Only telephone credit-card and reverse-charge calls outside of Europe can be made from Type 2 pay phones.

5. Reduced-rate international calls weekdays 10 p.m.—10 a.m. and all day Sunday.

Ireland *Telephones* 217

Telephone Tones You May Hear:

Kind	Seconds (0–10)	Description
Dial tone	▬▬▬▬▬▬▬▬▬▬	Low hum.
Ringing	■■　■■　■■　■■	2—short tones in 1 sec. and 2 sec. interval.
Add more money	▬	Single tone 10 sec. before time is up.
Busy	■■■■■■■■■■■■	0.4 sec. tone and 0.4 second interval.
or	♪ ♪ ♪ ♪ ♪	3 rising tones in 1 sec. and 1 sec. interval.
Out of order	♪ ♪ ♪ ♪ ♪	3 rising tones in 1 sec. and 1 sec. interval.

Italy
(including San Marino and Vatican City)
Country Code 39. Telephone: TELEFONO.

Pay phones are found at transport stations, airports, telephone "posti telefonici" offices, bars and cafes with a yellow telephone dial sign.

Phone Directories contain White and Yellow Pages. There is no English summary or international calling information. Find directories at SIP (telephone company) offices, hotels, shops, and about half of the phone booths.

Using Pay Phones: Use 1 gettone (telephone token, costs 200 lire) or 200-lire coin, or per pulse on a telephone card (scheda telefonica) per 6 minutes for local calls (in some areas, calls are not timed). Buy tokens and telephone cards (5,000, 10,000, 20,000 lire) at SIP offices, tobacco stores, bars and cafes. Some phones have token vending machines. Only some phones will take 100-lire and 200-lire coins as well as tokens.

How to make a call:

Coin and Gettone telephones:
1. Buy token(s) if needed.
2. Put in gettoni or coins (at least 1 for local call, 6 for long distance).
3. Pick up receiver.
4. Dial number.
5. If busy, hang up and try again immediately.
6. Add more tokens to extend call.
7. Unused coins or tokens will be returned when you push the red button halfway down the telephone box.

Card phones. (found at airports, main train stations, city centers, SIP and ASST offices, and rest stops on the autostrade):
1. Pick up receiver.
2. Insert card into blue box at the right of the telephone. (Tear off the corner tab from the card before first use.)
3. Dial number.
4. When call completed, hang up; card will be returned only if there are remaining units.
5. As you run out of units, to continue the call, you must replace the card with an

unused one when you see the flashing light.
Operator calls: some cost 1 gettone or unit; a few local operators and most international operators speak English.
Local information and directory assistance dial 12.
Long-distance information (no charge) dial 184.
Long-distance directory and long-distance operator dial 184.
International operator (no charge) for Europe and North Africa dial 194; rest of the world dial 170.
Emergency calls are free. Police dial 112, Fire dial 115, and Ambulance dial 113.
Long Distance Calls inside Italy, made from SIP offices, most coin phones with "Interurbano" or "Teleselezione" signs, and all card phones. Dial 0 + city code + subscriber number.

International Calls, made from SIP offices, "Teleselezione" or "Interurbano" pay phones. Dial 00 + country code + city or area code + number. To call Britain: dial 00 + 44 + area code + number.

Hotel Surcharge: No maximum percentage.

Things You Should Know: 1. Sometimes at the end of a timed local call, you'll be cut off. Adding coins or gettoni won't prevent cutoff.

2. You can get a busy signal at any time: before you dial, during dialing, and at the end of dialing. It means system overload—try again immediately.

3. You'll need a lot of gettoni for all but a short local call.

4. Phone numbers in a single city can have varying number of digits: for example numbers in Rome range from 4 to 7.

5. Reduced-rate long-distance and international calls 8 p.m.—8 a.m. and all day Sunday.

6. Italians answer the telephone with "Pronto".

7. Free calls are called "numero verde".

Telephone sounds you may hear:

Kind	Seconds	Description
Dial tone		0.6 sec. tone, 1 sec. interval, 0.2 sec. tone and 0.2 second interval.
Ringing		1 sec. tone and 4 sec. interval.
Busy		0.2 sec. tones and intervals.
Out of order		Busy or ringing tone.

Luxembourg
Country code 352. Telephone: TÉLÉPHONE.

Pay phones are found in front of or in post offices, train stations, the airport, on the street.

Phone Directories contain White Pages only, but some classified listings are included. Directories do not have an English summary or instructions for international calling. Entire country is in two volumes. Directories at Post Offices, most pay phones. Private Yellow Pages directory "La Ligne Bleu" is found at shops, hotels, and homes.

Using Pay Phones: Use 5-franc (F) coins from Luxembourg or Belgium for untimed local calls. Two types of telephones: one takes only 5F coins, for local calls only. Other type takes 1F, 5F, 20F coins, has world-wide automatic direct dialling.

How to make a call:
1. Pick up receiver.
2. Insert coin(s) (5F minimum).
3. Dial number.

Operator calls are free; many operators speak English.

Local information and directory assistance dial 017.

Long-distance operator dial 0010; for international directory dial 016.

International operator dial 0010.

Emergency calls cost 5F. Police, Fire, and Ambulance dial 012.

Long Distance Calls inside Luxembourg, made from post offices, all coin phones. Just dial the number, since there are no area or city codes.

International Calls, made from post offices (metered), hotels, some phone booths. Dial 00 + country code + city or area code + subscriber number.

To call Britain: dial 00 + 44 + area code + number.

Hotel Surcharge: No maximum percentage.

Things You Should Know: 1. In long-distance calls, you will hear a single short tone 20 seconds before money runs out. Add money or you will be cut off.

2. Reduced rate international calls 10 p.m.—10 a.m. every day.

Telephone sounds you may hear:

Kind	Seconds 0 1 2 3 4 5 6 7 8 9 10	Description
Dial tone	▬▬▬▬▬▬▬▬▬▬	Steady tone.
Ringing	▪ ▪	1 sec. tone and 4 sec. interval,
or	▪	1 sec. tone and 9 sec. interval.
Add more money	▪	Short single tone 20 seconds before cut-off.
Line busy	▪ ▪ ▪ ▪ ▪ ▪ ▪ ▪ ▪ ▪	½ sec. tone and ½ sec. interval.
System overload	▮▮▮▮▮▮▮▮▮▮▮▮▮▮▮▮▮▮▮▮	¼ sec. tone and ¼ sec. interval.
Out of order		Recording

Netherlands
Country code 31. Telephone: TELEFOON.

Pay Phones are found on the street, transport stations, airports, PTT telephone offices, department stores.

Phone Directories contain separate White Pages and Yellow Pages volumes. White Pages include classified listings, but no advertising. There is no English-language summary or international calling information. Yellow Pages have an English classified index inside the back cover and indexed city map at the front. Find directories at telephone offices, shops, hotels (White Pages only when not missing).

Using Pay Phones: Use 25-cent coin per untimed local call. Other coins accepted are 1 guilder, and, rarely, 2-1/2 guilders. For card phones, buy "Telefoonkaart" at post offices, telephone offices, some other shops; 20 units 5 guilders, 45 units 10 guilders, and 115 units 25 guilders.

How to make a call:

Coin phones:

1. Lift receiver.
2. Deposit money.
3. Dial number.
4. Unused coins will be returned.

Card phones: (rare, found in city centers, airports, and main transport stations).

1. Remove receiver.
2. Insert card into slot.
3. Dial number.
4. After the call, replace receiver.
5. Take card out (don't forget).
6. If card runs out while talking, press black button above touch pad, take out old card, and insert new card.

Operator calls cost 25 cents; almost all operators speak English.

Local information dial 004 (free), between 8:30 a.m. and 4:30 p.m., Monday—Saturday.

Local directory assistance dial 008.

Long-distance operator and directory assistance dial 0016.

International operator to make a call dial 0010.

International information dial 0018.
Emergency calls cost 25 cents. Police dial 22-22-22; Fire dial 21-21-21; Ambulance dial 555-5555. (Numbers may vary in rural areas.)
Tourist Information: Look under VVV in phone directory.
Long Distance Calls inside the Netherlands, made from post offices, almost all coin and card phones. Dial area code (starting with "0") + subscriber number.
International Calls from the Netherlands, made from coin phones accepting 1, 2-1/2-guilder coins, post offices. Dial 09 + dial tone + country code + city code + subscriber number.
To call Britain: dial 09 + dial tone + 44 + area code + number.
"Direct" calls: AT&T USA Direct dial 06 + second dial tone + 022-9111, costs 25 cents; Canada Direct (starts June 1, dialling code not available at press time); MCI Call USA dial 06 + second dial tone + 022-91-22.
Hotel Surcharge: No maximum percentage. Check before placing call.
Things You Should Know 1. Many White Pages have **no** instructions or information in them.
2. Reduced rate and international calling Mon.—Sat. 10 p.m.—10 a.m. and all day Sunday.

Netherlands   Telephones

3. Pay phones in restaurants, hotels, and other private places charge double or even triple for all calls.

In Amsterdam, 24-hour telephone office is open at "Telehouse", 46-50 Raadhuisstraat. (Fax and telex available, too.)

Telephone sounds you may hear:

Kind	Seconds 0 1 2 3 4 5 6 7 8 9 10	Description
Dial tone	▬▬▬▬▬▬▬▬▬▬▬▬	Steady tone.
Ringing	▬ ▬	1 sec. tone and 4 sec. interval.
Add more money	▬	1.6 sec. tone 15 seconds before line is cut off.
Busy	▮▮▮▮▮▮▮▮▮▮▮▮▮▮▮▮▮▮▮▮	¼ sec. tones and ¼ sec. intervals.
Out of order	♪ ♪ ♪ ♪ ♪	3 rising tones in 1 sec. and 1 sec. interval.
or	▄▀▄▀▄▀▄▀▄▀▄▀▄▀	2 alternating ½ sec. tones.

Norway
Country code 47. Telephone: TELEFON.

Pay Phones are found on streets, at transport station, Televerket (telephone calling) offices.

Phone Directories contain White and Classified White Pages. There is an English summary with international calling information near the front of the White Pages. Find directories at Televerket offices, hotels, shops, and in phone booths.

Using Pay Phones: Use 2 kroner per 3 minutes 8 a.m. to 5 p.m. weekdays (untimed at other times).

How to make a call:
1. Lift receiver.
2. Wait for dial tone.
3. Deposit coins and dial.
4. Unused coins will be refunded (if you're lucky).

Operator calls are free; many operators speak English.

Guaranteed English language operator dial 0115.
Local directory assistance dial 0180.
Long-distance operator dial 0111 and 0115.
Long distance directory dial 018.
International operator for Scandinavia dial 090.
Outside Scandinavia dial 093.

Emergency calls cost 2 kroner; numbers vary city by city, but 000 emergency number has been introduced in most cities. Oslo numbers: Rescue Police dial 66 90 50; Fire dial 144 55; Ambulance dial 20 10 90.

Long Distance Calls inside Norway, made from telephone (Televerket) offices, coin phones. Dial 0 + area code + subscriber number.

International Calls from Norway, made from Televerket calling offices, coin phones. Dial 095 + country code + city or area code + subscriber number.

To call Britain: dial 095 + 44 + area code + number.

"Dial Direct" numbers: AT&T "USA Direct" dial 050-12-011; "Canada Direct" (service expected in 1989; number not available at press time).

Hotel Surcharge: No maximum percentage.

Norway — Telephones

Things You Should Know: 1. Extra charge for operator if long-distance call can be dialed direct.
2. Reduced international rates 10 p.m.—10 a.m. and Sundays.
3. Accented vowel letters are listed after Z in telephone books.

Telephone sounds you may hear:

Kind	Seconds (0–10)	Description
Dial tone	▬▬▬▬▬▬▬▬▬	Steady tone.
Ringing	▪ ▪ ▪	1 sec. tone and 3 sec. interval.
or	▪ ▪	1 sec. tone and 4 sec. interval.
Add more money	▪	Single buzz 20 seconds before time runs out.
Busy line	▪▪▪▪▪▪▪▪▪	½ sec. tone and ½ sec. interval.
System overload	‖‖‖‖‖‖‖‖‖‖‖	¼ sec. tone and ¼ sec. interval.
Out of order	♪♪♪♪♪♪♪♪♪	3 rising tones in 1 sec.
or		Recording.

Poland
Country code 48. Telephone: TELEFON.

Pay Phones are found at post offices, transport stations, some hotel lobbies, outside walls of some buildings, phone booths.

Phone Directories contain White and Yellow Pages (separate volumes in Warsaw). Books are issued every five years or so. There is no English summary or international calling information. Find directories at post offices, hotels, shops.

Using Pay Phones: Use 5-zloty coin per untimed local call, for local calls only. Other coins phones accept 10-zloty and 20-zloty coins, can be used for long-distance calls.

How to make a call:
1. Pick up receiver, or with some phones, insert coin first.
2. Wait for dial tone.
3. Dial number.

Operator calls cost 5 zloty; few local and some international operators speak English.

Local information dial 911.

Local directory assistance dial 912.

Long-distance operator dial 900.

Long-distance directory assistance dial 912.

International operator dial 901.

Emergency calls are free. Police dial 997; Fire dial 998; Ambulance dial 999.

Tourist Information dial tourist information (Warsaw 21-36-73 or 27-81-31).

Long-Distance Calls inside Poland, made from post offices, from special long-distance phones. For major cities dial 0 + city code + subscriber number. For smaller cities dial 8 + city code + subscriber number. (You will hear routing tone while connection is being made.)

International Calls, made from post offices, hotels, private phones, but no pay phones. Dial 00 (for Austria, East Germany, Hungary, Great Britain, Soviet Union, Switzerland) or 80 (for Bulgaria, France, Italy, Spain, Sweden, Yugoslavia) + country code + city or area code + subscriber number. (You will hear routing tone while connection is being made.)

To call the Britain dial 00 + 44 + area code + number.
Hotel Surcharge: 10% and up.
Things You Need to Know: Sound quality is often poor.

Telephone sounds you may hear:

Kind	Seconds 0 1 2 3 4 5 6 7 8 9 10	Description
Dial tone	▬▬▬▬▬▬▬▬▬	Steady tone.
Ringing	▬ ▬	1 sec. tone and 4 sec. interval.
Busy	▪ ▪ ▪ ▪ ▪ ▪ ▪ ▪ ▪	½ sec. tone and ½ sec. interval.
Routing tone	▮▮▮▮▮▮▮▮▮▮▮▮▮▮▮▮▮▮	¼ sec. tone and ¼ sec. interval.
Out of order	♪ ♪ ♪ ♪ ♪	3 rising tones in 1 sec. and 1 sec. interval.
or		Recording.
or		Silence.

Portugal
Country code 351. Telephone: TELEFONE.

Pay Phones are found at post offices, bars, cafes, transport stations, a few booths in streets and squares.

Phone Directories contain White and Yellow Pages, separate volumes in Lisbon. There is no English summary or international calling information. Find directories in post offices, phone booths, hotels, and shops.

Using Pay Phones: Use 5 escudos ($) (increase possible during 1989) per 3 minutes for local calls, or phone card (credifone). Other coins accepted are 2$50 escudos, 25$ escudos.

How to make a call:
1. Pick up receiver.
2. Put in coin on ramp on top of phone and wait for dial tone (may take 15 seconds).
3. Dial number. Wait up to 10 seconds for ring.
4. If busy, hang up and try later (coin returned).

Using card phones, found in cities and transport centres. Buy cards (Credifone) at post offices, some other locations (often the nearest is shown inside the phone booth).

How to make a call:
1. Insert card in telephone.
2. Dial number when you hear dial tone.
3. After call, remember to retrieve card.

Operator calls cost 5$; a few local and many international operators speak English.

Information and local directory assistance dial 12. (Free if number is not listed in phone book—coin returned.)

Long-distance operator and directory assistance dial 090.

International operator dial 099 for Europe; dial 098 for elsewhere.

Emergency calls are free; Police and Ambulance dial 115; Fire calls are 5 escudos, number varies by town, Lisbon dial 32-22-22. Lisbon poison center dial 76-11-81, cost 10 escudos.

Tourist Information: Lisbon dial 57-50-86 or 36-33-14.

Long-Distance Calls inside Portugal, made from post offices, coin phones. Dial 0 + city code (which may include another 0) + subscriber number.

International Calls from Portugal, made from post offices, hotels, private phones.

Dial: For Europe 00 + country code + city or area code + subscriber number.

For elsewhere 097 + country code + city or area code + subscriber number.

To call Britain: dial 00 + 44 + area code + number.

"Dial Direct": "Canada Direct" (service to start June 1; number not available at press time).

Hotel Surcharge: 20% surcharge per call.

Things You Should Know: 1. Operators answer calls in order received—be patient and wait.

2. To make reverse charge calls, call 099 (for calls in Europe) and 098 (rest of the world) and ask for "Communicações pagaveis no destino".

3. You cannot use telephone credit cards in Portugal.

4. Mass telephone prefix changes for the year are listed at the beginning of White Pages.

5. Reduced costs for and international calls weekdays midnight—8 a.m. and all day Sunday.

Telephone sounds you may hear:

Kind	Seconds (0–10)	Description
Dial tone	▬▬▬▬▬▬▬▬▬▬	Steady tone.
Ringing	■ .... ■	1 sec. tone and 5 sec. interval.
Busy	■ ■ ■ ■ ■ ■ ■ ■ ■	½ sec. tone and ½ sec. interval.
Out of order	‖‖‖‖‖‖‖‖‖‖‖‖‖‖‖‖‖	0.2 sec. tones and intervals.
or		Busy tone.

Romania

Country code 40. Telephone: TELEFON.

Pay Phones are found in post offices, street booths, restaurants, hotels.

Phone Directories contain only White Pages. There is no English summary or international calling information. Directories are scarce, but can sometimes be found in post offices, hotels, and shops.

Using Pay Phones: Use 1 leu coin per 3 minutes local call.

How to make a call:
1. Pick up receiver
2. Deposit coin in slot.
3. Wait for dial tone.
4. Dial number.

Operator calls are free; no local and some international operators speak English.

Information dial 051.

Local directory assistance: public numbers dial 030, private numbers A-L dial 031, private numbers dial 032.

Long-distance operator dial 091.

Long-distance directory dial 031.

International operator dial 071.

Emergency calls; Police dial 055, Fire dial 081; Ambulance dial 061.

Tourist Information dial 14 51 60 (Bucharest); other cities vary.

Long-distance calls inside Romania, made from post offices, hotels, private phones. Dial city code + subscriber number.

International Calls from Romania, made from post offices, hotels, private phones. Dial access code + country code + city or area code + subscriber number. Special note: calls made from Romania are exorbitant, and cost per minute *rises* with length of call. First 3 minutes, 240 Lei; 4th to 6th minute, 120 Lei per minute; 7th to 10th minute, 160 Lei per minute; 11th to 21st minute 240 Lei per minute; above 20 minutes, 320 Lei per minute.

To call Britain: dial operator at 071.

Hotel Surcharge: maximum percentage unknown.

Telephone sounds you may hear:

Kind	Seconds (0-10)	Description
Dial tone	▬▬▬▬▬▬▬▬▬▬	Steady tone.
Ringing	▬ ▬	2 sec. tone and 4 sec. interval.
Busy	‖‖‖‖‖‖‖‖‖‖‖‖‖‖	3 tones and intervals per sec.
Out of order	▬‖‖▬‖‖▬‖‖▬‖‖▬‖‖	0.4 sec. tone and 6 - 0.1 sec. tones and 7 0.1 intervals. (1.7 sec. cycle.)
or	‖‖‖‖‖‖‖‖‖‖‖‖‖‖‖‖	⅛ sec. tone and 3 - 0.075 sec. pips and 4 - 0.075 sec. intervals. (⅔ sec. cycle).

Soviet Union
U.S.S.R.
Country code 7. Telephone: ТЕЛЕФОН

Pay Phones are found on the street (especially near underground stations), telephone calling offices.

Phone Directories do not exist in much of the Soviet Union. In Moscow, a small edition was printed in 1986; almost impossible to find. "Information Moscow", published in English every 6 months, is alternative to Moscow phone book (find it at hotel service desks, embassies, shops reserved for foreigners).

Using Pay Phones: Use 2-kopeck coin per untimed local call. Some phones accept 1- and 10-kopeck coins.

How to make a call:
1. Put coin(s) in slot before lifting receiver.
2. Wait for dial tone.
3. Dial number.
    (If there is a button marked "ОТВЕТ" (means answer), push it when you're answered to complete the connection.)
4. Coin returned if number is busy or no answer.

Operator calls cost 2 kopecks; most operators speak only Russian; many long-distance operators speak English.

Information and local directory assistance dial 09.

Long-distance directory dial 07.

Long-distance operator dial 8-196 (free).

International operator dial 8-194. In Leningrad dial 312-7383.

Emergency calls are free; Police dial 02; Fire dial 01; Ambulance dial 03.

Tourist Information: Intourist (Moscow): 203-6962. Intourist numbers in other cities are found in the brochure "Visiting the U.S.S.R.".

Long-Distance Calls inside the U.S.S.R., made from long-distance telephone offices (Peregovorny Punkt), hotels, private phones. Dial code varies depending on the city. Call 07 for information.

International Calls from the U.S.S.R, made from long-distance telephone offices (Peregovorny Punkt), hotels, private phones. No international or long-distance calls from pay phones.

Hotel Surcharge: Maximum percentage unknown.

Things You Should Know:

1. If no dial tone or is busy when you lift receiver, hang up and try again immediately.
2. From hotel rooms, local calls are often free.
3. If at a public phone and someone else is waiting to use it, limit your calls to 3 minutes.
4. It may take hours to place an international call.
5. If direct dialing a number in the Soviet Union from abroad, you must dial the "0" in the city code (example: Moscow 096).
6. If making a long-distance call from a telephone office, you must prepay the call.
7. When making an international call, if you are connected to a wrong number, you will still be charged.

Telephone sounds you may hear:

Kind	Seconds 0 1 2 3 4 5 6 7 8 9 10	Description
Dial tone	▬▬▬▬▬▬▬▬▬▬▬	Steady tone.
Ringing	▪ ▪ ▪	1 sec. tone and 3 sec. interval.
Busy	▪▪▪▪▪▪▪▪▪▪▪▪	0.4 sec. tone and 0.4 sec. interval.
Out of order		Silence.

Spain

Country code 34. Telephone: TELEFONO.

Pay Phones are found at the telephone company calling office (telefonica) in each town, major department stores, bars, cafes, booths on street.

Phone Directories contain White and Yellow Pages, separate volumes in large cities. Find directories at telephone company offices, hotels, and shops.

Using Pay Phones: Use 5 peseta (Pta) coin per 3 minutes local call. Other coins accepted 25, 50, and 100 Pta at long-distance phones. (The first card phones were installed in 1987.)

How to make a call:
1. Pick up receiver.
2. Wait for dial tone.
3. Dial number.
4. Deposit money at short tone.
5. During call, add more money quickly at short tone or you will be cut off.

Operator calls: few local operators will speak English, long-distance operators often can.

Information dial 098, costs 25 Pta.

Local directory assistance dial 003.

Long-distance operator dial 025-041 + regional code (See front pages of White Pages for map with regional codes).

Long-distance directory assistance dial 003, free.

International operator, free, dial:
- Europe: 008. (Will usually answer in French, but will pass you to an English-speaking operator.)
- Elsewhere: 005. (Operator will usually answer in Spanish, switch to English.)

Emergency calls cost 5 Pta; National Police dial 091; Municipal Police dial 092; Fire varies by city, see first pages of White Pages, look for "Bomberos" (Madrid and Barcelona dial 080); Ambulance varies by city, see beginning of White Pages.

Long-Distance Calls inside Spain, made from telephone company offices, coin phones marked "telefono interurbano" or "larga distancia" (these phones will accept 25, 50, and 100 Pta coins).

Dial 9 + area code (indicativo interurbano) + subscriber number.

International Calls from Spain, made from telephone company offices and coin phones marked "telefono interurbano". Dial 07 + high pitched dial tone + country code + city or area code + subscriber number.

To call Britain: dial 07 + high pitched dial tone + 44 + area code + number.

"Dial Direct": "Canada Direct" (service to begin June 1, 1989; access number not available at press time).

Hotel Surcharge: Maximum 25%, with a minimum of 15 Pta per call. You will be charged whether the call is completed or not.

Things You Should Know:

1. Long-distance calls may take 30 seconds after dialing to make connection.
2. Reduced international rates 10 p.m.—10 a.m. every day.

Telephone sounds you may hear:

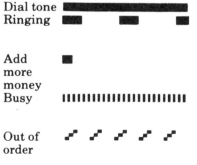

Kind	Description
Dial tone	Steady tone.
Ringing	1½ sec. tone and 3 second interval.
Add more money	Short tone 5 seconds before time is up.
Busy	0.2 sec. tone and 0.2 sec. interval.
Out of order	3 rising tones in 1 sec. and 1 sec. interval.

Sweden
Country code 46. Telephone: TELEFON.

Pay Phones are found at transport stations, shopping centres, restaurants, some on streets.

Phone Directories have White and Yellow Pages—but sometimes Yellow Pages are printed on white paper (separate volumes for Stockholm). There is an English-language summary with international calling information at end of introduction in White Pages. Find directories in phone booths, hotels, and shops.

Using Pay Phones: Use two 1-krona coins per 12 minutes local call.

How to make a call:
 1. Lift receiver.
 2. Insert coins, wait for dial tone.
 3. Dial number.

Operator calls cost 1 krona; all operators speak English.

Local information and local directory assistance dial 90-140.

Long-distance operator and directory assistance dial 90-140.

International operator for Scandinavia dial 0013; elsewhere dial 0019.

Emergency calls are free; Police, Fire, and Ambulance dial 90000, or at pay phones push red button below for instant connection to SOS operator (no coin required).

Tourist Information dial 221 840 (Stockholm).

Long Distance Calls inside Sweden, made from all pay phones, telephone calling offices, hotels. Dial area code + subscriber number. (Area codes are in front pages of directory.)

International Calls from Sweden, made all phones, telephone calling offices, hotels. Dial 009 + country code + dial tone + city or area code + subscriber number.

To call Britain: dial 009 + 44 + dial tone + area code + number.

"Call Direct": AT&T "USA Direct" dial 020-795-611; MCI "Call USA" dial 020-795-922; "Canada Direct" (Service to begin June 1, 1989; number not available at press time).

Hotel Surcharge: No maximum percentage.

Things You Should Know: 1. "0" is before 1 on dial telephones—not after 9.
2. Stockholm directory has good city maps in Business-to-Business directory (Företag).
3. Phone book listings A-Z, then å, ä, ö.
4. Reduced long-distance and international rates Monday to Friday 10 p.m.—8 a.m. and all day Saturday, Sunday, and Holidays.

Telephone sounds you may hear:

Kind	Seconds (0–10)	Description
Dial tone	▬▬▬▬▬▬▬	Steady tone.
Ringing	▪ ▪	1 sec. tone and 5 sec. interval,
or	▪	1 sec. tone and 9 sec. interval.
Busy	▌▌▌▌▌▌▌▌▌▌▌▌▌▌▌	¼ sec. tone and ¼ sec. interval.
Out of order	♪ ♪ ♪ ♪ ♪	3 rising tones in 1 sec. and 1 sec. interval.
or		Operator.

Switzerland

(and Liechtenstein), country code 41.
Telephone: TELEFON (German),
TÉLÉPHONE (French), TELEFONO (Italian).

Pay phones are found at train stations, airports, all post offices, most restaurants, on streets.

Phone Directories contain White Pages with classified headings are listed in alphabetical order. Yellow Pagers in only a few cities. There is an English-language summary and international calling information near the front of the book. Find directories at post offices, hotels, shops, and phone booths. Directories for all of Switzerland are found in all of these places.

Using Pay Phones: Use 2—20 centime (French) or rappen (German) coins per 4 minutes 6 a.m.—9 p.m. Mon. to Fri. (12 minutes all other times) per local call. Other coins accepted are 10, 20 centimes, 1/2, 1, and 5 franc. (Some coin phones only take 20-C coins.)

How to make a call:
1. Lift receiver, wait for dial tone.
2. Put in coins.
3. Dial number.
4. Watch money left on your call on the display: add more if needed.
5. Unused coins are returned.

Operator calls cost 40 centimes or rappen; almost every operator speaks English.

Local information and local directory assistance dial 111.

Long-distance directory dial 111.

Long-distance operator dial 114.

International operator dial 191 (no charge to place a call—coins returned).

International telephone rates dial 115.

Emergency calls cost 40 centimes or rappen; Police dial 117; Fire dial 118; Ambulance dial 144.

Tourist Information dial 120 (English recording); cost 40 centimes or rappen.

Long-Distance Calls inside Switzerland, made from all coin phones, post offices, and hotels. Dial 0 + city code (1 or 2 digits) + subscriber number.

International Calls from Switzerland, made from post offices, pay phones. Dial 00 + country code + city or area code + subscriber number.

To call Britain: dial 00 + 1 + area code + number. "Dial Direct": "Canada Direct" (service to start Feb. 1, 1988; number not available at press time).

Hotel Surcharge: No maximum percentage.

Things You Should Know:

1. No operator-assisted calls to another Swiss number are possible.

2. Operator-assisted international calls cost much more than direct-dialed.

3. Phone numbers printed on cards, letterheads, advertisements, etc. include the access code "0" as part of the area code.

4. Swiss area codes are in front of every phone book in the Red Pages.

Switzerland   *Telephones*   243

Telephone sounds you may hear:

Kind	Seconds 0 1 2 3 4 5 6 7 8 9 10	Description
Dial tone	▬▬▬▬▬▬▬▬▬▬	Steady hum.
Ringing	▪ ▪	1 sec. tone and 4 sec. interval.
Add more money		None—watch the display showing amount left.
Busy (line)	▪ ▪ ▪ ▪ ▪ ▪ ▪ ▪ ▪ ▪	½ sec. tones and ½ sec. intervals.
System overload	▮▮▮▮▮▮▮▮▮▮▮▮▮▮▮▮▮▮▮▮	¼ sec. tones and ¼ sec. intervals.
Out of order	♪ ♪ ♪ ♪ ♪	3 rising tones in 1 sec. and 1 sec. interval.
or		Recording.

Turkey

Country code 90. Telephone: TELEFON.

Pay Phones are found at post offices, hotels, large stores, on the street.

Phone Directories contain White and Yellow Pages, separate volumes in large cities. There is no English-language summary or international calling information. Find directories at post offices, hotels, and shops.

Using Pay Phones: Use small telephone token (jeton), cost 100 lira per 3 minutes local call. Use 500-lira tokens (normal jeton) forlocal and long-distance calls, and 1500-lira tokens (büyük jetonu) for long-distance and international calls. No other coins or tokens accepted, except some phones accept "telecards", bought at post offices (20 units, 1,925 lira; 30 units, 2,800 Lira; and 120 units, 11,400 lira.)

How to make a call:

Buy jetons or telecards at post offices, tobacconists.

Automatic telephones (yellow, pushbutton dial, has slots for all three types of jetons or one slot for telecard).

1. Check for red out-of-order light below pushbuttons: if lit, the phone is broken.
2. Lift receiver, insert jeton or telecard gently.
3. Wait for dial tone.
4. Dial number if a local call.
5. For long-distance calls, look for light at right of instructions. When it goes out, dial 9.
6. Wait for second dial tone, then dial.
7. For international calls, when light goes out, dial 99 + country code and number.
8. If light goes on and you hear tone, add more jetons.

Grey, black, or red dial phones: use "normal jeton" as above; for local calls only.

Operator calls are free; local operators speak only Turkish, many international operators speak English.

Local information and directory assistance dial 011.

Long-distance operator and directory assistance dial 031.

Extra-quick service at extra cost dial 091.
International operator dial 032.
Emergency calls cost 1 jeton; Police dial 055; Fire dial 000; Ambulance dial 077. Check front page of White Pages.
Long-Distance Calls inside Turkey, made from post offices, coin phones accepting large jetons (have lots of jetons) or telecards. Dial 9 + city code + subscriber number.
International Calls from Turkey, made from post offices, hotels, private phones, pay phones accepting 500 L and 1500 L jetons. Dial 9 + dial tone + 9 + country code + city or area code + subscriber number.
To call Britain: dial 9 + dial tone + 9 + 44 + area code and number.
Hotel Surcharge: No maximum percentage.

Things You Should Know:
1. Long-distance calls may require a long time to go through, especially if placed through an operator.
2. Reduced long-distance rates inside Turkey Saturdays, Sundays, and holidays. No reduced rates for international calls.

Telephone sounds you may hear:

Kind	Seconds (0 1 2 3 4 5 6 7 8 9 10)	Description
Dial tone	▬▬▬▬▬▬▬▬▬▬	Steady tone.
Ringing	▪ ▪ ▪	1 sec. tone and 3 sec. interval.
or	▬ ▬	2 sec. tone and 4 sec. interval.
Busy line	▪ ▪ ▪ ▪ ▪ ▪ ▪ ▪ ▪	½ sec. tone and ½ sec. interval.
System overload	▬||||▬||||▬||||▬||||	0.6 sec. tone, 4 tones and intervals of 0.2 sec.
Out of order		Ring, busy, or silence.

Yugoslavia
Country code 38. Telephone: TELEFON.

Pay Phones are found on the street, public places, transport stations.

Phone Directories contain White Pages only. Some directories have English-language summary and international calling section. Find directories in post offices, hotels, shops, and some phone booths.

Using Pay Phones: Use silver-coloured 20-dinar coin per 3 minutes local call. Some phones also accept silver-coloured 50- and 100-dinar coins. (Note: some phones require 50-dinar coin for a local call.)

How to make a call:
1. Pick up receiver.
2. Deposit coin(s), wait for dial tone.
3. Dial number.

Operator calls, usually free (coin returned); few local and many international operators speak English.

Local information dial 981.
Local directory assistance dial 988.
Long-distance operator dial 989.
International operator dial 981.
For calls that can't be direct-dialed call 901.

Emergency calls (free, no coin required): Police dial 92; Fire dial 93; Ambulance dial 94.

Long-Distance Calls inside Yugoslavia, made from post offices, hotels, and private homes. Dial access code + city code + subscriber number.

International Calls from Yugoslavia, made from post offices, hotels, and private phones. Dial 99 + country code + city or area code + subscriber number.

To call Britain: dial 99 + 44 + area code + number (but not possible from coin phones).

Hotel Surcharge: No maximum percentage known.

Things You Should Know:
1. Reduced long-distance and international rates all day Sunday.
2. There is no operator service from some telephones accepting 50- and 100-dinar coins.

3. Area code map for Yugoslavia is near beginning of the phone book.

Telephone sounds you may hear:

Kind	Seconds 0 1 2 3 4 5 6 7 8 9 10	Description
Dial tone	■ I■ I■ I■ I■ I	0.7 tone, 0.8 sec. interval, then 0.2 sec. tone, 0.3 sec. interval.
Ringing	■ ■	1 second tone, 4 second interval.
or	■	1 second tone, 9 second interval.
Busy	■ ■ ■ ■ ■ ■ ■ ■ ■ ■	½ sec. tone and ½ sec. interval.
or	IIIIIIIIIIIIIIIIIII	0.2 sec. tone, then 0.4 second interval.
Out of order	✦ ✦ ✦ ✦ ✦	3 rising tones in 1 sec. and 1 second interval.
or		Ringing tone.

Finding Public Toilets

Public toilets in Europe can be elusive, difficult to find, and cost money. When you do find one, it may be lacking such necessities as cleanliness, toilet paper, sink and soap or even a recognizable toilet. On the other hand, in some countries, such as Switzerland, Germany, and the countries of Scandinavia, cleanliness standards are often admirable.

Add over Europe, watch for the initials "W.C.", or water closet, the Victorian invention attributed to Thomas Crapper. (Other names, including one honoring the inventor, are numerous.)

All over Europe, women will often have to queue, since there won't be enough cubicles to meet the demand. Therefore, if you think you may need to use a toilet in a public place and there's no queue, it's probably a short-lived fluke; use it now.

Be Prepared!

Toilets in Europe are not alsays free or well supplied, so plan ahead. Small coins are often necessary: 2 to 5 - 10 pfennig coins in West Germany, 1 or 2 francs in France, 100 or 200 lire in Italy. Nominal sums, but if the stalls are coin operated, you'll usually need exact change.

Some flush handles are mere knobs you pull, push, or twist. Many are on the tops of the tanks.

In addition, you'll be wise to carry toilet paper or paper tissues; the more primitive toilets won't provide any.

In southern or Eastern Europe, you may get paper with the texture of sandpaper. Soap also may be nonexistent; you may want to carry your own or packets of disposable freshener tissues.

Sanitary towels are almost never found in toilets, but are widely available at pharmacies throughout Western Europe.

A new item in Europe (found in France, Germany, and the Netherlands) is the "Hygrolet", which is a toilet whose seat is covered with a strip of plastic. Just touch the button, and the plastic strip spirals around the seat, providing you with a plastic-wrapped seat untouched by human bodies.

Where to Find Toilets

Airports

Major airports usually have the cleanest and best maintained of all toilets in public facilities, and they're almost always free. They'll have toilet paper, sinks with hot and cold water, soap, and even outlets for electric shavers (though check current compatability with your shaver).

Train and Bus Stations

Most stations have public toilets, and in major cities you will have to pay to use them. Whilst cubicles are coin-operated, urinals aren't in cubicles, and so they are free. If they have an attendant (often an old dragon lady), any use costs.

Sometimes there will be only a plate on a stand or table by the door. A coin is expected but clearly not obligatory.

The presence of an attendant, however, guarantees neither cleanliness nor adequate supplies. Again, carry some tissues with you at all times.

In middle-sized stations, the toilet will usually be free and in the building; in small stations, the toilet may be an unmarked brick or concrete outhouse 50 yards or so from the station proper. If you ask for the "W.C." spoken in some variation of "toilette", you'll be pointed in the right direction. It may be locked, in which case you'll have to ask the station master for the key.

Museums, Castles, and Historic Monuments

These attractions usually have toilets. Often inadequate in number—particularly for women—they are frequently unmarked and likely to be in the basement or near the ticket vending window. You'll probably have to ask a guard or guide for directions.

Usually there will be an attendant to collect a fee. In France and southern Europe, cleanliness, toilet paper, and soap may be lacking.

Churches and Religious Shrines

Churches and religious shrines rarely have running water, let alone toilets. There are often street-side toilets near major tourist attractions such as Chartres, Notre Dame, and St. Paul's.

Usually monasteries such as Melk (Austria) and Fontenay (France) have toilets, well marked near entrances, and before ticket takers.

Department Stores

Large department stores almost always have toilets available to the general public. Usually they are well maintained and supplied. Some are free, and those which are pay toilets usually have an attendant.

As is usual in Britain, the toilets are on an upper floor in a back corner, often near the restaurant. Look on the store directory (usually near the escalators and lifts) or ask a sales person for directions. Most will be happy to point you in the right direction.

Hotels

Large hotels invariably have clean, well supplied free facilities, usually on the lobby floor, often near the lounge or restaurant. The trick here is to look as if you belong. While you may have to look around, just be completely self-assured. If you look as if you aren't a guest, the doorman or receptionist clerk may intercept you.

For example, the Paris Ritz, though well endowed with elegant, spotless toilets, lets no men in for any purpose without coat and tie unless they are bona fide guests.

While small hotels also have toilets, the toilets are less easy to find, and you're more likely to be questioned.

The chain hotels which cater to businessmen and tourists—names familiar to you at home—are the likeliest to be hassle free. At these hotels, you probably can ask the location of toilets from the concierge or the reception desk.

Offices

Office buildings, whether private or public, always have toilets somewhere, often available to visitors. Usually they're kept at an adequate standard of repair, cleanliness, and supply, since the patrons are local and can effectively complain.

A building with a number of different businesses is more likely to have readily accessible toilets than one occupied by a single company with a front-door receptionist.

Garages

Garages outside of central cities almost always have toilets. Some require coins, but most are free. Standards can be variable; prepare for the worst—lacking supplies, dirty, and smelly. Toilets along motorways are usually acceptably clean. While your patronage of the service station may be expected, you'll rarely be denied use of toilets anyway.

Check around the side, though fancier stations may have the toilets in through the lobby.

On main roads, many garages also provide public toilets. While most are free, cubicles in Germany may require several 10-pfennig coins to enter.

Bars, Cafés, and Restaurants

Bars universally have toilets available for patrons and passers-by. After all, bars dispense liquid refreshment. Bar toilets can be basic; have supplies ready. Since many bars in Europe cater mainly to men, women's toilets may not be provided, or there may be only one toilet for both sexes.

You need not purchase anything. If sensitive, go to a place with outdoor tables and pretend you're a patron.

In restaurants, practices vary. Few countries are as easy as Czechoslovakia, where many restaurants have toilets in the entry vestibule. Only a few are attended and require payment. In some other countries, the toilets are off the bar or lounge.

Street-side Toilets

Public Urinals (for men only)

Small cement street-side walk-in urinals are still found in some countries, though not as common as several years ago. They may range from doubles to eight or ten stalls. Invariably they are poorly maintained though very conveniently located.

Attended Urban Public Toilets

Major cities have public toilets, usually attended. They come in all qualities, including awful, dirty, and fragrant. They are usually clearly marked, frequently underground. There will usually be an attendant; a coin will be required. Cleanliness and supplies will vary widely. Attended public toilets almost invariably close at night.

The "Sanisette" or "Superloo"

A space-age item made in France and now being exported to Belgium and Britain is the Sanisette.

These are small oval buildings on pavements. When you deposit the correct coin (one Franc in France, 10 Francs in Belgium, and from two to 10 pence in Britain), curved sliding door opens up a compartment. A sign outside informs you that the toilet is cleaned, sanitized, and disinfected after each and every use.

As you enter and close the door you will find abundant toilet paper, and a clean sink with soap and towels. Usually, soft music plays in the background. The entire cabin may be wet from its most recent cleaning, however.

As you leave, the toilet is pulled into the innards of the building, and the cleaning begins with the whirr of brushes and the purr of machinery.

Take note: Maximum permitted use per coin is 15 minutes. (What happens when the time is up, however, is unknown.)

The Hole in the Ground (Squat) Toilet

While in northern Europe and will be easily recognizable, in southern Europe and France you will often find the squat or Turkish toilet. This is a ceramic pan resembling a stall shower floor with a hole in the middle and two slightly raised foot pads (or in Turkey, an oval ceramic bowl without foot pads) set into the floor.
If you've never used one, these instructions will probably save you some surprises.

Walk in and turn around so that your feet are on the foot pads, or at the edge of the oval bowl. Drop your trousers or raise your dress. Squat low. This posture will keep your clothes clean and dry, and is the most comfortable in the circumstances. They are surprisingly well designed for biological functions, in spite of your initial state of anxiety.

When you are done, do not flush until you have pulled your clothes back on and stepped as far away from the toilet as possible. This is because the flush of water completely floods the pan, and can send odd streams and sprays all over the compartment. Leave as soon as possible.

Be especially careful if there is no flush button, lever, or pull chain. Some of these toilets are on timed flushing cycles. Listen for the first gurgle of water coming down the pipes, and prepare to move fast to avoid getting wet.

This type of toilet, particularly at train and bus stations, may be the worst maintained of all. You'll almost always need your own toilet paper or tissues in these facilities.

The Bush at the Side of the Road

Often there won't be a public toilet in the countryside when you need it. Europeans seem to have no reservations about using whatever fields and forests exist. The small tufts of toilet paper scattered behind lay-bys give you the idea.

Toilet Word Key

Country	Language
Austria	German
Belgium	French
	Flemish
Bulgaria	Bulgarian
Czechoslovakia	Czech, Slovak
Denmark	Danish
Finland	Finnish
France	French
Germany	German
Great Britain	English
Greece	Greek
Hungary	Hungarian
Ireland	English
Italy	Italian
Luxembourg	French (officially)
Netherlands	Dutch
Norway	Norwegian
Poland	Polish
Portugal	Portuguese
Romania	Romanian
Soviet Union	Russian
Spain	Spanish
Sweden	Swedish
Switzerland	German
	French
	Italian
Turkey	Turkish
Yugoslavia	Various

Finding Public Toilets 257

Toilet Word Key (continued)

Toilet	Men	Women
Toiletten, W.C.	Herren	Damen
Toilette, W.C.	Messieurs, Hommes	Femmes, Dames
W.C.	Heren	Dames
Клозет	Мужчины	Женщины
Klozet	(M)	(Ж)
Toaleta, W.C.	Pani, Muzi.	Damy, Zeni
Toiletter, W.C.	Herrer	Damer
Pukeutuminen, W.C.	Ihmiset, Miehet	Nainen, Naisille
Toilette, W.C.	Messieurs, Hommes	Dames, Femmes
Toiletten, W.C., 00	Herren	Damen
Toilet, Loo, W.C., Convenience	Gentlemen, Men	Ladies, Women
Τοαλεττασ (Toaléta)	Ανδρων (Andrón)	Γυναικωυ (Ghinekón)
W.C.	Ferfi	Noi
Toilet, W.C.	Gentlemen, Men	Ladies, Women
Gabinetto, W.C.	Signori, Uomini	Signore, Donne
W.C. Toilette	Messieurs	Dames
W.C.	Heren	Dames
Toaletter, W.C.	Menn	Kvinner
Toaleta	Panovie	Panie
W.C.	Homen	Senhoras
Toaleta	Oameni	Femeile
Туалет	Мужчины	Женщины
(Tooalét)	(M)	(Ж)
Sanitarios, W.C., Servicios	Señores, Hombres, Caballeros	Señoras, Damas
Toaletter, W.C.	Herrar	Damer
Toiletten, W.C.	Herren	Damen
Toilette, W.C.	Messieurs, Hommes	Femmes, Femmes
Gabinetto, W.C.	Signori, Uomini	Signore, Donne
Tuvalet, W.C., 00	Baylara, Erkeklere	Beyanlara, Kadinlara
W.C.	Man's shoe	Woman's shoe

Lodging
Finding a Place to Stay

Almost unlimited choices for overnight rest await you, from the most luxurious of hotels through modest inns, bed and breakfast in private homes, to campgrounds and sleeping by the side of the road.

Many travellers, worrying about where to stay each night, reserve rooms well in advance in hotels they haven't seen. Some spend large amounts of money to stay at hotels whose names they know at home. Unfortunately, these are often the hotels with the least character and atmosphere and with above-average to the highest prices.

Through the judicious use of guidebook recommendations, hotel-finding services, and your own intuition, you'll always be able to find a place to sleep at night, even without reservations, and without sleeping under a bridge.

The following hints will make your choices easier, however:

1. Find your lodging by mid-afternoon. Many travellers don't even start looking until late afternoon. You won't need to worry about not finding a place if you arrive at your day's destination by late morning in cities and mid-afternoon in the countryside.

2. Look near a major railway station for hotels. They range from humble to at least mid-range in cost and amenities. Hotels on side streets will usually be cheaper than those on main access roads.

3. Ask the room-finding service to find you a place. These offices are most likely found in tourist information offices in train stations and airports. This is useful only if you arrive during business hours. You will usually be charged a small fee and may have to pay for the room right there, but you're assured of a bed for the night at a known cost. While it's a pig-in-a-poke situation, if you don't like your hotel that night, you'll be able to find another one tomorrow.

Generally airport offices are less busy and often have rooms after all the rooms listed with the train station office have been taken.

You may have to insist strongly to room-finding services to keep within your price range.

4. Use a guidebook you trust. Call early in the day or even the day before you arrive.

What's Your Choice?

Hotels

Hotels range from modest inns to converted palaces able to cater to virtually your every whim. Usually local law requires the price of the room to be posted; look for it on the inside of the door to the room to ensure it is the same as the receptionist told you. You will also be able to determine whether breakfast is included.

When looking for a room, you have every right to inspect it before you agree to take it. Many Europeans do as a matter of course: receptionists are used to this, and will either take you up or just give you the key.

If for some reason you don't like the room, ask to see another or try somewhere else. Unless you have made a reservation, you're under no obligation to stay. Just say thank you, or the local equivalent, and leave.

Baths, Showers, Sinks, and Toilets

Almost without exception, all rooms have a washbasin and mirror. Towels may be small and thin and there will rarely be a facecloth. Many small hotels don't provide soap; others give several tiny bars. When there are extras, consider taking them.

You may not find a toilet, a bath, or shower in the room. A room with shower or bath and toilet will cost as much as 50% more than a similar room without them. You will find the toilet and bath or shower down the hall. If the bath or shower door is not locked from the outside with a key, it is probably free. If it is locked and not being used, you'll have to ask the management for the key. You will be charged a small sum.

Shower curtains are infrequent in France and southern Europe—don't worry too much about water splashing all over the floor (some have floor drains).

The Bidet

Many hotel rooms, particularly in France and Italy, come with bidets, for cleaning yourself after you have used the toilet. Fill it up with water and sit on it to use it properly. (Some bidets include upward spray nozzles.)

Hotel Deposits

If you have reserved a room and paid in advance for it, the management is in many countries under no legal or ethical obligation to return any of it if for some reason you can't or won't stay in the hotel on the night you paid for.

Staying on the Train

Almost every European overnight train makes special provisions for sleeping, both in first class and second class. Some travellers—especially those with railpasses and tight schedules—use trains as hotels. For only a small charge, you can reserve a sleeper "Couchette". While this arrangement may not be quite as restful or roomy as a hotel or bed and breakfast inn, it neatly combines traveling and sleeping.

There are no showers and baths aboard; however, many major European railway stations have "Day Hotels" (particularly in Italy, where they are called "Albergo Diurno") to obtain inexpensively showers, baths, and even short-term room rental.

Bed and Breakfast (B&B)

The usual European bed and breakfast down to earth and quite modest in price. There may or may not be antiques, there may or may not be elegance, and, particularly at English seaside resorts, there may or may not be peeling paint, stuffy rooms, and lumpy mattresses.

Staying at B&Bs can be one of the best ways to meet the locals, since you're often treated as an honoured guest in the family home.

Your hosts will also be knowledgeable about nearby restaurants, since dinner is not usually included, though sometimes it is available at extra cost. Your hosts should also know of things to see in the neighbourhood, unique adventures, and public transport.

B&Bs abound in Britain, Ireland, Austria, and Germany. In France they're quite scarce; the few that do exist are mainly in the foreign-influenced holiday areas such as the Dordogne valley and Alsace.

In Eastern European nations such as Czechoslovakia and Hungary, you can often arrange lodgings on the spot through the official government tourist agencies such as Cedok and Ibusz. These lodgings are much cheaper than hotels, and will give you a far more accurate view of daily life than in the hotels open to tourists. This approach is not possible in East Germany or the Soviet Union, since all lodgings must be arranged and paid for far in advance, or Romania, where it is illegal to stay in a private residence unless closely related.

British B&Bs

Almost every major town and many minor ones have Tourist Information Centres which will book you a room for a small fee (often 75p or £1). Find Tourist Information Centres by following the lower-case "i" signs. You are likely to be matched with hosts who may share your interests, or at least your age and general demeanor. Costs may begin around £10 per person per night (depending on region), including a full breakfast.

Only a few bed and breakfasts in Britain have signs, so finding them along roadsides can be difficult.

Another solution in Britain is to use the annually updated AA/BTA guide, "Guesthouses Farmhouses and Inns in Britain", widely available in Britain. You can call ahead the same day for a room or reserve well in advance.

Irish B&Bs

You can find B&Bs throughout Ireland. Tourist information offices can call around to find you a room. Registered B&Bs can be found by looking for the Irish Tourist Board's green and white shamrock "Approved" sign. Sometimes you'll also find homemade signs on unregistered homes. Costs will begin at about 10 Irish pounds per person per night, almost invariably including a full breakfast.

Austrian and German "Fremdenzimmer" or "Zimmer Frei"

Austrian and German private homes with rooms for travellers are not neatly listed in a book. Local tourist offices (look for the "i" sign) can refer you, but often the best solution is to wander down a country road watching for signs reading "Fremdenzimmer" or "Zimmer Frei" (room available). The cost will be modest—often less than £10 per person, including breakfast.

These guest houses seem to be most densely packed into holiday areas such as the Austrian Alps and Bavaria. Often your hillside chalet room will have geranium-filled window boxes, a view of pine-clad mountains, and the breeze-borne scent of wildflowers and new-mown hay.

Dutch Pension or "Kosthuis"

When you're going to spend at least a few days in one place, you might stay at a pension, sometimes known as a "Kosthuis" which is like a boarding house. For more information, follow the blue and white VVV signs to the tourist information office in the town.

Scandinavia

Since the tourist season is short (summer), accommodations are at a premium. As a result, local tourist offices usually have extensive lists of private homes providing bed and breakfast.

Breakfast

The bed is only half of the arrangement. The other half will be the breakfast.

In Germany and Austria, it can include cheese, a boiled egg, and sometimes sliced luncheon meat, along with rolls or bread, jam butter, coffee, or pot of tea or hot chocolate. In the Netherlands, northern Belgium, and Scandinavia, it can also be substantial.

In France and southern Europe, it is almost always the continental breakfast—hard rolls (rarely croissants), butter, jam packets, and coffee (sometimes tea or hot chocolate).

Baths and Showers

Baths or showers are available at virtually all bed and breakfast establishments. In Britain, they are free and may be down the hall. On the continent, baths and showers often cost extra—a matter of a pound or two. Ask your host about bathing arrangements. (In most European languages, the word for shower is "douche", the word for bath is "bad" in German, "bain" in French, and "bagno" in Italian.)

Staying on a Farm

Many European farm families open their homes to travellers who will stay a week or two. These arrangements usually must be made in advance, and several services for arrangements exist. In addition, some services can arrange short-term rentals of vacation homes. For further information, contact the offices listed below.

Austria

Austria has a program of farm stays, called "Erholung auf dem Bauernhof", which lists hundreds of farms welcoming visitors. Many but not all are in the picturesque Tirol and Salzburger Land regions. Daily costs including breakfast range from 90 to 140 schillings per day. Information is available from Austrian National Tourist Offices, or directly from the "Holiday on a Farm Information Office" in each region of Austria.

Belgium

The picturesque Ardennes offer the largest concentration of farmstay holiday locations, but there are others throughout the country. Bed and breakfast range up to about 1000 francs per person per day, and farm chalets cost around 700 to 1200 francs per person per day. For information, contact:
Vacances à la Ferme/Fetourag A.A.B.
rue de la Science 21, Boîte 2
1040 Bruxelles, Belgium
Tel. (02) 230 72 95

Denmark

Many Danish farms welcome visitors, especially during the summer months. They are mainly in the Brande, Horsens, Varde, and Køge regions. Bed and breakfast range from about 200 Dkr per person per day to bed and three meals a day for about 200 Dkr. Further information is available from the Danish Tourist Board, or directly from:

Tourist Association Horsens
Det Gamle Raadhus
26 Søndergade
DK-8700 Horsens, Denmark
Tel. (05) 62 38 22, telex 61668

Finland

Finnish farms' visitor programs offer both farmstays with the family, and holiday cottages on working farms. Costs for bed and brakfast start around Finnish Markka (FIM) 100 per day; half-pension (two meals) from FIM 130, and full pension (three meals) from FIM 170. An annual booklet, "Farm Holidays in Finland", is available from Finnish Tourist Board offices. For information and reservations, contact:
Suomen 4 H-Iiitto
Boulevardi 28
SF 00120 Helsinki, Finland
Tel. (90) 645133

France

Gîtes Rurales, a non-profit-making French organization dedicated to staying on French farms puts out a yearly book, "French Farm and Village Holiday Guide", which is available from bookshops in Britain. The cost for bed and breakfast ranges from 90 to 160 F per person per night. Arrangements may be made directly with the farmer in some circumstances; in others you have to deal with a French regional office or the London office. For further information, contact:

Gîtes de France
178 Piccadilly
London W1
Tel. 01-493 3480
or

Fédération Nationale
des Gîtes Ruraux
rue Godot de Mauroy
75009 Paris, France
Tel. 47.72.20.20, ask for
"Tourisme Vert"

Germany (West)

Germany has a long tradition of farmhouse stays. A non-profit-making German organization, the "Deutsche Landwirtschaft Gesellschaft") publishes an annual colour guide listing hundreds of farms. The book is called "Urlaub auf dem Bauernhof".

You must make contacts or reservations directly; bed and breakfast costs start at DM 30 to DM 40 per person per night. The guide is published annually and available for DM 7 plus postage and packing from:
DLG-Verlag GmbH
Rüsterstrasse 13
D-6000 Frankfurt am Main 1
West Germany
Tel. (069) 716 83 41.

In addition to the national organization, some regional non-profit-making organizations also publish pamphlets and guides.

For the southwest, including the Black Forest, you can obtain the annual free brochure which includes descriptions, photos, prices, and a map. It is also called "Urlaub auf dem Bauernhof" from a non-profit-making organization that inspects and classifies farm and holiday homes.

For further information, contact:
Urlaub auf dem Bauernhof
Freidrichstrasse 43 (in person)
Postfach 5443 (by mail)
D-7800 Freiburg
West Germany
Tel. (0761) 271 33 91

Make arrangements through the office or directly with the farmer.

In the Rhineland in west-central Germany, including the main German wine regions, a similar non-profit-making organization publishes a booklet with hundreds of farms and vineyards welcoming guests. It has descriptions and prices (including the types of animals!) but no photos. It is free when sent outside of Germany and 40 pfennigs in Germany. The booklet is called "Ferien auf Bauern- und Winzerhöfen".

For further information, contact:

Fremdenverkehrsverband Rheinland-Pfalz e.V.
Postfach 1420
D-5400 Koblenz
West Germany
Tel. (0261) 3 10 79
Telex 862495

Great Britain

Britain is one of the most rewarding places to stay on farms. Many local tourist information centres will, upon request, find a farm B&B for you. They're usually quieter and the rooms tend to be larger than in town. Costs usually start at £10 per person per night.

You can obtain advance information about farm stays. Ask at travel information centres for the annual booklet, "Stay on a Farm", listing hundreds of farms in all parts of Britain (including England, Scotland, Wales, and Northern Ireland).

The Northern Ireland Tourist Board (address in the "Before You Go" chapter) produces a similar booklet called "Northern Ireland Farm and Country Holidays", 50 pence in Britain and free elsewhere. The booklet has photos and particulars of working farms scattered throughout Northern Ireland. Book directly with the farm.

In addition, the Farm Holiday Bureau publishes a detailed annual book of its' members farms, which includes over 1000. The "1989 Farm Holidays in Britain" is £3.50 from the Farm Holiday Bureau, or is also available from the British Tourist Authority (price may vary). The book includes illustrations, descriptions, and prices for over 1000 of farms in England, Wales, and Northern Ireland, and Scotland.

Book stays directly with the farmer; however the Group Vacancy Secretary may also help at the last minute. For further information, contact:
The Farm Holiday Bureau
National Agricultural Centre
Stoneleigh, Kenilworth
Warwickshire CV8 2LZ
el. (0203) 555100, fax (0203) 696900, telex 31697

Greece

Greece's farms, often in the back country but also on islands, offer various attractions for a holiday. Not as developed as farmstays in France or Britain, you may find it more refreshing for that very reason. The prices are reasonable, and vary by location. A few cooperatives in several regions organize the scheme.

For information and reservations, contact:

Agricultural
Cooopcrative of
Ambelakia
41000 Ambelakia
Greece

Agricultural Cooperative
of Petra
18008 Petra-Lesvos
Greece
Tel. (0253) 41238

Agricultural Cooperative of Chio
82100 Pirghi-Chios
Greece
Tel. (0271) 72496

Hungary

Hungary is a relatively new entry in the holiday on the farm theme, offering about 500 farm locations. Many farmstays are combined with nearby mineral hot springs. Costs are relatively reasonable. For details and reservations, contact:
Agroinform
Petöfi Sandor utca 17-19
H-1065 Budapest
Hungary
Tel. (01) 179800

Ireland

Ireland, long a country of warm welcomes and hospitality, has an active farmstay program, which runs rather like a bed and breakfast scheme. General costs are from £10 Irish per person per day for bed and breakfast. For further information contact the nearest Irish Tourist Board office.

Italy

Agriturist is an organization listing farms for holiday-makers. Farmstays in Italy can cost from a minumum of Lire 10,000 per person per night to over twice that. The Alps and Tuscany seem to have higher prices than the south. Agriturist can be contacted through many regional offices in Italy, or its headquarters. This organization also publishes a directory ("Guida dell'Ospitalità Rurale", 18,000 Lire) every two years that includes not only hundreds of farms welcoming tourists, but also includes a complete listing of the regional and local Agriturist agencies. Make arrangements directly with the farmer. For further information, contact:
Agriturist
Corso Vittorio Emmanuele 101
00186 Roma
Italy
Tel. (06) 65 12 342

Netherlands

Farm stays in the Netherlands are mainly camping on farms rather than home stays. A few farms have vacation cottages. In all, there are about 1500 participating farms. For further information, contact:
Central Farmers' Organisation
International Secretary
19 Prinsevinkenpark
2825 HK Den Haag
The Netherlands
Tel. (070) 526666

Poland

Prices in Poland's rural farms are low: for example, bed and one meal during the day can cost as little as 4,000 zloty. Families are welcomed. Most farm stays are available only from June through September. For information, contact:
Gromada
Wczasow pod gruszas
Ulica Podvale 23
00952 Warswawa
Poland
Tel. (022) 311211 through -5

Portugal

In Portugal, you can stay on a farm, and either engage in farm work or not. In either case, all homes are registered with the local Tourist Office. Prices are reasonable. For information, contact:

Ospatalità e vacanze lavoro
Segretaria de Estado de Turismo
Segretariado de Apoio ad Investidor
Avenida Antonia Augusto de Agular 86-9º
1004 Lisboa codex, Portugal
Tel. (01) 575040

Spain

The Spanish farm stay program was begun in 1957, and is available in most parts of the country. Information is available from most Spanish National Tourist Offices; ask for information about farm stays "Vacaciones en Casas de Labranza".

Switzerland

Swiss hospitality extends to the farm as well as the hotel industry. Swiss farm holidays cost from about Sfr 25 per person per night for bed and

breakfast. There are also farm chalets. For information in the French-speaking region, contact:
Fédération de Tourisme de la Suisse Romande
Office du Tourisme
CH-1530 Payerne, Switzerland

For information in the German-speaking region, contact:
Verkehrsverein Andermatt
Bahnhofplatz
CH-6940 Andermatt, Switzerland

Yugoslavia

Farm stays in Yugolavia are almost entirely in the northern region of Slovenia, near to Austria and Italy. Prices are reasonable, and the regional organisation inspects all farms. For information, contact:
Zadruzna Zveva Slojenije
Miklosiceva 4
61000 Ljubljana, Yugoslavia
Tel. (061) 211911

Home Exchanging

If you plan to stay in one area for an extended period, you may be able to exchange your home. A number of home exchange services exist in Britain. Contact the service(s) well in advance. Many services issue catalogues full of homes available for exchange. Many services charge for their catalogue and ask you to complete the arrangements yourself. Others make the arrangements themselves and charge a service fee. Screening of clients and homes varies from agency to agency.

A listing in a catalogue will clearly state if the exchange includes the use of a car and/or the care of gardens or pets. If you don't want to exchange, you can sometimes rent houses listed in the exchanges. Most services charge from £15 to £30 for catalogues; if they perform additional services, the charges are higher.

Home Exchange Services

Euro Exchange Club
New Barn House, Toft Road
Kingston, Cambridgeshire CB3 7NS
Tel. (022026) 2783

Publishes regular catalogues, free of charge. If you find an exchange through this service, you will be billed about £40. Mainly Denmark, France, and the Netherlands, plus scattered other locations.

Home Interchange Ltd.
8 Hillside
Farningham, Kent DA4 0DD
Tel. (0322) 864527

A member of the International Directory Group Association. Publishes a catalogue annually; make the arrangements directly with the listed parties.

INTERVAC Great Britain
6 Siddals Lane
Allestre, Derby DE3 2DY
Tel. (0332) 558931

Publishes a catalogue, which offer exchanges throughout Western Europe. Make arrangements directly with prospective exchange parties.

Worldwide Home Exchange Club
45 Hans Place
London, SW1X 0JZ. England
Tel. (01) 589-6055

Publishes an annual directory in January plus a supplement in April. The two volumes have about 800 listings from 30 countries. Directory includes sample contracts and checklists. Make your own arrangements directly with the other party. Some rentals are also included. A copy of the directory and listing of your home is about £15.

Home and Flat Rental

If you'd rather rent than exchange, your choices are exceedingly wide. Rentals generally are available only in Western Europe; in many parts of Eastern Europe, housing is in short supply or not considered suitable for short-term rentals.

Many frequented tourist areas in Western Europe have a wide selection of farms, chalets, houses, and flats for short- or long-term rental. Bear in mind that amenities can vary from place to place and region to region. The minimum term is usually one week, though in some areas it is up to one month in summer.

Various agencies have different ways to select rentals. You should ask how listings are chosen, what verification has been done of amenities and surroundings, and determine exact costs. Ask about transport: sometimes a car is included; sometimes access to sports facilities and accommodation for children may also be included. In London, many travellers have rented flats for a period of one week or more. The cost usually includes some maid service as well as a kitchen with pots, pans, and utensils. Note that many rentals in the south of France do not include any services, utilities, or even linens. On the other hand, maids as well as cooks are sometimes included in Portuguese rentals.

Generally, the entire amount of the rental is payable before you take possession.

The coasts of Spain and Portugal, the French and Italian Riviera, Tuscany, and the Alps have hundreds of rentals, ranging from cliff side apartments above Cannes to flats in Spain. In other areas, you can find fully-equipped manor houses, villas, and just about anything else you can conceive.

Costs per person for rentals are often less than for a hotel of equivalent quality, partly because you're not paying for expensive hotel staff, and because you're freed of hotel and restaurant meals.

Rental Agencies

A number of agencies offer you help in finding a suitable short-term home. In addition to the two on the Continent, there are many estate agents and specialists booking holiday rentals. Many are listed in the telephone book under "Holiday Accommodation". In addition, many travel agents are able to book holiday flats and houses. The following two do not have British offices.

Paris Séjour Reservation
90 avenue de Champs-Elysées, 3rd floor
75008 Paris
France
Tel. (1) 42.56.30.00, fax (1) 42.89.42.97
This rental agency offers about 300 apartments in Paris, ranging from studios to four-bedroom flats at prices from 250 to 1500 francs per night. If you are not able to reserve in advance, you can call or visit the Paris office when you arrive.

PEGO (Peter Godula)
Sägeweg 12
A-6700 Bludenz, Austria
Tel. (05552) 65666, fax (05552) 63801
Telex 52169
This firm issues a yearly English-language catalog of holiday homes and chalets, mainly in the Austrian Alps (Vorarlberg, Tirol, and Salzburg regions). The catalogue includes photos and terms for several hundred places.

Hostels

The youth hostel system provides an inexpensive network of places to sleep in almost every country in Europe. Despite the youth hostel name, there are no age limitations except in southern Germany. In fact, some of them are overrun by senior citizens' groups.

Most hostels are affiliated with the International Youth Hostel Federation (IYHF). To use affiliated hostels, you're supposed to have an IYHF card. Most hostels have curfews; the doors are locked at night, some as early as 10.30 p.m. and others as late as 2 a.m.

Hostels unaffiliated with the IYHF, usually only found in large cities, do not require a hostel card. These hostels, though similar, are usually less restrictive and often have no curfews.

Cards should be obtained from a hostelling organisation. The price for an annual card is £7 for adults (over 21), £3.60 junior (16-21), and £1.60 (from 5 to 15). Family memberships are £14. Lifetime memberships are £70. Non-residents of Britain can purchase guest cards at £1.25 per coupon (each valid for one night's stay at a hostel); after 6 coupons, the guest card is used as a regular hostel card. Prices may vary slightly in Scotland and Northern Ireland. Obtain the card from the youth hostel organisation in your region.

England and Wales

Headquarters
Youth Hostels
Association
Trevelyan House
8 St Stephen's Hill
St Albans,
Herts. AS1 2DY
Tel. (0727) 55215
Fax (0727) 44126
Telex 265258 YHAEW G

London office
YHA
14 Southampton Street,
Covent Garden
London WC2E 7HY
Tel. 01-836 8541
Telex 269330 YHATVL G

Scotland

Headquarters
Scottish Youth Hostels
Association
7 Glebe Crescent
Stirling FK8 2JA
Tel. (0786) 51181
Telex 779689 SYHA G

Northern Ireland

Headquarters
Youth Hostel Association
of Northern Ireland
56 Bradbury Place
Belfast BT7 1RU
Telephone (0232) 324733

Some affiliated hostels in Europe are rather casual about asking to see the card. Others will sell you a hostel card on the spot, though there may be an extra fee for this.

You can buy the International Youth Hostel Handbook, Vol. I (Europe and the Mediterranean, £3.50, £4 by post) from the youth hostel organizations, which lists all officially recognized IHYF hostels in Europe. This is important because many of the most pleasant ones are hidden in the countryside and are hard to find. Often those in cities can be found by asking at the local tourist information offices or by following the distinctive hostel logo (a leaning pine tree and house).

Hostels do have several disadvantages. All hostels close at least the sleeping areas during the day, and often the rest of the hostel as well. This makes it inconvenient if you want a midday rest or access to your luggage.

Hostel accommodation varies from four-bed rooms to a few vast barrack-like halls with dozens of beds. The sexes are usually strictly segregated in sleeping rooms and baths.

In cities, hostels can be inconveniently located and not always close to public transport.

Perhaps the worst problem an independent traveler faces (especially in summer) is tour group reservations. Youth and elderly travel groups reserve entire hostels well in advance and then arrive in tour buses. If all beds are full, you're out of luck. Making reservations for yourself is a problem, because you must usually make your reservations directly with each hostel, stating specific dates of your stay, and make full payment with vouchers with your reservation. (The International Youth Hostel Handbook lists those hostels with this requirement.)

Some hostels also have inadequate facilities, such as showers. If there are enough showers, there may not be any or enough hot water. In short, though hostels are inconsistent, most don't have the problems listed above. Though the hostel book doesn't do a complete job of telling you which ones are pleasant and which ones aren't, the book and travellers met along the way are your best hostel information.

Camping

Europeans are avid campers. A dense network of campsites has been created all across the continent. In Western Europe, many are privately owned and others are owned by city and town governments.

Many campsites are holiday retreats, where Europeans park caravans from year to year. More settled individual campsites include potted geranium plants and window boxes, television antennas, and occasionally a cuckoo clock.

There won't be picnic tables and chairs provided. Open fires are usually prohibited, so all cooking must be done on portable campstoves.

Most campsites are simply grassy areas, and people pitch tents or park caravans wherever space can be found. Campsites vary in size; you may be five or ten feet from your neighbours.

Showers may cost extra. Sometimes cold showers are free, but for hot showers you must either rent the key from the management, or drop coins every few minutes in the timer of a gas water heater.

At campsites, you are charged per person and per vehicle per day.

If you don't want to camp at campsites, in Western Europe, you are supposed to get the permission of the landowner to camp in fields and forests. In Eastern Europe, you are required to stay in official campsites. If you don't, you won't have the police stamps on your visa, and you may be held up at the border on your way out as the guards interrogate you about your movements.

Several camping guides exist: the Michelin camping guide of France is excellent. The most comprehensive camping guide for the entire continent, however, is the multilingual "Camping + Caravanning Europa" published in Germany easily obtained throughout Europe.

Many campsites require you to leave identification at the office as a guarantee of payment. Passports may be demanded unless you can offer a "Camping Carnet".

The carnet is obtainable from motoring organisations, and in Europe from motoring organisations, camping organisations, and many campsite registration offices.

Food and Drink

Your travels in Europe can be a gastronomic delight, as you enjoy the national cooking of the various nations. Meals are taken more seriously than in Britain, often comprising more courses and may last for hours.

There are many alternatives to restaurant fare. Picnics of savoury cold cuts, freshly-baked bread, colourful salads, and fruit of a sweenness and flavour matched only by that you pick yourself provide a tempting and economical alternative to a restaurant lunch or dinner.

The "sandwich" or "pannino imbottito" are the French and Italian incarnations of the sandwich.

The meals are, in the day's order:

Breakfast

The Full Breakfast

In most of northern Europe you will find a breakfast resembling the familiar one at home: orange juice or grapefruit; cereal; bacon, eggs, sausage, tomato, mushrooms and fried bread (or any selection therefrom); toast and marmalade; and tea and coffee. This breakfast is a filling, nourishing, high-cholesterol meal that should keep you going at least until lunch if not dinner. Breakfast is almost always included in the price of the room. In general, the smaller and more rural the establishment, the better the breakfast.

In all of France and some larger hotels in Britain, particularly in London, you will be offered the "Continental" breakfast (see below).

The Continental Breakfast

In most of southern Europe, the Continental breakfast reigns supreme, and the full breakfast is usually unknown and often unavailable even at an exorbitant price. The classic Continental breakfast consists of one or two rolls (including a croissant, if you're lucky), a pat of butter, jams and jellies in small plastic packets with peel-off covers, a single cup of coffee or a small pot of tea, or sometimes hot chocolate. If you're fortunate, you might get a small slice of cheese, or, in Eastern Europe, a slice of salami and pepper or cucumber.

In some countries, this modest breakfast is included in the price of the room. In others, particularly France and often Italy, it is usually a one- to four-pound per person add-on. Surprisingly, the most expensive hotels don't always charge the most. In France, the law states that you don't have to buy the hotel breakfast when you stay there overnight. Many hoteliers won't tell you this. Regulations vary elsewhere. Unless time and convenience are crucial, or you're a very timid traveller, try to tell the manager you don't want breakfast to avoid being charged. Polite firmness at the time of registration is the best approach.

In Germany, Austria, the Netherlands, and northern Belgium, the Continental breakfast is often augmented with a hard- or soft-boiled egg and a slice of cheese. Many mid-range to luxury hotels offer a buffet breakfast. The price of breakfast is usually included in the room.

In modestly-priced establishments, watch out for weak or heated-up coffee, yesterday's rolls, and postage-stamp sized paper napkins.

Alternatives to the Hotel Breakfast

Cheaper and better alternatives to a hotel breakfast exist. If you crave a strong, freshly-brewed cup of coffee to wake you up, go to local cafes or bars. The bar isn't the vile smoke-filled place you might expect: it is more like cafe.

The coffee will almost always be freshly-brewed for you and strong. You pay by the cup; no free refills are included. If you want another cup, you place another order and pay for it. Each cup may cost as much as a pound or even more. You can also order tea—which usually will be an inferior tea-bag blend, and often presented as a cup of hot (not boiling!) water with a tea-bag in the saucer.

Many bars and cafes have rolls or croissants to complete your Continental breakfast. Since bars and cafes depend on locals for patronage, the quality is usually far better than many hotels and much less expensive.

Even better bread and pastry than in the cafes and bars can be found in the multitude of local bakeries. These usually open at dawn or by 6 a.m., whichever comes first. You'll find bread still warm, croissants and brioche, and small batches of many kinds of pastry. You will probably not see "Danish pastries" covered with globs of pure sugar glazing, even in Denmark. The bakery products will usually be cheaper than in Britain.

A baker round every corner, and at least one in each hamlet who does lots of handwork to make small quantities, may be "inefficient production" from the jaundiced eye of the economist. It is, however, an enduring pleasure to locals and travellers alike.

You can get the best of a Continental breakfast by eating it as a progressive meal—that is, progress from lodgings to a cafe or bar (where in France you'll often find workers having their morning Cognac) for coffee, or tea. Next, go to a bakery for roll or pastry, and then on to the day's events.

You can also short-circuit this approach by buying some food the day before. You can even get an electric water heater for tea or instant coffee. Either buy one in Europe or buy converter plugs for the countries you're visiting. (Most European instant coffee is very good.)

Luncheon

The midday meal is the big meal of the day in Europe, particularly in the south. The gulped odds and ends crammed down in 15 or 20 minutes is rare. The large lunch—taking two hours or more—creates the perfect prelude to a siesta. As a result, major cities such as Rome or Madrid have four rush hours: early morning, one just before lunch and one just after, and late in the afternoon when workers head for home. On the other hand, virtually no one travels in the middle of lunch hours: it can be a real pleasure as you pass through almost empty streets.

In Britain, relatively reasonably-priced midday specials are offered by many restaurants that are far costlier at night. A few of Paris' most famous and expensive restaurants have begun to follow this custom as well.

Picnic Lunches

Lunch is the best time to have a picnic. Most of Europe has wide grassy areas along the roadside and many tranquil fields, pastures, and city park benches. But don't try to picnic in Venice's Piazza San Marco! You'll be fined 50,000 Lire if caught. The possibilities are limited only by your imagination—and by local supplies. The larder is full to overflowing throughout Western Europe. Eastern Europe presents, in contrast, cheap, excellent and widely available bread, alcoholic beverages, and sometimes little else.

East or West, you have to buy everything for your picnic before the lunch hour begins. Even many large food stores and supermarkets *may* close. Small shops and groceries almost always close. Once closed, often with the rattle of metal shutters, your only nourishment will be at an eating establishment such as a restaurant, cafe, or bar.

Buying will be an adventure: you go to the bakery for bread and pastry, to the delicatessen for meats and prepared salads, and to the grocers for drink and sometimes fruit. Queues may form just before closing time. Give yourself enough time to buy everything.

Your picnic will be much more pleasant if you have a beach towel or blanket to sit on. In most European city parks, it is forbidden to be on the beautiful lush grass. If you're permitted to be on it, the grass will either be scraggly, barely surviving, or very wet. In the countryside, the lush green appearance of distant fields becomes transformed upon closer view to tough grass and sometimes mud with a sharp pebble just where you sit down.

For a Nibble or Light Lunch

If you don't want a picnic, you can usually find a reasonably-priced snack at a cafe. This will often turn out to be the crusty equivalent of a sandwich, filled with ham, chicken, or other local products. You won't find squeezy bottles of mustard or ketchup on the table, though it is often available upon request.

The Evening Meal

The evening meal served in restaurants will be the very same as the luncheon in many countries such as Italy, France, and Germany. The cost will often be the same as well. Timing will vary by country: dinners may be served beginning at 6.30 p.m. and Scandinavia, 8 p.m. in France and Italy, and almost never before 10 p.m. in Spain. (In Spain, bars serve "tapas", small appetizer plates that keep your hunger at bay until dinner.) Dinner isn't rushed: it can be even more leisurely than lunch. One and a half to two hours isn't uncommon.

When a "Menu" Isn't a Menu

When you want to know what foods a restaurant offers, in Belgium, Denmark, France, Italy, the Netherlands, Spain, and Yugoslavia, do *not* ask for a "menu" unless you want the set meal. Many times the "menu" isn't shown on the regular bill of fare but rather on a separate sheet you may have to request.

What we call a menu is called "carte du jour" in French, "lista del giorno" in Italian, and "Speisekarte" in German. On it will be "a la carte" selections as well as the "menu(s)".

A la Carte

You compose an "a la carte" meal by choosing a procession of dishes from any of the food categories. Listings will often be broken down into appetizers, soups, pastas, meats, poultry, fish, sometimes vegetables, and desserts. Generally you are expected to order an appetizer, one main course, and usually a dessert.

Appetizers are first: the exact content will vary by country, by region, and by the style and elegance of the restaurant. In some countries, such as Italy, the appetizers (antipasti) will be a collection of a number of pickles, cold cuts, vegetables, and salami.

If soup and pasta are on the bill of fare, do not expect to order both without getting a quizzical look from the waiter.

If there is only one meat course, it can be any meat, or even a fancy salad or an omelette. It will in most cases include a garnish of vegetables.

If there are two main courses, fish is served first, and then the next will be meat. The second main course will never be fish. It will include meat, poultry, or game, and a garnish of vegetables, potatoes, noodles, or rice.

The next course can be salad, cheese, or dessert. (In Germany and Italy, salad may be served with the main course, too.) Many European salads are simple: lettuce, tomato, or cucumber dressed with oil and vinegar. The cheese tray in France offers you as many as two dozen choices from the 400 kinds produced in that country. You can try a taste of one or of all offered for the same price.

Next will be dessert. All of the better French and Belgian restaurants take great pride in their desserts and will offer you any or all of the dozen or more on the trolley or platter—and charge for only one!

Coffee—one cup, no free refills—is rarely served until after the dessert. In fact, ordering coffee will often be taken as a signal that you have finished eating, and a call for the bill with it as well.

Aside from this single circumstance, the bill is rarely brought in a restaurant until you ask for it.

The Set Meal (Menu)

If set meals (menus) are offered, they will be listed on the bill of fare at fixed prices. These are complete meals for less money than a la carte selections. A "menu" will at a minimum provide an appetizer, starter, pasta or soup, followed by a main course and dessert. Often you choose one of the two or three items offered for each course.

The most reasonably-priced "menu" is often called the tourist menu or *dagesnätter* in Sweden (lunch only), *menu touristique* (France), *menu turistico* (Italy and Spain), *table d'hôte* (Britain), and *Tagesmenu* in Germany. In some countries, reasonably priced two- or three-course lunches are offered. Establishments offering these special lunches are marked, usually by stickers at the door. In Denmark, a lunch of this type is known as *Danmenu,* in Norway (summer only) as a *Holiday Menu,* and in the Netherlands as a *Tourist Menu.*

Menus, or fixed price meals, always include tax in the price. In many, if not most, the service charge or tip will be included, too.

Other Meals

Tapas

Appetizer plates are served in Spanish bars to ward off hunger pangs until the 10 p.m. dinner. These "tapas" can provide enough nourishment to serve as a light dinner by themselves.

Snacks

Pastry, ice cream, coffee, fresh fruit and vegetables are sold almost everywhere. Cafes are good sources of snack food. Many of the rest of items can be bought from street vendors, kiosks, and stores.

Fast Food

For centuries, street vendors have been found all over European cities and towns. Hot dog vendors are still plentiful in Austria, Germany and Denmark. Belgium's favorite fast food is superb fried potatoes ("Friture" or "Frituur") served salted and with mayonnaise or mustard.

You can also find such familiar signs as McDonalds, Burger King, Kentucky Fried Chicken, and Wendy's. McDonalds, for example, has an outlet on Paris' Champs Elysées as well as a few locations scattered throughout Western Europe. Fish and chips to go are widely available, too.

Drinks with a Meal

Tap water

You may have to ask for tap water repeatedly, and will most likely get a small tumbler-full or very small carafe and a tumbler. Tap water is safe to drink except in Leningrad (U.S.S.R), Turkey, and Bulgaria.

Mineral Water

You can get mineral water virtually anywhere—it is universally available in bottles and widely accepted. You can get it fizzy or still—make your preference known. Many mineral waters are distributed only in the region of origin, making them a local pleasure.

Coffee

Coffee is not usually served during any meal except breakfast. Otherwise, it is served only with or after dessert. When requested early at lunch or dinner, it may be considered a signal to stop the meal and bring the bill immediately.

When you order coffee, you get a single cup. Refills will be brought in a new cup: you will be charged. Cream and sugar are served with coffee. Decaffeinated coffee is widely available in northern Europe, less so in southern or eastern Europe.

Since the coffee roasts and beans vary widely, be ready for different flavors. In France, you'll find "café filtre", which is brewed to order, and is strong.

In much of Europe, the most common form of coffee is espresso, which is strong and served in very small cups.

In Greece and the Balkan countries you'll be served Greek (in Greece) or Turkish coffee (in the rest of the region), which has the grounds still in it. It is so thick that a spoon can almost stand upright. It is also extremely sweet, unless you request otherwise. In some countries you'll get strong coffee with lots of hot milk such as "café au lait" in France or "cappucino" in Italy.

Some traveklers, unwilling to savour the different coffee flavours, buy a jar of instant before they leave home and drink that for their entire trip. However, instant coffee in Europe, particularly West Germany, is very good. (These travellers have to ask for the hot water.)

Tea

Tea is served at similar times as coffee, accompanied with sugar and cream, but only very rarely with lemon. Tea is usually made with tea bags.

Fizzy Drinks

Every country in Europe has fizzy drinks. Restaurants will often serve very small bottles. Coke, Pepsi, and Fanta are available in most places in Western Europe. In Eastern Europe, only one or the other will be available, often in tourist hotel dining rooms.

Beer

Even in the main wine countries such as France, Italy, and Spain, beer is widely available. The acknowledged beer strongholds are Germany, the Netherlands, Czechoslovakia, and Belgium. Beers, like mineral waters, rarely cross national boundaries even if they do leave their region of origin. Many beers are a localized luxury. There are lagers, dark beers, and ales.

Wine

Wine is always acceptable with meals in most countries. Entire books have been written about it, including which wine best matches certain foods. In general, you'll rarely go wrong to order red wine with red meat and cheeses, and white wine with everything else. Wine in the Soviet Union, however, is almost without exception too sweet to drink with meals.

Pre-Dinner Drinks

Before a meal, people usually order an aperitif such as vermouth, anisette, or in France a "Kir", which is white wine flavored with currant syrup. Most Europeans don't precede a meal with the standard British gin and tonic; in fact, outside of major hotels and tourist oriented restaurants, a dry Martini or Scotch may be difficult to find.

After-Dinner Drinks

Nationally produced liqueurs—especially local ones—are widely available. Foreign imports such as Scotch (everywhere except Scotland) or Cognac (everywhere except France) may be limited as well as very costly. *(Text continues on page 292.)*

Menu Key (Simplified Menu Reader)

English	French
"I would like . . . "	"Je voudrais . . . "
"the set meal."	"le menu."

Appetizers (Starters) — **Hors d'oeuvres**

Soup — **Potage, bisque, soupe, créme de . . .**

First course — **Entrée**

Fish, seafood — **Poissons, crustaces**
- Eels — Anguille
- Trout — Truite
- Pike — Brochet
- Salmon — Saumon
- Sole — Sole
- Oysters — Huitres
- Frogs' legs — Cuisses de grenouilles
- Lobster — Homard
- Snails — Escargots

Poultry — **Volaille**
- Chicken, cock capon — Poulet, coq, poussin, coquelet, poularde, chapon
- Duck, duckling — Canard, caneton, canette
- Goose — Oie
- Turkey — Dinde, dindonneau

Meat — **Viande**
- Beef — Boeuf
- Steak — Entrecôte, tournedos, biftec, steak
- Roast beef — Boeuf rôti
- Braised beef — Boeuf braisé

- Pork — Porc
- Ham — Jambon
- Cutlet or chop — Côte de porc
- Roast pork — Porc rôtie

- Veal — Veau
- Cutlet — Escalope
- Breaded veal cutlet — Escalope à l'anglais
- Veal stew — Blanquette de veau
- Liver — Foie

Menu Key (Simplified Menu Reader)

German

"Ich möchte . . ."

Italian

"Vorrei . . ."
"il prezzo fisso."

Vorspeisen
Suppe

Antipasti
Zuppa, Minestra,
Brodo

Primo Piatto

Fische, Krustentiere
Anguille
Forelle
Hecht
Lachs
Seezunge
Austern
Froschenkel
Hummer
Schnecken

Pesce
Anguille
Trota
Luccio
Salmone
Sogliole
Ostriche
Rane
Aragosta, gambero
Lumache

Geflügel
Huhn, Poularde, Kapaun

Ente, Junge Ente
Gans
Indian, Truthahn

Pollame
Pollo, capon

Anatra
Oca
Tacchino, pavone

Fleisch
Rindfleisch
Rindschnitzel, Steak

Rostbraten
Rindbraten

Schwein
Schinken
Schweinschnitzel
Schweinbraten

Kalbfleisch
Kalbschnitzel
Wienerschnitzel
Goulasch
Kalbleber

Carne
Manzo, bue
Bistecca, filetto

Arristo de manzo
Stufato di manzo (bue)

Maiale
Prosciutto
Costoletto, costarello
Lombata di maiale

Vitello
Costoletto, scaloppine
Milanesa
Osso buco
Fegato

Lamb	Agneau
Game	Gibier
Boar	Sanglier, marcassin
Venison, deer	Chevreuil, cerf
Hare, rabbit	Lievre, lapin

Side Dishes / Garnitures

Carbohydrates — **Fécules**
- Bread — Pain
- Potatoes — Pommes (de terre)
- Rice — Riz
- Noodles — Nouilles
- Dumplings — Quenelles

Vegetables — **Légumes**
- Beans — Haricots
- Cabbage — Chou
- Carrots — Carottes
- Mushrooms* — Champignons*

Many European mushroom varieties are considered distinct vegetables, separately named.

- Onions — Oignons
- Peas — Petits pois
- Marrows, courgettes — Courgettes

Salad — **Salade**
Cheese — **Fromage**

Dessert (Sweets) — **Dessert**
- Pancakes — Crêpes
- Cake — Gateau
- Pastry — Pâtisserie
- Fruit — Fruit
- Ice cream — Glace

Drinks — **Boissons**
- Tap water — Eau
- Mineral water — Eau minerale
- Beer — Biére
- Wine (white, red) — Vin (blanc, rouge)
- Milk — Lait**
- Coffee — Café
- Tea — Thé

**Milk is not generally served at meals.*

- tip included — Service compris
- Tip — Pourboire
- "The bill, please". — "L' addition, s'il vous plait".

Lamm	Agnello
Wild	Caggiagione
Wildschwein	Cinghialle
Hirsch	Selvaggina
Kaninchen	Lepre, coniglio

Beilagen — **Contorni**
Brot	Pane
Kartoffeln	Patate
Reis	Riso
Teigwaren	Pasta
Knödel	Gnocchi

Gemüse — **Verdure**
Grüne Bohnen	Fagiolini
Kohl	Cavolo
Karotten	Carote
Champignons*	Funghi*

Many European mushroom varieties are considered distinct vegetables, separately named.

Zweibel	Cipolle
Erbsen	Piselli
Zucchini	Zucchini

Salat — **Insalata**
Käse — **Formaggio**

Nachtisch — **Dolci**
Pfannkuchen	Crêpes, panzerotti
Torte	Torta
Gebück	Pasticceria
Obst	Frutta
Eis	Gelato, Cassata

Getranke — **Bevande**
Trinkwasser	Acqua
Mineralwasser	Acqua minerale
Bier	Birra
Wein (rot, weiss)	Vino (bianco, rosso)
Milch**	Latte**
Kaffe	Caffè
Thee	The

**Milk is not generally served at meals.*

Bedienungsinklusiv	Servizio incluso
Trinkgeld	Mancia
"Die Rechnung, bitte", or "Bezahlen, bitte."	"Il conto, per favore."

Smoking in Restaurants

Whilst some restaurants offer non-smoking areas, you are more likely to just have to suffer—or enjoy—the smell of cigarettes (notably stronger in France and Eastern Europe) and post-prandial cigars. There's usually not much you can do except move to another table.

Tipping

There are three tipping methods used in Europe, two of which include the tip in the bill.

Where a service charge is included in the price of the meal, there will be a notation on the bill of fare such as TTC, Service Compris, Servicio Incluido, Bedienungsinklusiv, etc. In this case, the price you see on the bill of fare will be the price on your bill.

In other establishments, prices do not include the tip but it is still added onto the bill. This is usually shown on the bill of fare by phrases such as the French "15% service non compris" or "15% service en sus", or equivalent phrases in other languages.

In most countries where the tip is included in the bill, it is also customary to leave a few coins, up to 5% in addition to the bill.

Where a tip is not included, the standard tip should be 10% to 15% of the total bill. Leaving more (unless truly extraordinary services have been performed) will only add to the waiter's unreasonable expectations.

Laundry
How You Can Keep Clothes Clean While Travelling

Doing your laundry is a necessary though unglamorous chore even at home. Keeping clothes clean while travelling in a foreign land is a special challenge. If you're constantly on the move, as many travellers are, the challenge is even greater.

There is, of course, the approach of an American couple met in Venice. "At home, we just bought extra underwear and a few other clothes, and packed them in an extra suitcase. At the end of each day, we put the dirty clothes in plastic bags in that suitcase. We'll clean it all when we get back home". Their hefty plaid extra suitcase was already stuffed with bags of dirty laundry, and they still had another week to go.

Another unique approach was taken by another American couple. They saved up all the old clothes they no longer wanted, put them in an extra duffle bag, wore them in Europe, and abandoned them when they were dirty.

There are a multitude of other approaches, of course, which fall into three main categories:

1. Using the hotel sink (a technical rule violation almost everywhere, though most guests and managements ignore the rule).

2. Finding and using a launderette.

3. Taking the laundry (and yourself) to the cleaners. Having the staff of a plush hotel take care of the laundry is a subcategory of this (and usually even less desirable, for reasons of slowness and extra cost).

If using this option, your clothes may not be treated in accordance with suggested care instructions.

The Hotel Sink

It's a rare hotel or B&B room in Europe that doesn't have a sink with hot and cold running water, even if the toilet and bath or shower are down the hall.

If you're properly prepared, you can do an acceptable washing job. You may occasionally have to carry your clothes damp in a plastic bag, but you *will* have your clothes with you. Finish drying them at your next stop (or in your car, if you're driving).

Synthetics and synthetic/natural fibre blends dry much more quickly than 100% natural fibres. If you use this method, plan on washing every day or two.

Laundry Supply Key and Check List

Many supplies are generally available at travel stores or haberdashery counters of large department stores. Many are also available at similar locations in Western Europe.

___Sink stopper plug. Some European sinks don't have stoppers (especially in Eastern Europe). Get the kind with flexible flat flanges.

___Elastic clothes line. It should have a hook or a suction cup at each end. Many are twisted double strands you pull open to hang your clothes in.

___Clothes pegs (optional). Plastic is lightweight and won't stain clothes.

Laundry

___Detergent. Buy single-use packets of cold-water soap, such as Woolite. You can buy detergent almost anywhere in Europe.

___Detergent container. Get a secure container to prevent powder from getting all over your possessions. A series of plastic bags, one inside the other, each sealed with a matal tie a is homely but effective container.

___Hangers. Inflatable hangers are preferable for wet shirts, blouses, etc.

___Plastic bags. Much of Europe is humid. Your clothes may not dry over night. Get some before you leave. More plastic bags are available in Europe when yours give out.

___Metal ties or rubber bands. Get them before you leave to seal plastic bags. In Europe, ties are rarely found, and rubber bands are scarce. Take extra rubber bands: they're invaluable for lots of other purposes.

What Not to Bring

1. Liquid detergent, bleach, or fabric softener. Containers are prone to leak or break, even when sealed inside a plastic bag. If you absolutely need liquid items to do laundry, buy them in Europe. Abandon liquids before flying: not all airplane holds are fully pressurized, which could result in leakage.

2. An iron. It's bulky and the electric current is different. Most hotel desks have irons for the use of guests. If you must take an iron, be sure to get an electric converter. Permanent press clothes are a better idea.

European Launderettes

The launderette with its sloshing machines is not always the common occurrence in Europe it is in Britain. You're especially lucky if you find one in southern or Eastern Europe. Some European launderettes will have a (sometimes required) service wash as well as offering self-service facilities.

See below for the Hot, Warm, and Cold Water Key to help you use machines or make your washing wishes known to attendants.

How to Find Launderettes

Launderettes are scarce, have unfamiliar names, and are often in unexpected locations. Rural villages will rarely have any.

Tourist information offices are *not* good places to ask for launderette locations. You can wander the city in search of a laundry facility, but there's a better way: the telephone book. Use the classified (Yellow) pages unless noted otherwise. Most have phones. A good map will help you find the way.

Launderette Word Key

Austria: *Waschereien* for laundries (Look under this listing for words "Waschsalon", or "Waschautomaten," or "Selbsbedienung" for self-service).

Belgium: French areas: *Salons-lavoirs* (Brussels Classification 7325).
Flemish areas: *Wassalons* (Brussels Classification 7325). (Check English-language Yellow Page index in other areas).

Denmark: *Møntvask.*

Finland: Finnish: *Pesulatoksia* for laundries (look for word "Itsepalvelupesula" for self-service).
Swedish: *Tvätt-och-Strykingrättningar* for laundries ("Sjalvbetjan" means self-service).

France: *Laverie automatique—libre service.*

Germany: *Waschsalons* or *Waschereien.*

Greece: *Laundries—Self Service* (in English language Blue Pages), or Αυτοματο πλυνοηριο (say "Automato Plintirio"), or Λωνδρι (say "Laundry") in the Greek classified pages.

Hungary: *Muszòsalon*

Ireland: *Laundries—Self Service.*

Italy: *Lavanderie a Gettone.*

Luxembourg: *Blanchisserie* (in White Pages).
Netherlands: *Wasserette* (listed in both Yellow and White pages).
Norway: *Vaskerier og stykerier* for laundries (look for words "Selvbetjenings-vaskeri", "Launderette", "Vaskeautomat", or "Myntvaskeri" for self service).
Portugal: *Lavandaria self-service.*
Soviet Union: (Ask Intourist.)
Spain: *Lavanderia* (not listed separately from full-service laundries; watch for the words "Auto Servicio" in the name or ad). Also check the White Pages under Lavanderia followed by washing machine manufacturers' names.
Sweden: *Tvätt* for laundries (look for words "Självtvätt" or "Tvättomat" for self- service).
Switzerland: German area: *Waschsalons.* French area: Yellow Pages *Blanchisserie* (for all laundries), then look for word "Salon-Lavoir" for self-service, or look in White Pages under "Laverie automatique—libre service." Italian area: *Lavanderie.*

Self-Service Laundries

Self-service laundries are most prevalent in northern Europe, particularly Scandinavia. If you find one with British or American-made equipment, instructions are enamelled in English on the inside of the machine lid. Other launderettes use European equipment. There are usually instructions, but not always in English. There are a few special quirks to watch out for.

Key to Better Self-Service Laundry Results

1. Have the right coins. Change machines are rare. You may have to go to a nearby shop to get change. Some machines require special tokens, available at the laundry, which require specific coins or combinations of coins. Check first.
2. Have your own detergent. You can't always count on there being any for sale. Even if there is, it will be expensive. However, in some laundries, you must use the soap provided

3. Check for a spin cycle. Not all European-made washing machines have spin cycles. When the wash and rinse are complete, your clothes will be *very* wet. A separate spin-dryer spins the water out of your clothes. Be sure that clothes are at the bottom of the drum, and evenly distributed. Spin-dryers frequently remove buttons or rip clothes with buttons. A separate coin will be required.

4. Watch the tumble-dryer temperature! Many dryers are permanently set for high heat. If you have drip dry or delicate clothes, take them out before they are bone dry or immediately when the machine stops.

Attended Launderettes

Some European launderettes have attendants, especially in southern Europe. In these places, you watch as the attendant runs the machine, or you can leave your clothes and collect them later. The operator usually (but not always) includes the detergent in the price. A few simple rules...

1. Specify washing and drying temperatures or your clothes will probably get a hot treatment: hot wash, hot rinse, and hot dry.

2. Be there at the end of the cycle to hang or fold your clothes. The attendant will usually not do this for you.

3. Bring your own hangers if you need them.

4. Don't plan to do your laundry during lunch. The attendant will probably close the shop for lunch.

The Full-Service Laundry

Full-service laundries are fairly common in Europe. Full-service laundries charge by the piece. Some may have minimum order requirements. In almost all cases, prices will be displayed. Be sure that you find out the total price of the service before you commit your clothes to them.

Hot, Warm, Cold Water Key

	Hot	*Warm*	*Cold*
Universal Color code	*Red*	no colour	Blue
Danish	*Warm*	Ikkesowarmt	Cold
Dutch	*Heet*	Warm	Koud
Finnish	*Kuuma*	Lämmin	Kylmä
French	*Chaud*	Tiede	Froid (F)
German	*Heiss*	Warm	Kalt
Greek	Ζεστοσ *(Zestos)*	Ζεστοσ (Zestos)	Κριοσ (Krios)
Hungarian	*Forò*	Meleg	Hideg
Italian	*Caldo*	Caldo	Freddo (F)
Norwegian	*Het*	Varm	Kald
Polish	*Goracy*	Ciepl	Zimny
Portuguese	*Quente*	Morna	Fria
Romanian	*Cald*	Várm	Frig
Russian	**Горячая**	**Теплая**	**Холодная**
Spanish	*Caliente*	Tepido	Frio (F)
Swedish	*Het*	Varm	Kall
Turkish	*Sicak*	Ilik	Soguk

Your clothes will not only be washed, they will usually also be ironed (even, sometimes, casual items like blue jeans). Shirts will often be starched. If you like your clothes spotless and incredibly crisp, the full-service laundry is the way to go. Most wash clothes in boiling water. Some fabrics will shrink with this treatment. Drip dry clothes will be ironed, too, sometimes collecting new creases in the process. Give temperature and ironing instructions to avoid these problems.

Prices will far exceed any other laundry method. Shirts and trousers may cost as much as £1 each, underwear up to a 60p apiece, and socks about 30p to 60p a pair.

A full-service laundry also takes time—usually two or three days. Express service may be available for a surcharge. Another drawback is that the laundry methods may not exactly follow either your recommendations or the label's.

Plush hotels will also arrange to do laundry. Often the laundry is farmed out to a local laundry, and you're charged the laundry's normal high price plus the hotel's surcharge. The hotel-arranged laundry can take the most time of all. Some hotels have quick but expensive in-house laundry service. Confirm charges and time before you entrust your clothes to the hotel staff.

Dry Cleaning

There may be one or two items in your travelling wardrobe that need dry cleaning. In a few countries, there are coin-operated dry cleaners that work like (and are often located in) coin-operated launderettes. You're likeliest to find self-service dry cleaning in Belgium, France, and West Germany.

Dry cleaning will be expensive if charged by the piece, and relatively cheap at self service operations charging by the load.

Full-service laundries also can perform dry cleaning, but it will rarely be same-day service. Hotels offer similar services at higher prices and are not necessarily quicker.

Finding Dry Cleaners

Find listings of dry cleaners in the telephone book (see the Dry Cleaner Word Key below). Tourist offices can sometimes help. Many dry cleaners are located in commercial shopping districts; you may find them during the normal course of your day.

Dry Cleaner Word Key

Austria: *Chemische Reinigung.*
Belgium: French area: *Nettoyage à sec* (Brussels classification 7335).
Flemish area: *Droogkuis* (Brussels classification 7335).
(Check index at front of Yellow Pages for classification number in other areas.)
Czechoslovakia: *Ryclo Clstiaren.*
Denmark: *Renseri* or *Kemisk rensning.*
Finland: *Kemiallisia Pesulatoksia.*
France: *Nettoyage à sec.*
Germany: *Chemische Reinigung.*
Greece: Καθαριστηριο (say "Kathiristírio").
Hungary: *Vegytisztitàs.*
Ireland: *Cleaners and launderers.*
Italy: *Lavandería a secco.*
Luxembourg: *Nettoyage à sec* (in the White Pages).
Netherlands: *Stomerij.*
Norway: *Renseri.*
Poland: *Czyszczenie Chemiczne.*
Portugal: *Lavandarias a secco.*
Spain: *Tintorería.*
Sweden: *Tvätt-Kemisk.*
Switzerland:
German area: *Chemische Reinigung.*
French area: *Nettoyage à Sec.*
Italian area: *Lavandería a secco.*
(In Yellow Pages, also check in the White Pages.)
Turkey: *Elbise temezliyici.*
Yugoslavia: *Hemisjsko ciščenje.*

Security

**Guarding Against Loss and Theft
(and What to Do if It Occurs)**

You, as a traveller, are an easy target. Your possessions are a desirable target to thieves since you are rich enough to travel and probably have your valuables with you. Foiling thieves consists mainly of travelling unostentatiously and keeping valuables hidden—and not taking irreplaceable valuables.

Keep all of your identification and valuables with you at all times. Don't put them in checked-in luggage on airplanes and trains. Don't leave them in hotel rooms; lock them in hotel safety-deposit boxes provided free to guests.

In some countries you may have to leave your passport at the hotel or campground desk for a few hours while the police make their routine checks. This is normal procedure in many countries (especially in Eastern Europe) and nothing to worry about. But don't forget to recover your passport.

Keeping a packet of papers and money on you can be difficult if you don't prepare. A number of systems to help you exist: money belts, purses, and pouches.

Many people use money belts worn under clothing. They are safe and satisfy many people, but money belts have some disadvantages: they are uncomfortable, some don't hold passports and traveller's cheques, and most important, the contents can be difficult to get at when you need them at border crossings, banks, etc.

Many Europeans (especially men) use pouches hung around their necks and under their shirt to keep their valuables safe.

Various styles exist; you will have to shop around to find the one that suits you. Another way to hide valuable documents is a shoulder holster, also worn under your clothes, and sold at travel supply shops.

Many women prefer bags, which are more exposed than either of the above possibilities. See the Clothing chapter (pages 47-56) for a thorough discussion of what makes a good handbag. If you use a bag for your valuables, wear it bandolier-style and keep it under your arm like a football, especially in crowds. In Italy (especially Naples and Rome) and Spain (especially Malaga and Valencia), and other large cities throughout Europe try not to walk on the road side of pavements unless you keep the bag away from the road.

Avoid keeping all of your valuables and identification all together. This way if some are lost or stolen, you aren't entirely without money or identification. For example, keep a copy of the identification page of your passport and traveller's cheque receipt in your luggage.

Swindles and Cons

Tourists are considered fair game and a rich prize for a variety of swindles and cons. Some of them can cost you your valuables, your money, and your common sense. (Don't end up thinking, "How could I have been so dumb?")

Some of the most common thievery methods are listed below. To a great degree, being a victim very much depends on odds and luck. You can improve the odds in your favor by being aware of them and watching out for them.

The Gypsy Kid Con

Roving groups of pathetic Gypsy children come begging for coins. While some tug at your clothes, others pick your pocket or rifle your bag. Your best defence is to try to ignore them, not to let them get too close, and to keep your eyes peeled. This con is most common in Italy, southern Spain, and Paris, but can be found elsewhere in southern and Eastern Europe, too.

If they keep approaching, the best defence is to start yelling at them (in any language) something like "Get Away!" They usually leave, since unwelcome attention from bystanders and local residents is the last thing they want to attract.

The Loaded Drink Con

If a debonaire stranger offers a drink, especially on a train, let him or her sample it first. Once in a while sleeping drugs are included—and you'll be robbed while you sleep.

The "Helpful Stranger" Con

If someone offers you a helping hand or free information, consider his or her motives. Are they being a front for someone? Are they acting in a company of thieves? Treat these offers carefully—some people are genuinely friendly but many have ulterior motives.

Foiling Pickpockets

Put a new thick rubber band snugly around your wallet. New rubber bands won't slide easily, and the pickpocket runs a greater risk of being discovered when your wallet won't slide easily.

Don't keep your wallet in a rear hip pocket: not only is it all too apparent to thieves, it is out of your sight. Front hip pockets are better, an inside coat pocket is better yet.

Preventing Luggage Theft

Don't take the most expensive designer luggage! (Why shout about how rich you are?) Lock the luggage or tape it shut.

Put distinctive markings on all your luggage—such as ribbons, tape wrapped around it, travel stickers, even bright lavender paint. Don't make it easy for someone to mistake your luggage for theirs. Watch for luggage switches, especially at airports.

Put clear, permanent identification on the outside and have another set inside, too. You may even want to sew it into soft and semi-soft luggage. Identification should have your name and phone number. If you can use a post office box instead of a street address, it will not give potential thieves a clue that your home might be unoccupied.

Keep your luggage in sight at all times, or check it into a locker, left luggage, or a hotel receptionist. Watch your luggage on trains and keep your valuables with you.

If you travel on a sleeping car on a train, lock your luggage and put it between you and the wall. In this way, potential thieves will think twice before rifling through it looking for valuables, and risking awakening you, the intended victim. Some travellers have even locked their luggage to the seats or luggage racks using a cable lock.

Don't entrust your luggage to strangers, no matter how tempting the prospect.

Avoid taking more luggage than you can carry.

Securing Your Room

In many European countries, you are expected to leave room keys at the desk when you are out during the day. However, sometimes, you may wish to take the keys (and their almost invariably large handles) along with you.

Other ideas are to turn on the television or a radio, and put a "Do Not Disturb" sign outside of the door. This way any thieves may believe the room is occupied and try another one.

You should, in any case, not leave easily portable valuables on night tables or the bed. Put your camera and other small valuables in your suitcase if not taking them along. Lock the suitcase, then put the suitcase in the closet or armoire. Bear in mind that many hotel door locks have see-through keyholes and are easily picked. Don't leave your valuables in view to tempt a thief.

Remember that all hotels have a safe for small valuables. Once you hand over the valuables, the management is legally responsible for them. Larger hotels often have safety-deposit boxes for the use of guests.

Preventing Car Theft

In cities, consider parking your car at parking garages attended 24 hours a day, or taking your car to the suburbs.

Take all valuables (especially cameras) and luggage with you, or at least make sure that nothing of value is visible. Put the valuable items in the boot. While it is true that thieves can break into boots, they are unlikely to do so without a clear knowledge that valuables lie inside.

Visible empty food shopping bags and newspapers don't cause that acquisitive urge to the same degree as cameras and luggage. However, it is wiser to hide them, too.

Leave the glove compartment door open with nothing visible. Then potential thieves know that there are no valuables there, and may try another car instead.

Money Exchange Problems

When you change money, know in advance how much you're supposed to receive. Count it at the counter before you turn to leave—even if the clerk or cashier counted it out in front of you. Don't be in a hurry; even banks in Switzerland have been known to make "mistakes".

Avoid buying money on the street from someone offering a great bargain. Note that in

Eastern Europe the black market is illegal, and if caught, penalties can be severe: long jail terms, confiscation of all your valuables, and worse. In Western Europe, there's generally no advantage to changing money on the street, but there are serious risks. Make sure you're not being given obsolete bills, play money, a single cleverly folded high-value bill covering low-value ones or plain paper, or are being set up for a mugging. If you insist on this type of dealing, keep your eyes open and count theirs before you hand over your cash. Best of all, don't deal with these types.

Overcharges and Shopping Cons

What is This Charge For?

Sometimes, for some reason especially in Italy, charges are added for items you haven't had. Ask for explanations when you need them. When caught, the clerk or waiter will gracefully shrug, and take it off the bill.

The Addition Error in the Bill

When you get a bill, add it up carefully. If you're not used to the change of currency from country to country, take a pocket calculator along. In an obvious but not obnoxious way, add the bill up and make sure it's right. If you can't read the bill, ask for a detailed explanation of every charge before paying.

Count your change, even if you aren't sure its right. (The vendor may not know that and will make it right.) Of course, sometimes it could also be an honest mistake: sometimes the error is in *your* favour.

Tax Refund Cons

When shopping and you want your Value Added Tax refund, you must get all the paperwork then and there. Don't believe it when they say, "Everything is taken care of at the _____" (fill in airport, train station, ferry port, etc.).

Street Vendors: What Are They Really Doing?

Watch out for swindling "something-for-nothing" cons from street vendors. Be especially suspicious if you're approached on the street rather than at a market.

You give them your something (usually money) and get nothing (or worthless items) back as they quickly vanish.

If "the deal" seems too good to be true, it usually is.

Buying "Genuine" Antiquities

Occasionally you will be offered a "genuine antique," such as a Greek bronze statue, various Roman remains, and so on. In spite of the appearance of being antique, few actually are. If you buy the item, buy it for its decorative value, not its supposed antique value.

If the item really is an antique, its export is usually illegal without special government permits. Many countries, particularly those in Eastern Europe, Greece, and Turkey are particularly harsh on those who try to take antiques out of the country without permission. (Sometimes the dealers have turned in the traveller!) They keep your money and receive a reward from the police as well.

Preventing Camera Theft

You can reduce the chances of losing or having your camera stolen with a few precautions. First and foremost, label the camera, its case, and a camera bag with your name, address, and phone number.

It is a good idea to have a second tag where you can write down your local address—such as a hotel, campsite, etc.

Learn to consider it as part of your clothing. Keep the camera strap on you at all times, especially in buses, on the underground, and on trains. When you sit down at a restaurant or other place, put the camera on the table, or at least on your chair—preferably in your way when you get up. Better, keep it in a nondescript bag unless actually taking a picture.

If you have a variety of camera equipment, you may wish to purchase special coats in place of a leather or metal camera case. Though heavy when full of equipment, they are less likely to be forgotten or stolen by thieves. These are available through camera stores.

Preventing Bag Theft

Bags are prime targets for thieves. Full of valuables, compact, and portable, bags are easy to snatch if not carefully guarded.

When walking, be sure that you hold on to the bag; if possible put it over your shoulder. Avoid clutch bags.

Be especially careful at airports, train and underground stations, and in crowds.

In pavement cafés and restaurants, keep it in your view. Make it impossible to leave without remembering it.

In any case, keep some money and identification in a place other than your bag, so that if it is stolen or lost, you're not totally destitute.

A Note on Honesty

Most people are very honest throughout Europe, and will try to return items you accidentally leave. You can help these well-meaning people promptly return anything you have forgotten if you label your possessions with a local address (such as a hotel), however temporary. This would cause many losses to become lost *and* found-and-returned items instead.

Remember! A little prudence can go a long way.

Don't let fear ruin your travels. After all, Europe is generally a safe place in which to travel.

When Loss or Theft Occurs . . .

If you lose some or all of your possessions, you obviously will try to recover or replace them. Notify anyone who can help or can limit your losses, and then try to continue.

If you lose some of your possessions, immediately call or return to the place you last had them. Surprisingly often, the item or items will be waiting for you. (This is the case even with valuable, unmarked items such as cameras, bags, coats, etc.)

If your items are stolen, report it to the police and get a report. It is true that in some places (Paris, Rome, Seville, and Madrid are reputed to be some), you will spend lots of time reporting it to officers uninterested in assisting you to recover anything. But this will not happen most of the time. If the theft occurred in a hotel room, report it to the management . . . but remember that the management is not usually legally liable for thefts from a room.

If you are mugged, the police will usually be more interested: you will still have to give statements and watch while a report is made out.

If your passport and traveller's cheques were stolen, take the police report to the embassy along with the photocopy of the passport page you should have, and to the traveller's cheque replacement office. It will provide a guarantee of authenticity to your claim.

If you don't speak the language, it will often be worth while contacting the consular services division of the nearest consulate or embassy first. (Thefts are so frequent in Rome, that the United States Consular Office gives theft victims a six-page handout to explain reporting procedures including instructions on what to do and where to report. Other embassies in other cities have similar instructions.) The consular staff should be able to explain the procedures to make your report to the police.

Your Embassy
How Can It Help You?

"Call the embassy!" may be one of your first thoughts in an emergency. The consular staff of your embassy can be of some help in protecting and assisting its own citizens abroad.

You should know the limits of an embassy's powers and services. For example, an appeal to an embassy will not get you out of any legal problems that occur—but will give you a list of qualified local lawyers and ensure that you're not being treated any worse than the locals.

The embassy's consular staff will render different services and provide different levels of help, depending on the subject and circumstances.

Consular officials do not provide the services of travel agents, tour guides, and bankers.

Missing Passports

If your passport is lost or stolen, contact the nearest embassy or consulate (see lists below for Britain).

Before you actually go, first call to find out how to file a missing passport report. Take the photocopy of the identifying front pages of your passport you should have put elsewhere in your belongings. This photocopy will dramatically speed the passport replacement process.

You must first report the loss to the local police, and only then to the nearest British consular offices.

In some cases, after obtaining a police report, you can return to Britain without your passport (by vehicle but not generally by air), and obtain a replacement when you have returned.

In other cases, you can obtain temporary travel documents, which will allow you to cross borders on the way back home. There is a fee for this service.

If you will be away for several weeks, you can take the police report to the consulate and request issuance of a new passport.

You are actually applying for a new passport and are required to pay the full fee. In addition, you must complete and sign a form, and provide information about that passport to the consular official. Required information includes the passport number, and date and place of issuance.

The renewal may take up to four weeks or longer, since an inquiry will have to be sent to Britain for a records search.

Legal Problems

Laws in foreign countries can differ greatly from those of your own. While in another country, you are fully subject to its laws. The legal philosophy of "innocent until proven guilty" often does not apply. Actually, in most nations, if you come to the attention of the police, you must disprove the legal presumption of guilt.

If detained, do not expect to be informed of your rights, and do not say anything. Most, if not all, of your statements can be used against you. Avoid signing any papers, especially if they are not written in a language you know.

If you run afoul of the law, you are subject to the same laws and jails as the local residents. The embassy's consular officials will, in most countries, be contacted by the government as the result of a consular agreement. However, you should ask the police to notify the nearest consular office of your arrest. You will be visited by a consular representative. He or she will try to ensure that you're not being treated any differently than anyone else. (In some countries, this will be small consolation. In some countries, prisoners must buy most food, blankets, and clothing.)

The consular official will not give legal advice, but will give you a list of local lawyers. You will have to hire and pay for your own lawyer. Do not expect (or hope for) release as a result of the embassy's knowledge of your plight. The embassy will, however, contact your family or other persons you designate.

Medical Problems

Your embassy can provide a limited amount of help with medical problems. It will, upon request, give you a list of English-speaking doctors or dentists, listed by speciality. It will not pay for any services or medicines, however.

Disorders and Disasters

If you find yourself in the midst of disorders, such as a revolution or civil war, or a disaster, such as an major earthquake, contact the embassy as soon as possible. The staff will give you the best available advice. In some situations, the staff will also assist with evacuations.

Death

In case of a death abroad, the embassy staff can provide advice. Staff members can also contact the next of kin.

In some circumstances, the consular staff can also be the conservator of possessions or an estate. However, you or your relatives must pay for funeral costs.

Taking bodies home can be the subject of great amounts of difficulty and large expense—much more than merely crossing the border when alive.

Registration

If you plan to stay in any country for an extended period, or are in a country where there is public disorder or any reason that you feel you could have problems, you can and are advised to register at the embassy or consulate. You can register in person or by mail or phone. Registration in person when you have your passport with you also provides proof of citizenship in case your passport is lost or stolen.

Voting

While on holiday and away from home, you can vote in all elections at home (parliamentary, European Parliament, and local). Before you leave, contact the Electoral Registration Officer in your area, and request form RPF9. This form lets you choose either to vote by post or to appoint a proxy to vote in your place. (Note: postal ballots cannot be sent outside the Britain.)

If you move outside of Britain and were registered as an elector during the five years before you move, you can vote as an "overseas elector" in parliamentary and European Parliament elections in the constituency in which you lived. Abroad, contact the nearest consulate; in Britain, contact:
Home Office Public Relations Branch
50 Queen Anne's Gate
London SW1H 9AT
Tel. 01-213 3000

National Holidays

Embassies and consulates are closed on all national holidays—both of the country you're visiting and of your own country.

Embassies Are Not Travel Agencies

If your hotel reservation isn't honoured, you need your airplane flight changed, or want tickets to a sold-out concert, do *not* contact the embassy. It will generally do no more to help you than to refer you somewhere else.

Likewise, if your baggage is mangled on the plane, or you were cheated in the flea market, or you need to cash a cheque, the embassy won't do much more than say, "Sorry!" and head you in another direction.

Money

When you run out of money, do not apply for a loan at the embassy or consulate. In general, it will not give you a loan. Rather, if you're in need, it will make (reverse-charge) calls to family, friends, or others who may be able to send money. The staff will also arrange for its transfer and payment to you.

The consulate can also cash cheques to a maximum of £50 on approved British banks (if the account is in credit), or when guaranteed by a guarantee card or Eurocheque card.

If you have a real emergency, are destitute, and have no one who will aid you, you may qualify for a "repatriation loan".

The repatriation loan is a little-known, under-funded program that provides a loan for your direct return home. Your passport is endorsed to prevent its future use (or have another one issued) until the loan is repaid in full. In general, repatriation loans, when granted, are given to destitutes, mental patients, or seriously ill individuals with no known relatives or others willing to handle their affairs. The consular staff makes the decision about whether you qualify for a repatriation loan, and the decision generally cannot be appealed.

British Embassies and Consulates in Europe

Embassies are usually in capital cities. There, the diplomatic representatives of the United Kingdom to other countries have offices. High commissions are similar to embassies, but are located only in Commonwealth countries.

The consular sections also provide services to British citizens. In some countries, consular affairs are handled in a separate building with a different address.

Consulates are located in other cities and function as branch offices.

Austria
British Embassy *Vienna*
Reisnerstrasse 40
A-1030 Wien
Tel. (0222) 731575/9
Telex 133410 BRITEM A

Belgium
British Embassy *Brussels*
Britannia House
28 rue Joseph II
1040 Bruxelles
Tel. (02) 217 9000
Telex 22703 BRITEM B

Bulgaria
British Embassy *Sofia*
Boulevard Marshal Tolbukhin 65-67
Sofia   Tel. 335361 and 2
Telex 22353
PRODROME SOFIA
Британское Посольство
Бульвар Маршал Толбухин 65—67
София

Czechoslovakia
British Embassy *Prague*
Thurnovska 14
12250 Praha 1
Tel. 53345/9, 533340 and 533370
Telex 121011 PRDM C

Denmark
British Embassy *Copenhagen*
Kastelvej 36-40
DK-2100 Købnhavn
Tel. (01) 26 46 00
Telex 19908 BRIEMBDK

Finland
British Embassy
Uudenmaankatu 16-20
SF-00120 *Helsinki* 12
Tel. (90) 647922
Telex 121122 UKHKISF

France
British Embassy
35 rue du Faubourg
St-Honoré   (Consular offices at 16 rue d'Anjou)
16 rue d'Anjou VIII
75383 *Paris* Cedex 08
Tel. (1) 42.66.91.42
Telex 650264 INFORM F

British Consulate-General
Bordeaux
15 cours de Verdun
33081 Bordeaux Cedex
Tel. 56.52.28.35, 56.52.89.51, and 56.52.48.86 and -7
Telex 570440 BRITAIN BORDX

Your Embassy 317

British
Consulate-General
11 square du Tilleul
59800 *Lille*
Tel. 20.57.87.90
Telex 120169 BRITAIN LILLE

British
Consulate-General
24 rue Childebert
69288 *Lyon* Cedex 1
Tel. 87.75.96.78/8
Telex 330254 BRITLYOF

British Consulate-General
24 avenue du Prado
13006 *Marseille*
Tel. 91.53.43.32 and 91.37.66.95
Telex 420307 BRITAIN MARSL

Germany, East (GDR)

British Embassy *East Berlin*
Unter den Linden
DDR 1080 *Berlin*
Tel. (02) 220 24 31
Telex 113172 BEBER DD

Germany, West (BRD)

British Embassy
Friedrich-Ebert-Allee 77
D-5300 *Bonn* 1
Tel. (0228) 234061
Telex 886887 BRINF D

British
Consulate-General
(West Berlin)
Uhlandstrasse 7/8
D-1000 Berlin 12
Tel. (030) 309 52 92/4
Telex 184268 UKBLN D

British
Consulate-General
Nordsternhaus
Georg-Glock-Strasse 14
D-4000 *Düsseldorf* 30
Tel. (0211) 43 42 81/5
Telex 8-584 855 BRIN D

British
Consulate-General
Bockenheimer
Landstrasse 51-53
D-6000
Frankfurt-am-Main
Tel. (069) 72 04 06
Telex 414932 UKFFT D

British
Consulate-General
Harvestehuderweg 8a
D-2000 *Hamburg* 13
Tel. (040)44 60 71
Telex 213562 BRHBG D

British
Consulate-General
Munich
Amalienstrasse 62
D-3000 München 40
Tel. (089) 44 60 71
Telex 529959 UKMUN D

Greece

British Embassy
1 Ploutarchou St.
GR-106 75 *Athens*
Βριτισ Πρεσβεια
1 Πλουταρκου
106 75 Αθνυαι
Tel. 7236211
Telex 216440 LION GR

Ireland

British Embassy
33 Merrion Road
Dublin 4
Tel. (01) 695211
Telex 93717 UK DB E1

Italy

British Embassy *Rome*
via XX Settembre 80A
I-00187 Roma
Tel. (06) 475 5441 and
475 5551
Telex 626119 UKEMB I

British
Consulate-General
Florence
Palazzo Castelbarco
Lungarno Corsini 2
I-50123 Firenze
Tel. (055) 263556
Telex 520270 UKCON I

British
Consulate-General
Naples
via Francesco Crispi 122
I-80122 Napoli
Tel. (081) 209227,
553320, and 582482
Telex 221464 UKCON I

Hungary

British Embassy
6 Harmincad Utca
Budapest V
Tel. (01) 182 888
Telex 224527 BRIT H

British Vice-Consulate
via San Lucifero 87
I-09100 *Cagliari*
Tel. (070) 662755

British
Consulate-General
Milan
via San Paolo 7
I-20121 Milano
Tel. (02) 8693442
Telex 310528 UKCON I

British
Consulate-General
Venice
C.P. 679
I-30100 Venezia
Tel. (041) 4227207/8
Telex 410283 UKCON I

Your Embassy

Luxembourg
British Embassy
14 Boulevard Roosevelt
L-2449 *Luxembourg*
Ville
Tel. 29864/6
Telex 3443 PRODRO LU

Malta
British High
Commission
P.O. Box 506
7 St Anne St, *Floriana*
Tel. 621 285/9
Telex MW 1249 UKREP
MALTA

Netherlands
British Embassy *The Hague*
Lange Voorhout 10
2514 ED Den Haag
Tel. (070) 645800
Telex 31600 BEMB NL

Norway
British Embassy
Thomas Heftyesgate 8
0264 *Oslo* 2
Tel. (02) 55-24-00
Telex 71575 UK OSLN

Poland
British Embassy *Warsaw*
Aleja Roz 1.00-556
Warszawa
Tel. (022) 281001/5
Telex 813694 PROD PL

Portugal
British Embassy *Lisbon*
35-39 Rua de Sao
Domingos a Lapa
1296 Lisboa
Tel. (01) 661191/5
Telex 12278 PROLIS P

British Consulate *Porto*
Avenida da Boavista
3072 4100 Oporto
Tel. (02) 684789
Telex 26647 UKOPO P

Romania
British Embassy *Bucharest*
24 Strada Jules Michelet
Bucuresti 70154
Tel. (0) 111634/6
Telex 11295 PRODRM R

Spain
British Embassy
Calle de Fernando el
Santo 16
28010 *Madrid*
Tel. (91) 419 0200
Telex 27656 INGLA E

British
Consulate-General
Edificio Diagonal
477 Avenida Diagonal
08036 *Barcelona*
Tel. (93) 322 2151
Telex 27656 BRBAR E

British
Consulate-General
Alameda de Urquijo 2-8
48008 *Bilbao*
Tel. (94) 415 7600 and
417 7722
Telex 32446 BRBIL E

British
Consulate-General Luis
Morote 6-3
Apartado Postal 2020,
Puerta de la Luz
35007 *Las Palmas*
Tel. (928) 262 508
Telex 95276 BRLTP E

Soviet Union (U.S.S.R.)
British Embassy
Naberezhnaya Morisa Toreza 14
121272 *Moscow*
Tel. (096) 231-8511/2
Telex 413341 BEMOS SU

Британское Посольство
Набережная Мориса Тереза 14
109072 МОСКВА

Sweden
British Embassy
Skarpogaten 6-8
S-115 27 *Stockholm*
Tel. (031) 670 140
Telex 19340 BRITEMB S

British
Consulate-General
Götgatan 10
S-411 05 *Goteborg*
Tel. (031) 11 327
Fax (031) 802761
Telex 802761 BSCGBG S

Switzerland
British Embassy
Thunstrasse 50
Postfach 265
CH-3000 *Bern* 15
Tel. (031) 44 50 21/6
Telex UKBUN CH

British
Consulate-General
Geneva
rue de Vermont 37-39,
6th floor
CH-1211 Genève 20
Tel. (022) 34 38 00 and
33 23 85
Telex 22956A UKGV CH

British Consulate-General
Dufourstrasse 45
CH-8008 *Zurich*
Tel. (01) 252 25 73
Telex 816467 UKZUR CH

Turkey

British Embassy
Sehit Ersan Caddesi 46a
Canyaka, *Ankara*
Tel. (041) 127 4310
Fax (041) 168 3124
Telex 42320 42320
PROD TR

British
Consulate-General
Mesrutiyet Caddesi 34
Tepabasi, Beyoglu
Istanbul
Tel. (011) 144 7545/9 or
144 7540
Telex 24122 BRITAIN
IST

Yugoslavia

British Embassy *Belgrade*
46 Generale Zdanova
11000 Beograd
Tel. (011) 645034, 645043 and 645055
Telex 11468 YU PROBEL

Open and Closed
Business Hours, Weekends, and Holidays

European business hours in many countries may be different to those in Britain; furthermore, they differ widely between countries as well, since they must account for different history, cultures, and attitudes.

The country-by-country key below provides details. However, several general rules are worth stating at the beginning.

Sundays

Sunday is a day of rest in most of Europe. As such, some things are virtually impossible to do on Sunday. For example, banks, post offices, many shops (including grocers) and restaurants are tightly closed every Sunday.

Frequently flea markets take place on Sunday, when there are few other entertainments.

However, Monday is the usual closing day in much of France.

National Holidays

National holidays can be a delight, often providing unexpected parades and pageantry. Holidays can also difficult for travellers, because trains and hotels are full to capacity, and sometimes more.

Religious holidays, particularly Christmas, are celebrated in most countries. When a country is part Catholic and part Protestant, such as West Germany, some religious holidays may be observed only in some sections of the country.

Common religious holidays found in more than one country are:

January 6: Epiphany

Maundy Thursday (Thursday before Easter)

Good Friday (Friday before Easter)

Easter Monday (Monday after Easter)

Ascension Day (five weeks after Easter during the week)

Eighth Sunday and Monday after Easter (Whit Monday; Corpus Christi)

August 15: Assumption Day (the biggest holiday of the year: try to avoid travel or finding lodgings immediately before or on this day)

November 1: All Saints' Day

Immaculate Conception Day (early December)

December 25: Christmas

December 26: Boxing Day or St. Stephen's Day.

Common holidays not of religious origin:

January 1: New Year's Day

May 1: Labour Day

Daily Business Hours

The climate as well as the culture determine when businesses, banks, and restaurants are open. For example, in Yugoslavia, most businesses are closed from noon until 4 or 5 in the afternoon.

In contrast, in Norway, businesses are open during the day, but often close relatively early.

When climates and cultures differ widely in a single country, there may be several different patterns.

Usually, banks are open for less of the day than other businesses.

Government offices, including post offices, are often on different schedules from shops or banks.

Department stores and sometimes supermarkets often remain open during lunch, when almost all other stores are closed.

Daylight Saving Time

In summer, most of Europe goes onto Daylight Saving Time. However, remember that each country starts on a different day in the spring and ends on a different day in the autumn.

Strikes

Europe has its share of strikes. In some countries, such as Germany, Switzerland, and all Communist countries, the likelihood of being inconvenienced by strikes is small to nonexistent. In others, such as Belgium, strikes are rarely a problem to travellers.

In still other countries, primarily Italy, Spain, and France, strikes can affect public transport. Whilst in Britain, strikes are usually for the duration of the dispute, in Portugal, Spain and France, strikes usually last for 24 hours.

Special Notes for Italy

Sometimes in Italy, strikes—particularly on railways—last only for one hour, or one day. It is rather a surprise to come to a halt in the middle of nowhere, while the train crews get off the train and joke among themselves. At the end of the hour, they all climb aboard, and the train is one hour late all the rest of the route.

Italian hotel and restaurant workers are also unionized, and as liable to one-day strikes as transport workers. When this happens, almost all middle-size and large hotels and restaurants are affected. In hotels, this means that you make the beds and that the bathrooms aren't cleaned. In restaurants, this means that they stay closed. Small family-run operations, since they are nonunion, remain open during strikes.

Business Hours & Holidays Key

Albania

Daily Business Hours
Banks: Open all day, 7 days per week. (You'll probably use Albtourist service desks in hotels.)
Government Offices: Post offices: 8 a.m.—10 p.m. 7 days per week.
Sundays: Many shops and offices are open.
National Holidays: January 1 and 2, January 11 (Republic Proclamation Day), May 1, November 28 (Independence Day), November 29 (Liberation Day).

Austria

Daily Business Hours
Shops: 8 a.m.—6 p.m. Monday to Friday, and Saturday morning; smaller shops often close from 12 to 2 p.m.
Banks: 8 a.m.—12:30 p.m. and 1:30—3:30 p.m., often open until 5:30 p.m. on Thursdays.
Government Offices: 8 a.m. to 4 p.m.
Sundays: Almost everything is closed except for hotels, some restaurants, and cafes.
National Holidays: January 1, January 6, Easter Monday, May 1, Ascension Day (five weeks after Easter), Whit Monday (eight weeks after Easter), August 15, October 26 (National Day), November 1, December 8 (Immaculate Conception Day), December 25 and 26.
Special Information: Many shops are open on Saturdays only until noon.

Belgium

Daily Business Hours
Shops: 9 a.m.—noon and 2—6 p.m. Monday to Saturday. In the Flemish (northern) part of Belgium, hours may vary slightly in the afternoon, from 1—5 p.m. Supermarkets are open until 8 p.m. Monday to Saturday.

Banks: 9 a.m.—12:30 p.m. and 1:30—4:30 p. m. (or sometimes 4 p.m.) Monday to Friday; a rew are open Saturday 9 a.m.—12:30 p.m.
Government Offices: 8:30 a.m.—noon and 2—5 p.m. Monday to Friday.
Sundays: Most shops and all offices are closed, except for hotels and most restaurants.
National Holidays: January 1, Easter Monday, Ascension Day, Whit Monday, May 1, July 21 (National Day), August 15, November 1, November 11 (Armistice Day), November 15 (Dynasty Day—government offices only), December 25 (and informally December 26).

Bulgaria

Daily Business Hours
Shops: 8:30 a.m.—7 p.m. Monday to Saturday (some closed from 1 to 2 p.m.).
Banks: 8 a.m.—noon Monday to Friday.
Government Offices: 9 a.m.—12:30 p.m. and 1—5 p.m. Monday to Friday.
Sundays: All shops are closed except for a few in resort areas. Hotels and most restaurants are open.
National Holidays: January 1, March 3 (Liberation Day), March 8 (Women's Day), May 1 and 2 (Labor Day), May 24 (Culture Day), September 9 and 10 (National Day), November 7 (Soviet Revolution Day).

Czechoslovakia

Daily Business Hours
Shops: 9 a.m.—6 p.m. Monday to Friday; some shops close from noon until 2 p.m. Some shops close at noon Saturday, the rest are closed all day Saturday.
Banks: 8 a.m.—2 p.m. Monday to Friday and 8 a.m.—noon on Saturday.
Government Offices: 8:30 a.m.—5:15 p.m. Monday to Friday.
Sundays: Almost everything is closed except hotels and restaurants.
National Holidays: January 1, Easter Monday, May 1, May 9 (National Day), December 25-26.

Denmark

Daily Business Hours
Shops: 9 a.m.—5:30 p.m. Monday to Saturday (all close at noon on Saturday).
Banks: 9:30 a.m.—4 p.m. Monday to Friday, and until 6 p.m. on Thursday.
Government Offices: 8 a.m.—4 p.m. Monday to Friday.
Sundays: Virtually everything is closed except restaurants, hotels, and entertainments.
National Holidays: January 1, Maundy Thursday, Good Friday, Monday after Easter, Two weeks after Easter (Common Prayers Day), May 1 (afternoon only), Ascension Day, Whit Monday, June 5 (Constitution Day), December 24 (afternoon only), 25, and 26, and December 31 (afternoon only).

Finland

Daily Business Hours
Shops: 9 a.m.—5 p.m., but 8 p.m. on Monday and Friday and 2 p.m. on Saturday.
Banks: 9 a.m.—4 p.m., Monday to Friday.
Government Offices: 8:30 a.m.—4 or 4:30 p.m. Monday to Friday.
Sundays: Almost all shops closed: hotels and restaurants are usually open.
National Holidays: January 1, Epiphany, Good Friday, Easter Monday, April 30 and May 1, Ascension Day, Whit Saturday, Midsummer Eve and Midsummer Day, All Saints' Day, December 6 (Independence Day), December 24, 25, and 26.

France

Daily Business Hours
Shops: 9 a.m.—12:15 p.m. (food stores and bakeries 6 or 7 a.m.—12:15 p.m.) and 2—6:30 p.m. Monday to Saturday. Many shops are closed on Monday, especially in the provinces, but are sometimes open on Sunday.

Banks: 9 a.m.— noon or 12:30 p.m.; 2 or 2:30—4 or 4:30 p.m. (varies regionally), Monday to Friday, and some on Saturday 9 a.m.—1 p.m.

Government Offices: 8 a.m.—noon and 2—5 p.m., Monday to Friday.

Sundays: Many food shops and, in the provinces, other types of shops are open on Sunday but closed on Monday.

National Holidays: January 1, Easter Monday, May 1, May 8 (Victory Day), Ascension Day, Whit Monday, July 14 (Bastille Day), August 15, November 1, November 11 (Armistice Day), December 25.

Special Information: August is a holiday month: many businesses and shops are closed, and government offices are minimally staffed. The better restaurants in major cities are often closed as well.

Germany, East (GDR)

Daily Business Hours

Shops: Variable but generally 10 a.m.—7 p.m. in Berlin and 9 a.m.—6 p.m. elsewhere. Late closings on Thursdays (8 p.m.), Only large shops are open on Saturdays, and everything is closed on Sundays.

Banks: 8—11 a.m. Monday to Friday.

Government Offices: 8 a.m.—4 p.m. Monday to Friday.

Sundays: Everything is closed except hotels and restaurants.

National Holidays: January 1, Good Friday, Whit Monday, May 1, October 7 (German Democratic Republic Day), December 25 and 26.

Germany, West

Daily Business Hours

Shops: 8 a.m.—noon and 1 or 1:30 p.m.—6 or 6:30 p.m., and 8 a.m.—2 p.m. on Saturdays. Large department stores stay open during lunch hours. Stores are also open until 9 p.m. one weekday evening (varies city by city).

Banks: 8:30 a.m.—1 p.m. and 2—4 p.m. Monday to Friday, and until 5:30 on Thursday.
Government Offices: 8 a.m.—5 p.m. Monday to Friday.
Sundays: Virtually everything is closed on Sunday except hotels, restaurants, and a few shops in main railway stations, and autobahn rest stops.
National Holidays: January 1, Good Friday, Easter Monday, May 1, Ascension Day, Whit Monday, June 17 (German Unity Day), Prayer Day (mid November), December 25, and 26.
Regional Holidays: November 1 (in Catholic areas only).

Great Britain

Daily Business Hours
Shops: 9 a.m.—5:30 p.m. Monday to Saturday.
Banks: 9:30 a.m.—3:30 p.m. Monday to Friday (closed 12:30—1:30 p.m. in Scotland).
Government Offices: 9 a.m.—5 p.m. Monday to Friday.
Sundays: Virtually everything is closed except hotels and restaurants, and local grocer "corner" shops. Some of the large open-air flea markets and street markets are only open on Sundays.
National Holidays: January 1, Good Friday, Easter Monday, first Monday in May (May Day), last Monday in May (Spring Bank Holiday), first Monday (Scotland only) or last Monday in August (rest of Great Britain—Summer Bank Holiday), December 25 and 26.
Regional Holidays: January 2 (Scotland only), March 1 (St. David's Day—Wales only).
Special Information: Early Closing (EC): In most towns (but not cities), all shops close early one day per week, usually at noon. Several of the hotel and restaurant guides list Early Closing days in each town listing.

Greece

Daily Business Hours
Shops: 8 a.m.—2:30 p.m. Monday, Wednesday, and Saturday and 8 a.m.—1:30 p.m. and 5:30—8:30 p.m. Tuesday, Thursday, and Friday.
Banks: 8 a.m.—2 p.m. Monday to Friday. (A few are open for foreign exchange only on Saturday.)

Government Offices: 8 a.m.—1:30 p.m. and 4:30—7:30 p.m. Monday to Friday and 8 a.m.—1:30 p.m. Saturday.
Sundays: Many shops are closed, but restaurants and tavernas are open. The flea market in Athens is open on Sunday mornings.
National Holidays: January 1, January 6, Shrove Monday (Monday before Lent), March 25 (Independence Day), May 1, Good Friday, Easter Monday, August 15, October 28 (National Day), December 25 and 26.
Regional Holidays: A number of festivals take place before Lent as part of Carnival. Navy Week, at the end of June and beginning of July, is a waterfront festival, especially on some of the Aegean islands.

Hungary

Daily Business Hours
Shops: 10 a.m.—6 p.m. Monday to Friday and 10 a.m.—3 p.m. on Saturday. Smaller shops often close during lunch. Food shops are open 6:30 a.m.—7 p.m. Some shops are open Thursday until 8 p.m.
Banks: 8:30 a.m.—3 p.m. Monday to Friday.
Government Offices: 8:00 a.m.—4:30 or 5 p.m. Monday to Friday.
Sundays: Virtually everything is closed except restaurants, hotels, and places of entertainment.
National Holidays: January 1, April 4 (Liberation Day), Easter Monday, August 20 (Constitution Day), November 7 (Soviet Revolution Day), December 25 and 26.

Ireland

Daily Business Hours
Shops: 9 a.m.—5:30 p.m. Monday to Saturday.
Banks: 10 a.m.—12:30 p.m. and 1:30—3 p.m. Monday to Friday (5 p.m. Thursday).
Government Offices: 9:30 a.m.—5:30 p.m. Monday to Friday.
Sundays: Virtually everything is closed except hotels and restaurants, and some tourist attractions in summer.
National Holidays: January 1, March 17 (St. Patrick's Day), Good Friday, Easter Monday, first Monday in June (June Bank Holiday), first Monday in August (August Bank Holiday), last Monday of October (Halloween), December 25 and 26.
Special Information: Early Closing (EC): Most Irish towns have Early Closing Day one day a week, usually Thursday or Wednesday, but occasionally Monday or Tuesday. On this day, most shops in town close about 1 p.m.

Italy

Daily Business Hours
Shops: 8:30 a.m.—12:45 p.m. and 3—7 p.m. Monday to Fridays and Saturday mornings.
Banks: 8:30 a.m.—1:30 p.m. Monday to Friday.
Government Offices: 8:30 a.m.—1:45 p.m.; post offices and SIP telephone offices also open 3—5:30 p.m.
Sundays: Virtually everything is closed except hotels, restaurants, entertainments, and outdoor vendors and flea markets.
National Holidays: January 1, Easter Monday, April 25 (Liberation Day), May 1, August 15, November 1, December 8 (Immaculate Conception Day), December 25 and 26.
Special Information: In many but not all towns, everything is closed one week day (Closing Day) except restaurants and hotels. Some hotel and restaurant guides state which day.

Luxembourg

Daily Business Hours
Shops: 9 a.m.—noon and 2—6 p.m. Monday to Saturday.
Banks: 8:30 a.m.—noon and 1:30—4:30 p.m. Monday to Friday (some remain open 9 a.m—4 p.m.).
Government Offices: 9 a.m.—noon and 2—5 p.m. Monday to Friday.
Sundays: Almost everything is closed except for restaurants and hotels.
National Holidays: January 1, Shrove Tuesday, Easter Monday, Ascension Day, Whit Monday, May 1, June 23 (Grand Duke's Birthday), November 1 and 2, December 25 and 26.
Regional Holiday: Schobermess, the Luxembourg Fair (variable, but twice a year in spring and autumn).

Netherlands

Daily Business Hours
Shops: 8:30 or 9 a.m.—5 or 5:30 p.m. Monday to Saturday. Many shops are closed Monday morning. Some shops remain open until 9 p.m. Thursday or Friday (depends on city).
Banks: 9 a.m.—4 p.m. Monday to Friday.
Government Offices: 8:30 a.m.—5:30 p.m. Monday to Friday.
Sundays: Virtually everything except hotels and restaurants is closed.
National Holidays: January 1, Good Friday, Easter Monday, April 30 (Queen's Day), Ascension Day, Whit Monday, December 5 (St. Nicholas' Day), December 25 and 26.
Special Information: Many stores stay open at least part of Good Friday.

Norway

Daily Business Hours
Shops: 9 a.m.—5 p.m. Monday to Friday and 9 a.m.—1 or 2 p.m. Saturday.

Banks: 8:15 a.m.—3 p.m. Monday to Friday, and until 5 p.m. on Thursday.
Government Offices: 9 a.m.—4 p.m. Monday to Friday.
Sundays: Almost everything is closed except hotels and restaurants.
National Holidays: January 1, Maundy Thursday, Good Friday, Easter Monday, May 1, May 17 (Independence Day), Ascension Day, Whit Monday, December 24 (afternoon only), December 25 and 26, December 31 (afternoon only).

Poland

Daily Business Hours
Shops: 9 a.m. (sometimes 11 a.m.)—7 p.m. Monday to Saturday.
Banks: 9 a.m.—noon or 2 p.m. Monday to Saturday.
Government Offices: 8 a.m.—3 p.m. Monday to Friday and 8 a.m.—1:30 p.m. Saturday.
Sundays: Almost everything is closed except restaurants and hotels.
National Holidays: January 1, Easter Monday, May 1, May 9 (Victory Day), Corpus Christi (Thursday date varies), July 22 (National Day), November 1, December 25 and 26.

Portugal

Daily Business Hours
Shops: 9 a.m.—1 p.m. and 3—7 p.m. Monday to Friday, and Saturday 9 a.m.—1 p.m. Shopping centers are open daily (including Sunday) 10 a.m.—midnight.
Banks: 8:30—11:45 a.m. and 1—2:45 p.m. Monday to Friday.
Government Offices: 9 a.m.—1 p.m. and 3—5 p.m. Monday to Friday (Occasional variations outside of Lisbon and Oporto.)
Sundays: Most shops close.
National Holidays: January 1, Shrove Tuesday, Good Friday, April 25 (Liberty Day), May 1, June 10 (National Day), August 15, October 5

(Proclamation of the Republic), November 1, December 1 (Independence Day), December 8 (Immaculate Conception Day), December 24 and 25.
Regional Holidays: Lisbon: June 13 (St. Anthony's Day), Oporto: June 24 (St. John's Day).

Romania

Daily Business Hours
Shops: 8 a.m.—noon and 4—8 p.m. Monday to Saturday, and sometimes Sunday mornings.
Banks: 9 a.m.—noon and 1—3 p.m. Monday to Friday and Saturday morning.
Government Offices: 8 a.m.—4 p.m. Monday to Saturday.
Sundays: Most shops and restaurants are open, especially in resort areas.
National Holidays: January 1 and 2, May 1 and 2, August 23 and 24 (National Days). Informally, also December 25, though most shops remain open.

Soviet Union, U.S.S.R.

Daily Business Hours
Shops: 9 a.m.—7 p.m., closed one hour during lunch (often 2—3 p.m.). Large department stores stay open during lunch. Food shops and bakeries are usually open 7 a.m.—7 p.m.
Banks: 9 or 10 a.m.—5 or 6 p.m. (closed one hour during lunch).
Government Offices: 9 or 10 a.m.—5 or 6 p.m. (closed one hour during lunch).
Sundays: Most shops and many restaurants are closed.
National Holidays: January 1 and 2, May 1 and 2, May 9 (Victory Day), November 7 and 8 (Days of the Revolution), December 5 (Constitution Day).
Special Information: Many shops may not have much to sell; if there's a long queue, it may have something of value to Soviets only.

Spain

Daily Business Hours
Shops: 9 or 10 a.m.—1 p.m. and 4—7 p.m. (winter) or 5 p.m.—8 p.m. (summer) Monday to Friday and Saturday mornings.
Banks: 9 a.m.—2 or 3 p.m. (1:30 or 2:30 p.m. in summer) Monday to Friday and 9 a.m.—12:30 p.m. Saturday.
Government Offices: 9 a.m.—1:30 p.m. and 4 p.m.—7 p.m. Monday to Friday.
Sundays: Many shops are closed but flea markets and public amusements and many restaurants are open.
National Holidays: January 1, January 6, March 19 (St. Joseph's Day), Maundy Thursday, Good Friday, May 1, Corpus Christi (date is variable), July 25 (St. James' Day), August 15, October 12 (Columbus Day), December 8 (Immaculate Conception Day), December 25.
Regional Holidays: Each city has a patron saint: during the patron saint's festival, all work comes to a halt for several days.
Special Information: 1. Evening meals don't begin until 10 p.m. and most restaurants don't open for dinner until 7:30 p.m. or later.
2. When holidays come during midweek, they often stretch to include the nearest weekend. (Please see Food & Drink chapter.)

Sweden

Daily Business Hours
Shops: 9:30 a.m.—6 p.m. Monday to Friday and 9 a.m.—1 p.m. (sometimes 4 p.m.) Saturday. Some stores (Närbutiker) are open 7 a.m.—10 or 11 p.m. Monday to Saturday in cities and towns.
Banks: 9:30 a.m.—3 p.m. Monday to Friday and also 4—5:30 p.m. Thursday.
Government Offices: 9 a.m.—5 p.m. Monday to Friday.
Sundays: While most shops are closed, some bakeries, florists, and vendors are open, as are most restaurants.

National Holidays: January 1, January 6, Good Friday, Easter Monday, May 1, May 28 (Ascension Day), Whit Monday, June near but not usually on the solstice (Midsummer Day), October 31 (All Saints' Day), December 25 and 26.

Switzerland

Daily Business Hours
Shops: 8 a.m.—12:15 p.m. and 1:30—6:30 p.m. Monday to Friday and 9 a.m.—4 p.m. Saturday. Large department stores stay open during lunch.
Banks: 8:30 a.m.—4:30 p.m. Monday to Friday.
Government Offices: 8 a.m.—noon and 2 p.m.—6 p.m. Monday to Friday.
Sundays: Almost everything is closed, except for hotels, restaurants, and garages.
National Holidays: January 1 and 2, Good Friday, Easter Monday, Ascension Day, Whit Monday, August 1 (Independence Day), December 25 and 26.
Regional Holidays: Almost every canton has at least one local holiday during the year.

Turkey

Daily Business Hours
Shops: 9 a.m.—1 p.m. and 2:30—7 p.m. Monday to Friday and 9 a.m.—1 p.m. and 1:30—8 p.m. Saturday.
Banks: 9 a.m.—noon and 2—5 p.m. Monday to Friday.
Government Offices: 9 a.m.—noon and 2—5 p.m. Monday to Friday.
Sundays: Many but not all shops are closed.
National Holidays: April 23 (National Day), May 1, May 19 (Youth Day), May 27 and 28 (Constitution Days), August 30 (Victory Day), October 29 and 30 (Declaration of the Republic Days).
Special Information: Ramadan is the ninth month of the Muslim calendar, and lasts 30 days. During Ramadan, little food or drink is served from dawn to sunset.

Yugoslavia

Daily Business Hours
Shops:
   Winter: 8 a.m.—1 p.m. and 4—7 p.m. Monday to Saturday.
   Summer: 7 a.m.—noon and 5—8 p.m. Monday to Saturday.
Banks:
   Winter: 8 a.m.—noon and 4—7 p.m. Monday to Friday.
   Summer: 7—11 a.m. and 5—8 p.m. Monday to Friday.
Government Offices: 7 a.m.—2 p.m. Monday to Saturday.
Sundays: Most shops are closed, but some self-service food stores in cities are open.
National Holidays: January 1 and 2, May 1 and 2, July 4 (Partisan Day), November 29 and 30 (Republic Days).
Regional Holidays: Bosnia-Herzegovina and Croatia, July 27; Macedonia, August 2 and October 11; Montenegro, July 13; Serbia, July 7; Slovenia, July 22-23
Religious Holidays: Easter and Christmas are unofficially celebrated in the northern Christian republics; Ramadan is unofficially celebrated in the southern Muslim republics.
Special Information: Business hours vary slightly from region to region.

Shopping
What are the Good Buys?

You can find a world of things to buy in Europe. Each country has its specialities, which are widely available locally, though often unknown or very expensive elsewhere. Some items, particularly crafts, are regional. Sometimes the regions are very small. For example, in Provence near Arles, gnarled olive wood trunks are carved into freeform fruit bowls of exceptional beauty. But 50 miles or farther away, you'll never find them.

If you find items you want because they are unique, or you won't have the time to come back and get them, buy them because you may never see them again. (Of course, you may see something better later, but that is a matter of chance and not likely.)

Prices vary greatly, but often prices within a country are fixed, regardless of the store of purchase. This is particularly true for well-known trademark items such as Baccarat crystal or Lladró porcelain. Whether the price is less than near your home depends very much on the product. Be sure to price things you may want to buy at home before you go, because in many cases there are no savings at all.

There is a wealth of art and antiques. However, while there is generally no restriction on purchase, you must get export licences for art in many countries.

In Eastern Europe, virtually anything older than 1950 is considered an antique, which requires a rarely given export license.

Fine Arts and Antiques

Export of old fine arts such as painting and sculpture is carefully regulated in Britain, France, Greece, Italy, Spain, and Turkey.

In France, you apply for an export permit from the Customs office if the item is valued over 100,000 francs. The items then must be approved by Customs and an official of the National Museums of France. In Spain, the process is similar: the curator is from the Prado Museum. Italy also requires approval from the ministries of culture, education, interior, plus a national museum curator.

In Italy and Spain, if the permit is denied, the museum can purchase the work—at a valuation they decide on. In France, permission can be denied without any desire to purchase. In these countries, you should insist that the sale is "contingent upon issuance of an export permit".

In Britain, export permits are required for art, antiques, and collectors' items and motor vehicles over 50 years old valued at over £16,000. Lesser limits apply in some cases: photographs more than 60 years old (£400); representations of British historical personages (£4000); all archaeological items recovered in Britain, and architectural and engineering drawings made by hand. If a museum wants the art, it will have to buy it for the amount you paid for it. Otherwise you will be granted the export permit.

Details and step-by-step procedures of the export permit process for Britain and France are found in "Manston's Antique Markets" guides for those countries.

For further information about purchases and removal of fine art and antiques contact:

France
Direction Générale des
Douanes et Droits
Indirects
182 rue Saint-Honoré
75001 Paris
Tel. 42.50.35.90

Great Britain
Department of Trade
and Industry—Export
Licensing Branch
Millbank Tower
London SW1P 4QU
Tel. (01) 211-4620

Greece
Ministry of Culture
Supervisor of Prehistoric
and Classical
Antiquities
Museum Section
Aristidou 14
101 86 Athens
Υπουργειο Πολιτισμου
Δ/νση Προιστ. & Κλ.
Αρχ/Των.
Τμημα Μουσειων
Αρισειτδου 14
101 86 Αθηναι
Tel. 324 3015

Italy
Ministero dei Beni
Culturali ed Ambientali
Ufficio Esportazione
Opere d'Arte
Via Cernaia 1
00185 Roma
Tel. (06) 461457

Spain
Ministerio de Cultura
Paseo de la Castellana 39
Madrid 16
Tel. (91) 455 5000

There are few if any problems in the export of art from Belgium, the Netherlands, West Germany, or Switzerland. In these countries, if you buy it, you can generally take it. In all cases, you must be able to provide a "Declaration of Exportation" if requested to Customs when you leave the nation of purchase.

Aside from antiques and fine arts, every country in Europe has specialities you can buy and take home. Here a few specialities, listed by country.

Shopping Specialities Key

Austria: Jaeger outfits for men and women, jewellery, down pillows, quilts, and comforters.

Belgium: Diamonds, chocolate, lacework.
Bulgaria: Folk art, such as painted and carved wooden plates, embroidered tablecloths.
Czechoslovakia: Crystal, hand woven carpets. (If you buy crystal elsewhere than a Tuzex shop, you may have to pay a 100% export duty when you leave Czechoslovakia, however, inspection is spotty.)
Denmark: Fine design: jewelry, silver, stainless steel, porcelain, furniture, furs, smoking pipes and tobacco products, women's furs.
Finland: Furs, Marimekko designs, wood products.
France: Perfume, crystal, Limoges porcelain, fashions, kitchenware.
(West) Germany: Sensible kitchen gadgets, cuckoo clocks, mechanical products, motor vehicles.
Great Britain: Woollens, raincoats, Wedgwood and other porcelain, books.
Greece: Copper and enamel ware, ouzo, furs (in Kastoria). (Be sure that the furs you buy aren't on the British Customs protected species list, however.)
Hungary: Folk art such as handwoven carpets and embroideries, Herend porcelain, paprika.
Ireland: Aran hand-knit sweaters, Waterford crystal, Belleek porcelain.
Italy: Leather goods, gold jewellery, faience pottery.
Monaco: Postage stamps.
Netherlands: Diamonds, wooden shoes, Delft ware.
Norway: Ski sweaters.
Poland: Folk art, vodka.
Portugal: Hand-painted tiles, woven goods, straw, and pottery.
Romania: Folk embroidery.
Spain: Toledo metalware, leather goods.
Sweden: Crystal, furnishings.
Switzerland: Knives, linens, watches, chocolate.
Turkey: Rugs, copper ware, onyx, brass.
Yugoslavia: Folk art such as weaving, carved wooden plates, wickerwork, wine barrels, crystal. etc.

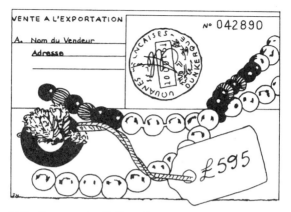

Value Added Tax Refunds

Value Added Tax (VAT) is charged in every Western European country, plus Hungary and Yugoslavia in Eastern Europe, as well. In many countries, you can receive a refund of the amount of VAT if you complete the proper paperwork. If British residents request a VAT refund where they purchase goods, they may have to pay VAT to British Customs when they return home.

In some countries, VAT is lower than it is in Britain (for example, the maximum in Luxembourg is 12%, and in Germany is 14%). It is not worth the effort to obtain a refund, only to have to pay more to British Customs.

It may be worth obtaining a refund, however, with some purchases in some countries, such as France, where VAT can be as high as 33%.

Each country sets a minimum amount that purchasers must spend to collect a refund. Sometimes the requirement is set per single item (as in Italy), while more genertally it is total purchase amount in the same shop. In addition, shops are free to impose additional requirements. Most minimums are around £50.

European Community (EC) and Non-EC Countries

If you buy in any EC country, VAT paid abroad offsets any potential British VAT tax payment you have.

If you buy outside the EC, you should always request a VAT refund when you purchase goods. You will have to pay British VAT when you return to Britain (if your purchases are over the duty-free allowances).

Non-EC countries that offer tax refunds are Austria, Finland, Norway, Sweden, and Switzerland.

Some countries, whether or not in the EC, do not offer VAT refunds. These include Greece, Hungary, Portugal, and Yugoslavia.

General Procedures

Each country's procedures for refunds are a bit different. They are very precise, and failure to follow them exactly will usually result in failure to receive the refund you expected.

In general, a three- or four-part form must be filled out by the shop assistant at the time of your purchase. Be sure you have the business name, address and phone, and assistant's name either on the form or elsewhere in case there is a problem.

If you don't have the paperwork completed when you leave the shop, you will not get a refund from that establishment.

When you go shopping, take your passport or passport number, since it is almost always required to complete the form.

When purchasing goods in non-EC countries, that country's customs officials stamp the forms and you receive your refund either at the border, or later by cheque or credit to your credit card account.

When purchasing goods in EC countries, British Customs stamps the forms in the correct places. You keep a copy yourself. You must post another back to the shop. One or two more copies are kept by Customs.

You may have to pay British VAT (usually 15%). You also may have to pay British customs duty and excise tax.

You will recieve the refund as a cheque or a credit to your credit card account.

Non-EC Residents

Residents of countries outside the EC (including Australia, Canada, New Zealand, and the United States) may not know about or be familiar with the Value Added Tax, a sort of national sales tax. They are able to receive VAT refunds on many purchases of goods, but not generally on services and items consumed or used before export. In general, non-EC residents must have the forms stamped by customs officials in the country of purchase. One copy of the form must be sent back to the shop, which then sends the refund as a cheque or a credit to a credit card account. Be sure to keep your copy in case you have problems.

How Your Refund Will Be Paid

Refunds are usually mailed to your home address by cheque. Sometimes the refund is credited through your bank into your account or credit card account. When buying, be sure you have the following banking information with you: your bank name and address, and your account number. The routing code (the computer readable numbers at the bottom of your cheque) contains much of this information.

Expect to wait up to three months for refunds to arrive. Inform your bank to watch for these credits to your account.

In other cases, if the store participates in a "Tax Free" plan (look for the "Tax Free Shopping for Tourists" sticker) you get a cheque at the store with the amount of refund on it. It becomes valid when stamped by Customs; then it can be cashed at exchange booths or banks at borders, or later through your bank.

Refunds on Services and Consumed Items

Tourist Travel

You cannot generally receive a refund on any costs (goods and services) associated with non-business travel, such as hotel rooms, car rentals, meals, tickets, or telephone calls.

Business Trips

If you visit other European Community (EC) countries at least in part for a business purpose (such as attending a trade show, meeting with a prosepective business associate, or looking for certain types of merchandise for resale), you may be able to reclaim some or all of the Value Added Tax paid for travel expenses and services, including hotels, meals, transportation, and trade show expenses.

Each country has its own complex and different rules: for example, in Germany, you must submit the original receipts with your forms; in France, you must hire a French firm to process the paperwork for you. These firms process these claims for a percentage of the refund.

Information about these rules can be obtained from each country's govenment office for collecting the tax.

Value Added Tax Refund Key

Austria

Tax name: Mehrwertsteuer (Initials MWST).
Tax rates: Minimum: 20%, or 16.66% of the sales price.
Maximum: 32%, or 24.24% of the sales price.
How to determine in advance if a store gives tax refunds: The Austrian National Tourist Office has a booklet about Tax Free Shopping. Some stores have a sign reading "Tax Free Shopping". In any case, you can ask at the store if there is no other marking.

Minimum Purchase: 1001 Austrian Schillings (AS) at each store.
Procedures at the store:
1. When purchasing, ask for refund.
2. Store clerk must fill out form U-34, "Ausfuhrbescheinigung für Umsatzsteuerszwecke".
3. You will have to present your passport.
4. Clerk will retain one copy, give you remaining ones, with envelope to return stamped papers to store.
Procedures when leaving Austria:
1. Stop at Austrian customs (Zollamt) on your way out.
2. Present form U-34 with receipt attached.
3. Have goods ready for inspection. (They should not have been used.)
4. Austrian customs will stamp all copies of the form.
5. Give store's return envelope to customs officer. It will be returned to the store. (Be sure it has postage on it.)
5 Alternative. Send the original stamped copy back to the store yourself, after you have left Austria. (Be sure to keep a copy of everything you post.)
You can receive cash refunds when leaving, at ÖAMTC offices (the Austrian Auto Club) at main international road frontier crossings. To receive this refund, the form U-34 must have the Club's blue imprint. For a small fee (sliding scale 10%-4%, minimum AS 40), the Club frontier office will give you a cash refund. Customs officers cannot refund money. In addition to road crossings, the ÖAMTC has offices at the Vienna airport and Salzburg and Kufstein railway stations.
You cannot receive a refund if you are unable to follow procedures when leaving Austria. No customs stamp, no refund.
You will receive the refund as cash at the border from ÖAMTC, as a credit to your current or savings account (be sure the paperwork includes your bank and account number), international money order sent to your home, or an Austrian cheque drawn in schillings.

Belgium

Tax name: *French:* Taxe sur la Valeur Ajoutée (TVA); *Flemish:* Belasting Toegevoegde Waarde (BTW).

Tax rates: Maximum: 25% for "luxury" items, plus 8% non-refundable "luxury tax", but most items are 19%.

Minimum purchase requirement: 3000 Belgian francs in one store.

How to determine if a store gives tax refunds: Ask the store staff.

Procedures at the store:

1. Complete the refund form.
2. The merchant will keep one copy and give you the rest.
3. Be sure you get a self-addressed envelope from the store. (Buy stamps for it if the store doesn't put them on.)

Procedures at customs:

British Residents:

1. Have British Customs stamp the forms, and post them back to the shop yourself.
2. Wait a month or two for the refund to arrive.

Non-EC residents: when leaving Belgium:

1. Submit filled-out form to Belgian customs for signature and stamp. Be prepared to show the items you bought.
2. Give stamped envelope to customs to mail, or mail it yourself.

If you are leaving Belgium by train, there are usually no customs officers on the train. You may have to check-in your luggage and have the station customs officials stamp the forms.

If you leave by plane or ferry, there are customs officials at the airport or docks.

If you drive across the border, there are customs offices at main road border crossings.

3. Wait a month or two for the refund to arrive.

You cannot receive cash refunds when leaving Belgium.

Tax cannot be refunded if you are unable to follow Customs procedures.

You will usually receive the refund as a cheque in Belgian francs.

Denmark

Tax name: Mer Omdaetnings Afgift (MOMS).
Tax rate: 22% (or 18.03% of selling price including tax).
How to determine if a store gives tax refunds: Often stores have a clearly visible red and white sign reading "Danish Tax Free Shopping".
Minimum purchase requirement: 600 Danish kroner (including tax) at one store.
Procedures at the store:
A. If merchandise is sent outside of the Common Market or Scandinavia, or delivered to Kastrup airport, fill out paperwork at store. No tax will be charged, but you will have to pay any shipping charges.
B. 1. Fill out the refund form at the store. Most stores catering to tourists or with the Danish Tax Free Shopping sign have the form.
2. The store will charge a 3% service fee to process the refund (maximum charge 350 Dkr).
Procedures for Customs:
British residents:
1. Declare goods to British Customs. They will stamp and sign paperwork.
2. If you have a cheque, you must negotiate it with your bank.

If you have forms, you must post them back to the shop and wait for payment by cheque or credit to your credit card account.
Non-EC residents:
1. Declare goods at the Danish border, ferry port, or airport and get each copy of the form(s) stamped by customs officers.
2. Give an addressed envelope and all except one copy of the form to the customs officer or send it back to the store yourself.
You cannot receive cash refunds at the border when leaving Denmark, except at Kastrup Airport near Copenhagen.
The tax cannot be refunded if you are unable to follow procedures when leaving.
Your refund will be as a cheque sent to you in Danish kroner, or as a direct deposit made to your bank account.

Finland

Tax name: Liikevaihtavero (LVV).
Tax rates: 16% on most purchases, but refund is 11% of purchase price.
Minimum purchase requirement: 150 Finnish Marks (Fmk).
How to determine if a store offers tax refunds: The store will usually have the "Finland Tax-Free Shopping" logo displayed. If not, ask an assistant.
Procedures at the store:
1. Tell the store you want a "Tax-Free" refund when you buy.
2. You must present your passport, proving that you live outside of Scandinavia.
3. The store staff will fill out the Tax-Free Export Receipt and Shopping Cheque.
Procedures when leaving Finland:
1. Take the tax-refund form and merchandise to the Tax-Free Service Office found at airports in Helsinki, Turku, Mariehamm, Vaasa, or Rovaniemi, road crossings to Sweden, Norway, and the Soviet Union, and on some ferries (check before you board).
2. Show the receipt, present the cheque, and be ready to show the merchandise. (Do not open the package until you receive your refund.)
3. You will receive your refund in cash on the spot in Finnish marks, even if you charged the purchase on a credit card.
You cannot get the refund if you are unable to follow procedures when you leave Finland.

France

Tax name: Taxe sur la Valeur Ajoutée (TVA)
Tax rate: 18.6% on most items, 33% on luxuries.
Minimum purchase requirement: 1200 French francs in one store, though some stores may require a higher amount.
How to determine if a store gives tax refunds: Ask if the store offers "détaxe". Many but not all stores in Paris offer tax refunds, but fewer stores in the provinces refund tax.

Procedures at the store:
1. Make it clear you want refund (ask for "détaxe" and be sure you receive a "Fiche de Douanes").
2. A four-part form called "Vente a l'exportation" must be filled out in the store.
3. You will have to present your passport or give the passport number.
4. Pay full amount, including tax.
5. Get stamped envelope preaddressed to the store.

Procedures for Customs:
British residents:
1. Have British Customs sign and stamp the form.
2. Send the shop's (pink) copy back to the shop. Retain the green copy for your records.

Non-EC residents:
A. *Normal procedure:* refund to your home or account.
1. Take all your forms and purchased merchandise to French customs (Douane) officers. Note: If leaving by train (except to Britain), take care of this before you board. Get a customs official in the baggage area to stamp the forms. You will probably be required to check-in the luggage containing the goods. No on-train customs officers will stamp the forms.
2. At night, you may have to rouse an official.
3. Have each copy stamped and initialled by customs.
4. Customs official will keep white and pink copies.
5. Give customs official the return envelope.
6. Keep the completed green copy.

B. *For refund in cash* (only available at Charles de Gaulle, Orly, and Nice international airports during airport bank branch hours):

Follow steps 1, 2, and 3 immediately above. At this point, have customs give you a "Bon de Remboursement Aéroport", which you must take to the bank in the airport to cash.

Note: Be sure to allow plenty of extra time if you use this procedure, since these offices are usually understaffed. Your refund must be made before you leave, since the "Bon" is only good at the airport bank.

C. Use a credit card.
Follow steps 1, 2, and 3 above. When you pay, have separate charge slips made up for the price of goods and for the amount of tax. Some shops will make the second charge slip a credit to be processed when your customs-stamped paperwork is returned to them. Others will make the TVA an additional charge that will not be made if the customs-stamped paperwork is returned to them in a reasonable time.

Tax cannot usually be refunded if you are unable to follow procedures when entering Britain (or non-ECs countries when leaving France), but you can try by returning the form by registered mail to the store when you arrive in Britain.

You can receive the refund as a sterling cheque drawn on either a British bank or a French bank, a French franc check drawn on a French bank, a credit to your bank account (give them the name of your bank and account number), or a credit to your credit card.

Germany, West

Note: Because the maximum tax rate is 14%, it is not usually worth while for British residents to request VAT refunds.)
Tax name: Mehrwertsteuer (MWST).
Tax rate: Minimum: 7% (books and groceries); Maximum: 14% (almost everything else)
Minimum purchase requirement: set by each store; a small service charge may be levied.
How to determine if a store gives tax refunds: Ask the store staff, though a few stores have a "Tax-Free" sign or sticker at the door.
Procedures at the store:
1. Present your passport.
2. Assistant will fill out an Export and Buyer's Certificate (Ausfuhr- und Abnehmerbeschienigung), including a description of the merchandise and its price.
3. Obtain a stamped and addressed envelope.
4. Give the seller your bank's address and account number.

Procedures for Customs:
British residents:
1. Have British Customs sign and stamp the form.
2. Send the shop's copy back to the shop. Retain one copy for your records.
3. Wait for the refund.
Non-EC residents:
1. Be sure you have a copy of the certificate to keep; make a photocopy if necessary.
2. Take the form to the German customs office (Zollamt), or find a customs officer when you leave. Have the purchases available for inspection.
3. Customs officer will stamp all copies of the form, and take the preaddressed, stamped envelope and post it to the store.
You cannot receive cash refunds when leaving West Germany.
You can receive a tax refund if you aren't able to follow procedures if you take the certificate and merchandise to the German consulate. The staff will sign and stamp the certificate, which you will have to mail to the store.
You will receive the refund as a direct deposit made to your bank account or, rarely, a credit to a credit card account, or a cheque in Deutsche marks.

Great Britain

Note: Only people who permanently reside outside the EC can obtain Value Added Tax refunds.
Tax name: Value Added Tax (VAT).
Tax rate: 15% on most items.
No minimum purchase requirement, though many stores impose their own. Stores are permitted to levy a service charge. (Example: Harrods has a minimum £70 purchase, and charges £2 for processing the refund.)
How to determine if VAT refunds are offered: ask the sales person, or look for the "Tax-Free Shopping" sticker near the door.
Procedures at the store:
1. The store staff must fill out the "Value Added Tax Retail Export Scheme" form.

2. You must show your passport.
3. Sign the "Declaration by the Customer" on the form.
4. Get pre-addressed (and usually stamped) envelope.

Procedures when leaving Great Britain:
1. Take form and merchandise to H.M. Customs and Excise counter or office at the airport or ferry terminal.
2. Customs officials may view merchandise and will stamp papers. Give official the return envelope to send to the store.
3. Get the customer's copy of the form for your records.

Note for air travellers: Due to the way Heathrow and Gatwick airports are laid out, you must check-in luggage before you can have your paperwork stamped. Carry your purchases in your hand luggage or hope the official doesn't want to see anything you've checked-in in your luggage. Check the computerised display board at Gatwick for exact location of the office.

You cannot receive cash refunds at the airport or ferry terminal when leaving Britain.

If you fail to get British customs to stamp your paperwork before you leave Britain, you can still get a refund if you have the refund form.
Procedure:
1. Get a customs duty receipt or a copy of your customs declaration from your own country, or a customs stamp on the refund form.
2. You can also get a Chief of Police or Notary Public at home to stamp Box B of each copy of the VAT form. This certifies that the goods were exported from Britain.
3. Mail the stamped and signed forms (except the customer's copy) to the seller as in the normal procedure.

You will receive the refund in the form of either a cheque drawn in pounds sterling or a credit to your credit card (if originally charged).

Ireland

Tax name: Value Added Tax (VAT).
Tax rates: Minimum: 10% (clothing), though almost everything else is 23%.
No minimum purchase requirement, though many stores set a minimum purchase of about £50. Stores may charge a service fee (about £2) for processing the refund.
How to determine if VAT refunds are offered: Ask the store staff; stores are not required to offer refunds.
Procedures at the store:
1. Obtain an invoice which includes your name, address, describes the merchandise, and shows the amount of VAT paid.
2. Before leaving Ireland, make a copy of the invoice if you don't have one made by the store.
Procedures for Customs:
British residents:
1. Have British Customs sign and stamp the form.
2. Send the shop's copy back to the shop. Retain one copy for your records.
3. Wait for the refund.
Non-EC residents:
1. At customs (whether airport or ferry port), present the invoice to customs for stamping and initialling. Also, ask them to stamp the copy you keep.
2. Post the original stamped and initialed invoice back to the store, or a central value-added tax refund clearing house (address on the invoice).
You cannot receive cash refunds at ferry terminals when leaving Ireland, but you can receive cash refunds in Irish pounds at Shannon and Dublin airports. Look for the "Cashback" office.
You cannot receive a refund if you are unable to follow procedures at British Customs (or, for non-EC residents, when leaving Ireland).
You will receive the refund either as a cheque (usually in Irish pounds), a money order, a credit to a credit card account, or cash at Shannon airport. If you pay in cash, the credit can still be in the form of a credit card credit if you leave the account number with the merchant.

Italy

Tax name: Imposta Valore Aggiunto (IVA).
Tax rate: 18% to 30%, depending on the item, but refund is 13%.
Minimum purchase requirement: 250,000 lire for each single item or set. Some stores will combine all items as a "set"; others will not.
How to determine if a store gives tax refunds: Every store is legally required to offer tax refunds. (Legal Authority: Art. 38-quater—Sgravio dell'imposta per i viaggiatore stranieri, 16 D.P.R. 30-12-1981.)
Procedures at the store:
1. Obtain an invoice, which includes your name, address, passport number, and a description of the purchase. Be sure to get two copies, and the export forms. If you are to receive credit on your credit card, be sure that a credit slip is imprinted.
Procedures for Customs:
British residents:
1. Have British Customs sign and stamp the form.
2. Send the shop's copy back to the shop by registered mail (to guarantee it is received). Retain one copy for your records.
3. Wait for the refund.
Non-EC residents:
1. Show both copies of the invoice and the merchandise to Italian customs at the "Ufficio della Dogana" when you leave Italy. (There is no special tax-refund office.)
2. Italian customs will stamp the invoice and return it to you.
3. Send the original stamped invoice to the store by registered mail (to guarantee it is received).
4. The store must receive the invoice by post within three months of the purchase or you will not receive a refund.
5. The store is required to send the refund within 15 days of the day it receives the stamped invoice.
You cannot receive cash refunds when leaving Italy.

The IVA tax cannot be refunded if you are unable to follow procedures at British Customs (or, for non-EC residents, when leaving Italy).

Your refund will be most often an Italian cheque in lire, bank draft, or, in rare occurrences, a credit to your credit card account.

Note: Due to the state of the Italian post office, you should allow a good deal of time to receive your refund.

Luxembourg

Note: Because the maximum tax rate is 12%, it is not usually worthwhile for British residents to request VAT refunds.)

Tax name: Taxe sur la valeur ajoutée (TVA).

Tax rates: 3%, (mainly food), 6% (mainly food and books), and 12% (almost everything else).

Minimum purchase requirement: 15,800 F.

How to determine if a store offers refunds: Ask the store staff whether tax refunds ("détaxation") are offered.

Procedures at the store:

1. The store will give you an invoice describing the purchase and amount of TVA tax.
2. Be sure to keep a copy of the invoice.

Procedures for Customs:

1. Present the receipt to British Custom, (or, if a non-EC resident, the customs officer at the Bureau des Douanes when you leave Luxembourg, Belgium, or the Netherlands. You will have to show your passport.
2. Send the stamped invoice to the store.
3. If you are leaving by train from Luxembourg City, take the invoice and goods to the customs office (Bureau des Douanes) at the right side of the Gare Centrale station. They will stamp the invoice, and you can take the stamped invoice back to the store and collect a refund on the spot.

You cannot receive a TVA tax refund if you are unable to follow procedures when leaving.

You will the receive the refund as a credit to your credit-card account, or credited to your checking account at home, unless you receive an immediate refund before you leave (see #3 above).

Netherlands

Tax name: Belasting Toegevoegde Waarde (BTW).
Tax rates: Minimum: 6% (only on food), maximum: 20%, plus luxury tax, only on cars.
Minimum purchase requirement: 300 Guilders in one store.
How to determine if a store gives tax refunds: Ask the store staff, or look for "Tax Free for Tourists" sticker.
Procedures at the store:
1. The store staff will complete a form, listing the item, price, and your name, address, and passport number, or sometimes give you a check with the refund amount. The check becomes valid when stamped by customs.
2. Be sure you get an envelope addressed to the store as well, or the refund service agency.
Procedures at Customs
British residents:
1. Have British Customs sign and stamp the form.
2. Send the shop's copy back to the shop. Retain one copy for your records.
3. Wait for the refund.
Non-EC residents:
1. Dutch customs officers must sign and stamp all copies of the form. Sometimes when leaving by train, there will not be any customs officers on the train, especially when going into Belgium. In this case, check-in your bags and get the stamps at the station.
2. Send the form back to the store from another country.
You can get cash refunds when leaving at Schiphol airport and major road border crossing with "Grenswisselkantoren" banks if you have a check. You'll be given a voucher by customs to exchange at the airport bank.
The BTW tax cannot be refunded if you are unable to follow Customs procedures.
You will usually receive the refund as a cheque, usually payable in guilders, or in cash at borders.

Norway

Tax name: MOMS.
Tax rates: Minimum: 16.67%
Minimum purchase requirement: 1000 kroner in one store.
How to determine if a store offers tax refunds: The store will usually have the Norway Tax-Free logo displayed, either as a sticker at the door or as a placard or poster. If it is not shown not, ask an assistant.
Procedures at the store:
1. Tell the store you want a "Tax-Free" refund when you buy.
2. You must present your passport, proving that you live outside of Scandinavia.
3. The store staff will fill out the Tax-Free Export Receipt and an attached Shopping Cheque. **Procedures when leaving Norway:**
1. Take the tax-refund form and merchandise to the Tax-Free Service Office found at ports, airports, and on some ships, and at Kastrup Airport in Copenhagen, Denmark.
2. Show the forms and be ready to show the merchandise.
3. You will receive your refund in cash on the spot in Norwegian kroner, even if you charged the purchase on a credit card.
You cannot get the refund if you are unable to follow procedures when you leave Norway.

Spain

Tax name: Impuesto de Valór Añadido (IVA).
Tax rates: 7% to 33%, depending on type of merchandise.
Minimum purchase requirement: 25,000 pesetas at one store.
How to determine if a store offers tax refunds: Ask the store staff. You can only apply for a refund if you take the goods with you. If you have the store ship the goods to your home, tax is not charged.
Procedures at the store:
1. The store staff must complete the form, "Desgravación Fiscal a la Exportación de Mer-

cancias Adquiridas por Residentes en el extranjero". You must present your passport.

2. Be sure you have the form and return envelope when you leave the store.

Procedures for Customs:

British residents:

1. Have British Customs sign and stamp the form.

2. Send the shop's copy back to the shop. Retain one copy for your records.

3. Wait for the refund.

Non-EC residents:

1. Take the form to the window or office marked "Desgravación Fiscal" or the customs office at the frontier.

2. Customs officers will stamp your forms, mail the blue copy back to the store in the provided envelope, give you the yellow copy, and keep the other copies. (At Madrid's Barajas airport, the window is on the concourse of the departures level. Allow about a half hour to take care of this before check-in.)

You cannot receive cash refunds when leaving Spain.

The tax can be refunded if you aren't able to follow procedures when leaving Spain. You must mail the blue copy of the completed form back to the store from Britain. (An official postmark should be stamped in the box reserved for the customs stamp to provide proof of exportation.)

You will usually receive the refund as a Spanish cheque in pesetas.

Sweden

Tax name: MOMS.

Tax rate: 23.46%, but refund is 14%.

Minimum purchase requirement: None, but most stores require a purchase of at least 200 Swedish kronor.

How to determine if a store offers tax refunds: The store will usually have the Sweden Tax-Free logo displayed as a sticker near the door or a poster. If not, ask an assistant.

Procedures at the store:

1. Tell the store you want a "Tax-Free" refund when you buy.
2. You must present your passport, proving that you live outside of Scandinavia.
3. The store staff will fill out the Tax Free Export Receipt and a Shopping Cheque.

Procedures when leaving Sweden:
1. Take the tax refund form and merchandise to the Tax-Free Service Office found at ports, airports, and on some ships. (At Arlanda airport, the counter is on the check-in level, another is in the transit hall. Refunds are only given in the transit hall. Allow up to an extra hour for this chore.)
2. Show the forms and be ready to show the merchandise.
3. You will receive your refund in cash on the spot in Swedish kroner, even if you charged the purchase on a credit card.

You cannot receive the refund if you are unable to follow procedures when you leave Sweden, except at Kastrup airport in Copenhagen, Denmark. Make your purchases within seven days of your departure from Sweden, to guarantee your refund. (While reasonable allowances over seven days can be made, refunds are not guaranteed.)

Switzerland

Merchandise Turnover Tax:
German: Warenumsatzteuer (WUST).
French: Impôt sur le chiffre d'affaires.
Italian: Imposta sulla ciffra d'affari.

Tax rates: 5.6% to 8.4% (food, newspapers, livestock, and utility service are tax free).

Minimum purchase: 500 Swiss francs in one store.

How to determine if tax refunds are offered: Ask the store staff.

Procedures at the store: Store staff will complete the paperwork, and give you forms, a receipt, and further instructions.

The refund will usually be a Swiss franc bank cheque, or a credit to your credit-card or bank account.

Flea Markets and Street Markets

You can find almost anything at Europe's street markets and flea markets. Hidden amidst the junk are more than a few jewels.

Flea markets range from indoor collections of private shops to rowdy street scenes offering everything from antiques to old clothes, tools, and other used items.

Street markets offer fresh produce, shoddy new clothes, cheap kitchen gadgets, entertainment, and sometimes even live chickens and farm animals.

Many markets overlap in their offerings, including fruit, vegetables, and clothes as well as junk.

Almost every city, town, and many villages have street markets, usually on one or two days of the week. Most people in town know which days are market days and where they are located.

Another easy way to find out is to watch the "No Parking" signs in squares and on wide streets for prohibitions from about 6 a.m. to 2 to 4 p.m. on specific days. During those times, the area becomes a street or flea market.

On market day in some towns, such as Sarlat-le-Canéda in the Dordogne valley of southwestern France, virtually the entire centre of town becomes a market, one of the most exciting in one of the most beautiful settings in Europe.

Larger cities have more than one market, each with its own speciality. Often city markets are held daily.

Know what you're looking for or you may not get good buys. For example, there are sometimes solid silver pieces mixed in with the silver plate—but if you don't know European silver hallmarks, you may get stuck with virtually worthless plated ware at sterling prices. At a flea market, you are most likely to find solid silver cheaply if the hallmark is from another country than the one you're in. Judge other speciality items with the same knowledge.

Of course, if you just *like* the item, buy it and enjoy it!

At any street market, the local currency's cash is the only welcome medium of exchange.

Bargaining—Prices at the Flea Market

Bargaining is expected in all flea markets, except those selling food and new items. Generally, you'll fare better by offering about half the asking price, and expect to pay about two thirds to three quarters. You can try walking away—the sellers may concede and call you back just as you pass out of earshot. But don't let the game keep you from your purchase. You may never see it again if you don't return.

Flea Market Key: Locations and Times

The following Flea Market Key is just a sampling of the flea and street markets of Europe. (For more information, including shipping, antiques export and customs regulations, as well as hundreds of flea markets, antique fairs, and auctions, please see "Manston's Antique Markets" for Britain and France.

Austria

Vienna. Flea market (Flohmarkt) at Naschmarkt, near Mariahilferstrasse, west of the Opera house. Saturday mornings. Especially good during the summer.

Belgium

Antwerp. Flea market (Vogelmarkt, literally bird market) at Oudevaartplaats, near the Nationale Bank building in the city centre. A large flea market, food market, and flower market, plus animals and birds. Sunday mornings.
Antwerp. Vrijdagmarkt, (literally Friday market) an outdoor antique and used furniture auction at Vrijdagmarkt near the Plantin-Moretus Museum in central Antwerp. Wednesday and Friday mornings. One of the most interesting in Europe.
Antwerp. Antique market at Lijnwaadmarkt, Saturdays from about 10 a.m. to 6 p.m.

Brussels. Flea market (marché aux puces) at Place du Grand Sablon, near the Art Museum (Musèe d'Art). Antiques, including silver, paintings, and old arms (such as swords and crossbows). Saturdays from 9 a.m. to 3 p.m. and Sundays from 9 a.m. to 1 p.m.
Brussels. Daily flea and street market at Place de Jeu de Balle, on rue Blaes (south of Grand Sablon). A junkier flea and street market. Daily from 8 a.m. to about 1 p.m., best on Wednesday and Saturday..
Brussels. Huge Sunday morning produce, and clothes, and used items market all around the Gare du Midi (Zuidstation). Used bicycles are sold in the median of the Boulevard du Midi.

Ghent (Gand). Food and produce market at St. Michaelsplein. Sunday mornings.

Liège. Flea and street market (La Batte) on the left bank of the Meuse between Place Cockerill and Pont Maghin. Saturdays from 9 a.m. to 2 p.m. Possibly the best single market in Belgium.

Denmark

Copenhagen. Israels Plads flea market, near the Norrepost S-tog station and botanical gardens. Saturdays from May to September from 8 a.m. to 2 p.m.

Copenhagen. Flea market behind the Fredericksberg Rådhus near the Fredericksberg S-tog station. Summer Saturday mornings, early, but no set opening time.

Copenhagen. Frelsens Haer indoor antique market, at Høhusgade 5. Lots of booths and small shops. Tuesdays, Wednesdays, and Thursdays, 1 p.m. to 5 p.m., Fridays, 1 p.m. to 6 p.m., Saturdays 9 a.m. to 1 p.m.

Finland

Helsinki. Street market in central market square. Food and souvenirs but few antiques. Daily 7 a.m. to 2 p.m. except Sundays. Also 3:30 to 8 p.m. in summer.

France

Aix-en-Provence. Flea, antique, and street market at the place de Verdun in the city centre. One of the most picturesque markets in France. Tuesday, Thursday, and Saturday from 8 a.m. to about 1 p.m.

Dijon. Food market in the old market hall in place du Marché in the old town. The hall is reminiscent of famous the old Les Halles market in the center of Paris. Clothes and other items around; antiques on the adjoining place de la Banque. Tuesdays and Saturdays from 6 a.m. to about 12:30 p.m.

Lyon. Flea market (marché aux puces) on rue Tita Coîs in the northeast suburb of Vulx-en-Velin. Take Metro to Cosset and walk. Saturday and Sunday mornings.

Lyon. Flea market (marché aux puces de la Feyssine) along the Rhône. Antiques and collectables are inside the oval building. Saturday and Sunday mornings.

Lyon. Brocante Stalingrad. Lyon's antique trades centre, where the Parisian dealers buy, on boulevard Stalingrad in the Villeurbanne district. Thursday, Saturday, and Sunday.

Paris. Flea market (marché aux puces) at Porte de St. Ouen and Porte de Clignancourt, near the Metro stops of the same names. This market is huge, probably the largest in Europe. Thousands of small shops and booths, street tables, with junk, clothes, antiques. Know what you're buying and bargain or don't pay much. These people are wise to tourists! Sunday is the best day. Saturdays, Sundays, and Mondays from dawn to dusk. The best pickings are just before dawn from the street stands.

Paris. Smaller flea market at Porte de Vanves near the Metro station of the same name. More relaxed, less sophisticated, delightful tree-shaded setting. Saturdays and Sundays, dawn to 7 p.m.

Paris. Flea market at Porte de Montreuil, near the Metro station of the same name. Large, open, dusty, and windblown. The best antiques and collectables are along the west fence; kitchenware, clothes, and odds and ends towards the east. Saturdays, Sundays, and Mondays from 7 a.m. to 7 p.m.

Paris. Smaller flea market in a poor neighbourhood at place d'Aligre, near the Ledru Rollin Metro station. Poor selection, low prices. Every day.

Paris. Le Village Suisse, a modern several-story gallery of several hundred tiny elegant antique shops southeast of the Eiffel tower. Open 10 a.m. to 7 p.m., closed Tuesdays and Wednesdays.

Paris. Flower market. Retail flowers at the place Louis-Lépine, Île de la Cité, Daily 8:45 a.m. to 6 p.m.

Paris. Bird market at place Louis-Lépine, Île de la Cité, Sundays morning to mid-afternoon.

Paris. Book market. Bookstalls along the Quais des Seine, from the Louvre to near Notre Dame. Lots of prints and old books. Prices are negotiable, but still often more expensive than Britain. Daily morning to afternoon.

Paris. Stamp market. Avenue Gabriel at avenue Marigny (near the Rond-Point) near the Champs Élysées-Clemenceau Metro station. Thursdays, Saturdays, and Sundays, 10 a.m. to dusk.

Paris. Rungis-Les Halles. The wholesale food market for the Paris region that was moved from the colourful but cramped 19th-century cast-iron marvels at Les Halles in the centre of Paris. Go on Autoroute A6 to the Rungis-Les Halles exit just north of Orly airport. When you drive in, you must pay an entrance fee equivalent to several pounds. Clean, organized, architecturally undistinguished, but the products are the show. Hundreds of acres of fresh fruit and vegetables (such as matchstick-size string beans laid parallel in the crates), halls of flowers larger than football fields, hundreds of hanging sides of beef and other meats, fields of cheeses, and warehouses of wines and spirits. Wholesale only: you need a wholesalers' permit to buy. Often you sample free cheeses and wines. 11 p.m.—8 a.m. You will not meet many tourists here!

Sarlat-le-Canéda. Street market in village centre. Virtually the entire village becomes a marketplace of food, clothes, junk, and gadgets. Saturdays, dawn to afternoon.

Tours. Flea market at place des Victoires, between the Halles food market (open daily) and the Pont Napoleon. Neighbourhood is partly urban renewal, partly broken-down, partly impeccably restored antique homes. Wednesdays and Saturdays from early morning to midafternoon.

Note: for a complete listing of flea markets in France, please see "Manston's Antique Markets and Auctions of France".

Germany (West)

Frankfurt. Flea market (Flohmarkt) at the Schlachthof on the south bank of the Main River east of the Sachsenhausen district. Saturdays from 8 a.m. to about 3 p.m. (Also see Offenbach.)

Munich. Flea, antique market, and carnival (Auer dult), a huge selling festival on Mariahilfplatz, across the river Isar from the Frauenhoferstrasse U-Bahn station. The last week in April and July and the first week in October, all day.
Munich. Flea market (Flohmarkt) Saturday and Sunday at 128 Dachauerstrasse. The largest market in the region; finds possible for the early bird. Saturday and Sunday mornings, beginning at dawn.

Offenbach. Flea market (Flohmarkt) along the bank of the Main. Best market in the Frankfurt region, on a delightful tree-shaded riverside promenade. Lots of brass, glass, some furniture.

Great Britain

Birmingham. Flea market every Tuesday, Thursday, and Saturday at St. Martin's Market, immediately across the street from Bull Ring Centre in the city centre. Occasional huge Wednesday antique markets as well.

Brighton. Flea market, on Upper Gardiner Street the railway station, Saturday mornings. Brighton is one of the centres of the antiques trade in Britain, and there are dozens of antique shops in the area.

London. Few cities can rival London in the number of its street and flea markets. There is one somewhere every day of the week.
London. Monday to Friday. Leadenhall Street, near Bank underground station. General street market. Dawn to afternoon.
London. Monday to Saturday. Camden Passage near Angel underground station. Street and flea market (antiques and junk especially on Wednesday), plus scores of exclusive antique shops. Dawn to dusk.
London. Saturday and Sunday. Camden Lock. Street musicians, jugglers, food makers, and

craftspeople in a delightful canal side setting. Nearby, The Stables, north along Chalk Farm Road, are packed with stall-sized shops offering used merchandise of all types, including one of the best selections of collectables in Britain, especially strong in Art Deco.

London. Monday to Saturday. Portobello Road, near Ladbroke Grove and Notting Hill Gate underground stations. Street and flea market (antiques and junk especially on Saturday). Lots of small shops as well as street stalls, high-priced junk as well as high-priced antiques; well picked over. Though a few gems may lurk, it is a tourist attraction as much as a market, with prices to match. Know what you're buying and watch out for pickpockets!

London. Tuesday, Thursday, Friday, and especially Saturday. Greenwich Antiques Market, nearest to Elephant & Castle underground station.

London. Friday only. New Caledonian (also called Bermondsey), nearest to London Bridge underground station. Flea market possibly with London's best collection of antiques. Treasures lurk here. Dealers predominate as buyers as well as sellers until 7 a.m. Dawn to afternoon.

London. Sunday only. Petticoat Lane, which during the rest of the week is Middlesex Street, near Aldgate underground station. The quintessential London street market, with lots of cheap new junk, sleazy toys, clothes, food, and music. 7 a.m. to mid-afternoon.

London. Sunday only. Chapel Market, Islington, near Angel underground station. Street market with a bit of junk thrown in.

Note: for a complete listing of markets in Britain, please see "Manston's Antiques Fairs and Auctions of Britain."

Greece

Athens. Flea market at the east end of the Plaka district. Especially lively on Sunday mornings.

Italy

Arezzo (Tuscany). Antique market (Mostra mercato dell' antiquariato) takes place in the arcaded medieval Piazza Grande and surrounding streets and alleys. The first weekend of every month. Saturdays and Sundays, dawn to late afternoon.

Milan. Flea market (Fiera di Sinigaglia) on Via Catalafini. Saturdays from 8 a.m. to dusk. A long, narrow paved strip in a neighbourhood of drab apartment buildings.

Rome. Flea market at Porta Portese. Clothes, antiques, junk, tourist souvenirs, and almost anything else you can think of. Antiques are about one kilometre south of the entrance gate. Chaotically crowded; beware of pickpockets, particularly groups of Gypsy children. Sundays from dawn to about 1 p.m.

Turin. Antique fair and market (Mostra mercato dell' antiquariato) in the elegant Palazzo Nervi the 2nd and 3rd weeks of April. This is one of the largest antique shows in Italy, possibly in Europe.

Netherlands

Amsterdam. Flea market and street market at Waterlooplein market on Rapenburgerstraat, near where the Amstel and Nieuwe Herengracht meet. Some stands are old railroad cars. Daily from about 7 a.m.

Rotterdam. Flea market and street market on the square under the Blaak Station, across from the public library. Wednesday and Saturday mornings.

Portugal

Barcelos (about 30 miles north of Oporto). A street and craft market at the Campo da Fiera, a quarter-mile square in the centre of town graced by a beautiful fountain. Lots of handicrafts, such as the famous Portuguese roosters, embroidered lace and copper ware; a food market; live poultry; and assorted odds and ends. Thursdays from 7 a.m. until midafternoon.

Lisbon. Flea market (Fiero da Ladra) behind the S. Vicente de Fora church. Know what you're buying and be prepared to bargain. Tuesdays and Saturdays, early morning until about noon.

Spain

Madrid. A huge flea market (El Rastro) along the Ribera de Curtidores and the alleys and streets around it. Street market Sunday mornings, though dealers' shops and indoor covered galleries are open during the week. Everything from genuine antiques to used electric appliances, clothes, books, records, and junk of every type. Know what you're buying and watch out for pickpockets (especially Gypsies).
Madrid. Stamp market. Plaza Mayor. Sunday mornings until about noon.

Switzerland

Basel. Flea market at Petersplatz. One of Switzerland's best markets. Sundays, April— November, starts about 6:30 a.m.

Geneva. Flea market at Plain de Plain Palais. Get there early, the good stuff goes fast. Wednesdays and Saturdays promptly at 6 a.m.

Zurich. Flea market at Burkliplatz, where Bahnhofstrasse meets the lake. Saturdays May to October from 7 a.m. to midafternoon.

Cultural Pursuits

Performing Arts

Europe offers you an exciting and varied array of symphony, opera, and theatre. You'll also find everything from singers and Chilean guitarists in the subways of Paris, to the magnificent circuses of Eastern Europe.

London Theatre

London is famous for its thriving year-round theatre. The theatre district is centered on Shaftesbury Avenue near Piccadilly Circus. Other theatres are throughout the city.

Ticket costs depend on the play and the seat. Musicals cost between £7 and £20 for large productions, while less extravagant theatres offering plays may charge between £4 and £10. Theatre box offices sell tickets at cost, and are usually open about 10 a.m. Tickets can also be obtained from ticket agencies, listed in the phone book under Theatre Booking Agents. In Britain, many agencies charge the price of the ticket plus 21%.

Curtain time is as early as 7 p.m. for evening performances, so be sure you ask for exact information when buying your tickets.

Tickets to smash hits may be difficult to obtain at the last minute. Some tickets are returned to the box office, and the house's special house seats are sold just before the play at the original cost to anyone waiting. For hit plays, the queues form hours in advance. However, ticket touts also hover around just before the play begins.

Half-Price Tickets

The Half-Price Ticket Booth in Leicester Square, in the theatre district, offers tickets valued at more than £5 or more at half price plus a £1 service charge. Tickets are sold only on the same day as the performance. (You won't get a seat to a smash hit here.) The office is open from noon to 2 p.m. for matinee tickets and 2:30 to 6 p.m. for evening tickets.

Theatre on the Continent

Theatre is as prevalent in major continental cities as in London. However, English-language performances are rare, except in Vienna, where the English Theatre mounts frequent English-language productions.

Information is best obtained on the spot from tourist information offices, from weekly or monthly programmes put out by cultural affairs offices, and from newspapers.

Opera

Opera has long been a European favorite. La Scala of Milan is world famous, as are the opera companies of Paris, Vienna, and Berlin, among many others.

Most European opera houses are relatively small, and tickets may be difficult to obtain at the last minute. In this case, you can often purchase standing room tickets an hour or two before the performance. The price of standee tickets may be just a pound or two, though the comfort level will be low and the sight lines less than ideal.

You can rent opera glasses at opera houses.

Music

Most European countries give great emphasis and often large subsidies to music. It has been said that Austria spends more on music than on the armed forces! The capitals and large cities of almost every country support at least one symphony orchestra, as well as innumerable chamber groups and ensembles.

Obtaining current information is difficult from a distance. Many tourist information offices have free schedules of musical events and can advise you about getting tickets.

Tickets usually must be paid for in cash and are sold at the box office. Some cities have ticket agents. Computerized ticket-purchasing services are rare.

Ticket prices are especially low in Eastern Europe, where music is highly subsidized. However, tickets to the most popular cultural events, such as the Bolshoi Ballet, must usually be obtained through the government tourist office, and reserved well in advance.

Evensong—Church Concerts

Anglican churches in England, particularly in large cities, offer a rare opportunity to enjoy religious music at the daily evensong. Check in churches for the schedule.

Also, many churches offer daytime organ recitals. St. Paul's in London has recitals on a regular schedule.

On the continent, there are also performances in churches, but most of them are in conjunction with church services.

If you're lucky, you will occasionally come across the organist practising early in the morning or early in the afternoon. However, this is rare in churches where there are significant numbers of tours, which seem to take precedence over music.

Season and the Summer

Most European orchestra seasons run from late September or early October to May. During the summer, there are many other places to enjoy music: chamber performances and, especially, summer festivals.

The European Association of Music Festivals functions as an information centre for these festivals. Its main office is:

Association Européenne des Festivals de Musique
122 rue de Lausanne
CH-1211 Genève 21, Switzerland
Tel. (022) 32 28 03
Telex 289917 AEFM CH

A free schedule of festivals is put out each year by the Association, listing the major music festivals, and is available from the above address. Tickets and information can be obtained from each festival organizer.

Schedules and ticket information can also be obtained in Britain from:

Specialised Travel Ltd.
4 Hanger Green
London W5 3EL
Tel. 01-998 1761
Telex 887863 STPR G

A list of official representatives in other countries is available from the Association.

Museums and Museum Passes

Europe's museums range from the well-known riches of the Vatican, Louvre, and the Tate Gallery to small, less known museums focusing on local artists and history. Most standard guidebooks list the museums.

Many museums throughout Europe are closed on Mondays. Often admission prices are reduced on Sundays or one day during the week.

Note: Pickpockets frequently work crowded museums, particularly on free or reduced-price admission days. Guard your valuables carefully.

Passes

Some countries or cities offer special passes that, for a one-time charge, will give you unlimited entry to dozens of museums, estates, and other cultural sites, and sometimes free or reduced price transportation.

Denmark

The Copenhagen Card. This card provides free transport in the Copenhagen area and free admission to almost all museums and the Tivoli Gardens. Validity is from 1 to 3 days. Contact the Danish Tourist Board for information. This card is sold widely in Copenhagen at tourist information and transport information offices.

France

La cARTe. This card provides free or reduced-price admission to over 60 national and municipal museums in Paris and the surrounding region, including the Louvre, Centre Pompidou, Musée d'Orsay, and Versailles. The card costs 100 francs, and is sold at all participating museums and Paris regional offices of the Credit Agricole (CA) bank.

Great Britain

Great Britain has four different and partially overlapping cards.

The Great Britain Heritage Pass. This card gives you free entry to more than 500 historic houses, castles, and gardens. When you get the card, you also get a directory of where you can use it. The card is valid for 15 days or one month. Do not date the card until you first use it.

Buy the card in Great Britain from:

Tourist Information Centre Victoria Station Forecourt London SW1	British Travel Centre Lower Regent Street London SW1

or

London Tourist Information Offices.

Buy the card in North America from BritRail Travel International Offices in New York, Chicago, Los Angeles, Toronto, and Vancouver. On the European continent, ask the British Tourist Authority for local vendors.

Historic Buildings and Monuments Commission for England Card. This one-year card provides free entry to all monuments and sites of the Historic Buildings and Monuments Commission, such as Hampton Court and the Tower of London, as well as some castles in Scotland and Wales.

Buy the card at the ticket office of the first site you visit. The ticket is half price for children and senior citizens.

National Trust Card This one year membership card provides free entry to all National Trust (England) and National Trust for Scotland sites. There are individuals, family, junior, and life memberships.

The card is available from:

The National Trust Membership Department P.O. Box 39 Bromley, Kent BR1 1NH Tel. (01) 464 1111	The National Trust 36 Queen Anne's Gate London SW1H 9AS Tel. (01) 222 9251

The less expensive (particularly for families) *National Trust for Scotland Card* offering identical privileges in England, Wales, and Northern Ireland as well as Scotland is available from:

The National Trust for
Scotland
5 Charlotte Square
Edinburgh EH2 4DU
Tel. (031) 226 5922

The National Trust for
Scotland
12 Sherwood St.
London SW1V 7RD
Tel. (01) 437 1012

Historic Houses Association Card. This one-year card provides free entry to about 250 privately owned historic houses, including some of those in the The Great Britain Heritage Pass programme. This card is available from:

Historic Houses
Association
38 Ebury Street
London SW1W 0LU

or P.O. Box 21
Letchworth,
Hertfordshire SG6 4ET
Tel. (01) 730 9419

Italy

There is no nationwide museum pass.

The Netherlands

National Museum Card. This annual card (January 1—December 31) gives you free entry to about 400 museums in the Netherlands, including Amsterdam's Rijksmuseum. The card is available in the Netherlands from all local tourist offices (VVV). It is not available outside the Netherlands. The price 21 guilders, but is lower for those under 25 (18.50 guilders) and senior citizens (13.50 guilders).

Holland Culture Card. This annual card (about £10) looks like a credit card, and a provides free Museum Card (see above). In addition, it also provides entry to artists' studios, and a 50% discount on first-class train tickets inside the Netherlands. You can also use it to obtain tickets for concerts and other performances using the KLM Airlines computer without a service charge. The Holland Culture Card is available only from KLM airline or Netherlands National Tourist Offices.

Holland Leisure Card. This annual card (about £6) includes 55% discounts on first class train tickets, 25% discounts on Avis rental cars, and 30% discount on Dutch domestic flights. It is available through the Netherlands Board of Tourism offices outside of the Netherlands.

Sweden

Three cities—Gothenborg, Malmö, and Stockholm—issue transport and tourist cards.

Göteborgskortet. This 3-day card provides free entry to most museums, the Liseburg park, and a free sightseeing tour of the city. Buy it at the Tourist Information Office at Kungsportsplaatsen 2. Reductions are offered for children.

Malmökortet. This 3- or 7-day card gives free public transport, free entry to most museums, and various other discounts. Buy it at the Tourist Information Office at Hamngatan 1, near the railway station.

Stockholmskortet. This card provides free entry to most Stockholm museums as well as free public transport. Buy it at the Tourist Office at Hamngatan 27.

Reading in Europe
Finding English Language Books, Magazines, and Newspapers

Looking for the day's news, a novel, or reference book on the continent?

You'll have to look harder than in Britain or Ireland. When you find an English-language book or periodical to buy, you will often pay much more for it than you're accustomed to.

You can, however, find enough English-language reading in most countries if you know where to look. This chapter includes city-by-city and country-by-country listings with locations of English-language libraries, bookstores, and newspapers.

Newspapers and Magazines

English-language newspapers can be found at street newsstands in major cities and tourist areas throughout Western Europe. Most of them are either British or locally produced. British papers are often one day old, and are widely available. Locally produced papers are often oriented to the tourist and expatriate community.

In Western Europe, you can usually find British newspapers at newsstands and kiosks in major cities, transport terminals, and airports, though often it will be yesterday's edition.

Newspapers commonly found include The Times, The Telegraph, and The Guardian. The tabloids are not found as frequently.

The Financial Times is also widely distributed.

Magazines are also available, though the selection is likely to be smaller than at home. Some will be available the same places English-language newspapers are sold, and in English-language bookshops as well.

News in Eastern Europe is quite different. Western publications are virtually unavailable in almost all of the East Bloc countries. When available, they will be only at the newsstands inside the hotels reserved for foreigners, and can be up to two weeks old. The only current English-language newspapers and magazines are likely to be those issued in the country you're in, or Communist newspapers imported from both Eastern and Western Europe. Sometimes they are left in stacks in the foreigners' hotel lobbies, and are free for the taking. These Eastern newspapers are very different to those you're used to, both in the type of the stories and their slant. There is much less advertising, if any.

Books

English-language books are much harder to find than newspapers and magazines. In general, you are more likely to find English-language books in the small countries of northern Europe such as the Netherlands and Scandinavia. There are also a few bookshops thinly scattered in cities in the rest of Europe as well.

Finding English-language books to buy in the East Bloc will be difficult and the selection limited.

English-language books, whether new or used, are almost always more expensive than at home, in part because costs of import are high and the volume is low.

Reading in Europe

English-Language Libraries

Great Britain maintains a network of English-language libraries operated by the British Council, a quasi- governmental nonprofit agency. They have British books and periodicals. Many have both nonfiction and some particularly good fiction sections. These libraries are marked (BC) in the listings. While primarily designed for local residents (who are able to check out books), they also welcome travellers. They resemble a small-town public library, with standard reference works, nonfiction and fiction sections, and a limited selection of periodicals. These libraries are marked (BC) in the listings.

The United States Information Service of the United States government also maintains a network of English-language libraries in most major cities of Europe. These are marked (USIS) in the listings.

All USIS and all British Council libraries are open to anyone for reading room and reference use. If you will be staying in one location for an extended period, you can qualify for a library card to obtain check-out privileges at either or both of these libraries. Sometimes a small card fee is charged at the British Council libraries.

In addition, public libraries are scattered around, particularly in northern Europe. Some of them have English-language sections, particularly at universities.

(Key to English-language bookshops and libraries starts on the next page.)

Key to English-Language Libraries, Bookshops and Some Newspapers in Europe

Austria

Vienna
Libraries

Amerika Haus
Bibliothek (USIS)
Friedrich Schmidt-Platz
2 (behind the Rathaus
at the American
consular offices)
A-1010 Wien
Tel. 31 55 11

British Council Library
(BC)
Schenkenstrasse 4
(behind the Burgtheater)
A-1010 Wien
Tel. 533 26 16
Telex 132521 BC VIE A

Bookshops

The British Bookshop
Wiehburggasse 8
A-1010 Wien
Tel. 512 19 45

Wilhelm Frick
Buchhandlung
Graben 27
A-1010 Wien
Tel. 533 99 14 and
533 99 15

Leopold Heidrich
English Bookshop
Plankengasse 7
Tel. 52 72 87

Shakespeare &
Company, Booksellers
Sterngasse 2
A-1010 Wien
Tel. 535 50 53/4

Belgium

Brussels
Libraries

The American Library
(USIS)
Square du Bastion 1-C
(at the Porte de Namur
Pre-Metro stop)
1050 Bruxelles
Tel. (02) 512 21 29

British Council Library
(BC)
Brittania House
Rue Joseph II 26
1040 Bruxelles
Tel. (02) 219 36 00
Fax 230 83 79
Telex 24743 BCBEL B

Bookshops

W.H. Smith   71-79 boulevard Adolphe Max (near de Broukere Metro)
1001 Bruxelles
Tel. (02) 219 27 08

La Route de Jade Travel Bookstore
rue de Stassert 116
1050 Bruxelles
Tel. (02) 572 96 54
Some books in English, lots of maps.

The Strathmore Bookshop   131 rue St. Lambert (behind shopping center)
1200 Bruxelles
Tel. (02) 771 92 00
Metro: Roodebeek, then south through shopping center

House of Paperbacks
813 Chausée de Waterloo
1180 Bruxelles
Tel. (02) 343 1122
(tram 90 + 23 to Churchill)

The English Shop (Le Magazin Anglais)
1384 Chausée de Waterloo
Uccle, 1180 Bruxelles
Tel. (02) 374 9839

Czechoslovakia

Prague
Library
British Council Library at the British Embassy (BC)
Jungmannova 30
110 00 Prague 1
Tel. 22 45 01, 22 45 50, telex 122097 BCC Z C

Denmark

Copenhagen
Libraries

American Library(USIS)
Dag Hammerskjølds Alle 24 (also the U.S. Embassy)
DK 2100 København
(Open 12-5 p.m., 12-6:30 on Monday)
Tel. (01) 42 31 44

British Council Library (BC)
Møntergade 1 (near the east end of the Strøget)
1116 København K
(Open 9:30—4:30)
Tel. (01) 11 20 44
Telex REF BC0Ø23
265451 MONREF G

Bookshops

Boghallen
Rådhusplads 37
Tel. (01) 11 85 11

Arnold Busck
International Boghandel
Købmagergade 49
DK-1150 Køabenhavn K
Tel. (01) 12 24 53

Magasin du Nord
Kongens Nytorv 13
1095 København K
Tel. (01) 11 44 33
(book department on
first floor)

Illums
Østergade 52
Tel. (01) 14 40 02
(book department on
ground floor)

Nordisk Boghandel
Østergade 16
DK-1100 København K
Tel. (01) 14 07 07

Erik Paludan Boghandel
Fiolstr. 10
Tel. (01) 15 06 75

Magazine
Copenhagen This Week (published monthly!) Free four-colour glossy with information about cultural events in the centre pages, and street and transport maps. Widely available in Copenhagen.

Finland

Helsinki

Libraries

America Center Library
(USIS)
Kaivokatu 10A
00101 Helsinki 10
Tel. 176599

British Council Library
(BC)
Erottajankatu 7B 00130
Helsinki 13
Tel. 640505
Telex 123936 BCHEL SF

Bookshops

Akateeminen
Kirjakauppa
Keskuskatu 1
00100 Helsinki
Tel. 121 41
Fax 121 4441
Telex 125080 AKAHE

Suomalainen
Kirjakauppa
Branches throughout
Helsinki; call 65155 to
locate nearest one.

France

Bordeaux
Library
British Council Library (BC)
c/o British Consulate General
15 cours de Verdun
33000 Bordeaux Cedex
Tel. 56.52.28.35

Lyon
Library
British Council Library (BC)
c/o British Consulate General
24 rue Childebert
69288 Lyon Cedex 1
Tel. 78.37.59.67

Lille
Library
British Council Library (BC)
c/o British Consulate General
24 square de Tilleul
59019 Lille
Tel. 20.52.87.90

Marseille
Library
British House
24 avenue du Prado
13000 Marseille
Tel. 91.54.29.43
or 91.33.48.02

Paris
Libraries
British Council Library (BC)
9 rue de Constantine
75007 Paris
Tel. 45.55.95.95
Telex 250912 BRICOUN

Centre de Documentation Benjamin Franklin (USIS)
2 rue St. Florentin
75008 Paris
Tel. 42.22.22.70

Bookshops
Brentano's
37 ave. de l'Opéra / 8 rue Danielle Casanova
75002 Paris
Tel. 42.61.52.50
Metro: Opéra

Shakespeare & Co.
37 rue de la Bûcherie
75005 Paris
Metro: St. Michel
Used books only

Galignani
224 rue de Rivoli
75001 Paris
Tel. 42.60.76.07
Metro: Tuileries

W.H. Smith
The English Bookshop
248 rue de Rivoli
75001 Paris
Tel. 42 60 37 97
Metro: Concorde

NQL Nouvelle Quartier Latin
78 blvd. St. Michel (near Luxembourg Gardens)
Tel. 43 26 42 70
Metro: Luxembourg

Germany East (DDR)

Berlin
Library
British Council Library (BC)
Unter den Linden 32/34   DDR-Berlin 108
Tel. 220 2431, fax 312 1064, telex 113171 GBBER DD

Germany, West (BRD)

Bonn
Library (USIS)
American Embassy
Deichmannsaue 29
D-5300 Bonn 2
Tel. 33 91

Berlin
Libraries
Amerika Haus Berlin
(USIS)
Hardenbergstrasse
22-24
D-1000 Berlin 12
Tel. 8 19 79 05

British Council Library
(BC)
Hardenbergstrasse 20
D-1000 Berlin 12
Tel. 31 01 76
Fax 312 1064
Telex 185814 BCGB D

Bookshops

Buchexpress
Habelschwerater Alle 4
Tel. 8 31 40 04

Marga Schoeller
Bucherstube GmbH
Knesebekstrasse 33
D-1000 Berlin 12
Tel. 881 11 12, 881 11 22

Cologne (Köln)

Libraries
Amerika Haus Köln
(USIS)
Apostelnkloster 13/15
D-5000 Köln 1
Tel. 24 13 67

British Council Library
(BC)
Hahnenstrasse 6
D-5000 Köln 1
Tel. 23 66 77
Fax 2064455
Telex 888 1147 BCGK D

Frankfurt

Library
Amerika Haus
Frankfurt (USIS)
Staufenstrasse 1
D-6000 Frankfurt am Main 1
Tel. 72 33 37

Bookshop
British Bookshop
Börsenstrasse 17
D-6000 Frankfurt 1
Tel. 28 04 92

Freiburg

Library
German-American Institute
Kaiser Joseph Strasse 266
D-7800 Freiburg

Hamburg

Libraries
Amerika Haus Hamburg
(USIS)
Tesdorpfstrasse 1
D-2000 Hamburg 13
Tel. 44 46 30

British Council Library
(BC)
Rothenbaumchausee 34
D-2000 Hamburg 13
Tel. 44 60 57
Fax 447114
Telex 2162557 BCHB D

Hannover
Library
Amerika Haus
Hanover (USIS)
Prinzenstrasse 9
D-3000 Hannover 1
Tel. 32 13 98

Heidelberg
Library
German-American
Institute
Sophienstrasse 12
D-6900 Heidelberg 1

Munich (München)
Libraries
Amerika Haus München
(USIS)
Karolinenplatz 3
D-8000 München 2
Tel. 59 53 69

British Council Library
(BC)
Bruderstrasse 7/111
D-8000 München 22
Tel. 22 33 26
Telex 528446 BCGM D

Bookshop
Anglia English Bookstore
Schelling 3
D-8000 München 3
Tel. 28 36 42

Nürnberg
Library
German- American
Institute
Gleisbuhlstrasse 13
D-8500 Nürnberg

Saarbrücken
Library
German-American
Institute
Berliner Promenade 15
D-6600 Saarbrücken

Stuttgart
Library
Amerika Haus Stuttgart
(USIS)
Friedrichstrasse 23A
D-7000 Stuttgart 1
Tel. 292-330

Tübingen
Library
German-American
Institute
Karlstrasse 3
D-7400 Tübingen

Great Britain

Public libraries
Britain has an excellent public library system. A library can be found in almost every medium size town

or city. Check the telephone book and look under libraries, or ask at the local tourist information office.

Bookshops
There are so many bookshops in London that you can buy books about them. Many are on Charing Cross Road. In the rest of Britain, bookshops abound, particularly in university towns such as Oxford.

Newspapers
A wide variety of newspapers is sold in every city, town, and almost every village. Almost all of the London newspapers also have wide distribution throughout Britain.

Magazines
The weekly magazines Time Out and What's On, 90p each, are probably the best source to find out about London's current entertainment and cultural events. You can buy them at almost every newsstand in London.

Greece

Athens
Libraries

American Library
(USIS)
22 Massalias Street (at
right angles to
Akademius)
22 Μασσαλιαζ
101 44 Athens
Tel. 778-9407

British Council Library
(BC)
17 Plateia Philikis
Etairias
Kolonaki Square
17 Πλατεια Φιλικηζ
Εταιριαζ
(Πλατεια Κολῶυακιου)
10673 Athens
P.O. Box 3488
102 10 Athens
Tel. 36 33 211 and
36 06 011
Telex 218 799 BRIC GR

Bookshops

Eleftheroudakis
4 Nikis (near Syntygma Square)   105 63 Athens
Ελεγθεροδακης
Νικηζ 4
Tel. 32 21 231

Pantelides
11 Amerikis (near the Academy)
Παντελιδης
Αμερικης 11
Tel. 644 8547

Reymondo's International Bookstore
18 Voukourestiou (near Syntygma)
Tel. 364 8188
18 ςουκουρεστιου

Newspapers
The Athens News and the Athens Daily Post, published daily. Sold in news kiosks and in hotels. Also, The Week in Athens, published weekly, is found at tourist information offices and main hotels. Lists current cultural events and a useful hodgepodge of information, including a map of central Athens inside the back cover. The Athenian magazine is published monthly, 250 Drachmas.

Thessaloniki (Salonika)
Libraries

American Center Library (USIS)
34 Metropoleos Street
34 Μετροπολεος

British Centre Library (BC)
9 Ethnikis Aminis 9
(corner of Tsimiski)
541/10 Saloniki
P.O. Box 10289
Εψνικης Αμυνις
Tel. 235 236/7
285 570/1
Telex 412974 BCSLGR

Hungary

Budapest
Library
British Council Library (BC)
Harmincad Utca 6
Budapest V
Tel. 182 888
Telex 224527 BRIT H

Newspaper
The Daily News/Neueste Nachricten. This bilingual (English-German) daily newspaper publishes the party line. Can be found in some news kiosks, but is sometimes free in the lobbies of the foreigners' hotels (such as the Intercontinental, Hilton, and Gellert). The main Western-oriented hotels newspaper stands sometimes have the London Times, International Herald Tribune, and other Western newspapers.

Italy

Florence

Library
Biblioteca dell' Instituto Britannico
Palazzo Lanfredini
Lungarno Guicciardini 9
50010 Firenze
Tel. 228 40 31

Bookshops

Feltrinelli
Via Cavour 12/20
50129 Firenze
Tel. 29 21 96 and 21 95 24
Large English-languge section.

Libreria BM
Borgognissanti 4
50123 Firenze
Tel. 29 45 75
All English language.

Marzocco
Via Martelli 22
Tel. 29 85 75.
Has an English section.

Paperback Exchange
Via Fiesolana 31red
Tel. 247 81 54
Almost all English-language and will trade.

Milan (Milano)

Libraries

Biblioteca Americana (USIS)
Via Bigli 11/A
20121 Milano
Tel. 79 50 51 -5

British Council Library (BC)
Via Manzoni 38
20121 Milano
Tel. 782018, 782016, 781749, fax 475 6641
Telex 311084 BRICON I

Bookshop
American Bookstore
via Camperio 16 at Largo Cairoli
20123 Milano
(Metro: Cairoli)
Tel. (02) 870944
All English language

Naples (Napoli)
Library
British Council Library (BC)
Palazzo d'Avalos
via dei Mille 48
80121 Napoli
Tel. 414876, 421321, telex 710460 BRICON I

Rome (Roma)
Libraries

Biblioteca Americana
(USIS)
Via Veneto 119a
00187 Roma
Tel. 46 742

British Council Library
(BC)
(Biblioteca Britannica)
Palazzo del Drago
Via delle Quattro
Fontane 20
00184 Roma
Tel. 475 66 41
Fax 475 4296
Telex 622231 BRICON I

Bookshops

Anglo-American
Bookshop
Via delle Vite 57
00187 Roma
Tel. 679 52 22

Economy Book & Video
Center
Via Torino 136
00184 Roma
Tel. 4746877
Many used books—they
will trade!

The Lion Bookshop
Via del Babuino 181
(near the Spanish steps)
00187 Roma
Tel. 360 97 27

Newspapers
International Daily News, sold at newsstands in tourist-frequented areas. This Week in Rome lists

entertainment and tourist-oriented and cultural events. Get it at tourist information offices and some newsstands.

Luxembourg

Bookshop
The English Shop (Le Magasin Anglais)
Allée Sheffer 19
L-2520 Luxembourg
Tel. 2 49 25

Newspaper
Luxembourg News Digest, weekly; sold at some newstands (80 F) or free in major hotels. Strictly local and expatriate news. Tel. 97 00 52

Netherlands

Amsterdam
Library
British Council Library (BC)
Keizersgracht 343
1016 EH Amsterdam
Tel. 22 36 44, telex 16599 BCAMS NL

Bookshops

Allert de Lange
Boekhandel BV
Damrak 62
1012 LM Amsterdam
Tel. 246744 *and*
P.C. Hooftstraat 57
1071 BN Amsterdam
Tel. 6628075

American Discount Book Center
Kalverstraat 185
1012 XC Amsterdam
Tel. 25 55 37
and 23 53 36

English Book Club
Leidsestraat 52
Tel. 26 32 37

English Book Shop
Lauriergracht 71
1016 Amsterdam
Tel. 26 42 30

Athenaeum Boekhandel
Spui 14-16
1012 XA Amsterdam
Tel. 22 62 48

Scheltema Holkema
Vermeulen B.V.
Koningsplein 20
1017 BB Amsterdam
Tel. 26 72 12

Robert Premsela
van Baerlestraat 78
1071 BB Amsterdam
Tel. 6624166

The Hague

Library
American
Documentation Center
(USIS)
Korte Voorhout 2
2521 EK Den Haag

Bookshop
American Discount Book
Centers
Spuistraat 72
2511 BE Den Haag
Tel. 64 27 42

Norway

Oslo

Libraries
U. S. Reference Center
(USIS)
Drammensveien 18
0255 Oslo 2
Tel. 44-20-63

British Council Library
(BC)   Fridtjof Nansens
Plass 5
0160 Oslo 1
Tel. 42 68 48
Telex 79421 BRICO N

Bookshops
Tanum-Johan Grundt
Karl Johans Gaten 43
0107 Oslo
Tel. 42 93 10

Olaf Norlis Bokhandel
Universitetsgaten 24
Tel. 42 91 35

Poland

Krakow
Library
Biblioteka Amerykanski
(USIS)
Konsulate Stanow
Zjednoczonych
Ulica Stolarska 9 (in the
U.S. consulate)
31043 Krakow
Tel. 229400

Poznan
Library
Biblioteka Amerykanski
(USIS)
Konsulate Stanow
Zjednoczonych
Ulica Chopina 4
Tel. 59586

Warsaw
Libraries
British Council Library (BC) Al Jerozolimskie 59 (in the British embassy) 00697 Warszawa
Tel. 287401/3
Telex 812555 BRIN PL

Biblioteka Amerykanski (USIS)
Ambasada Stanow Zjednoczonych
Aleje Ujadowskie 29/31
(in the U.S. embassy)
Tel. 229-764

Portugal

Coimbra
Library
Casa de Inglatera (BC)
Rua de Tomar 4
3000 Coimbra
Tel. 39 23549, 39 33437, 39 36705
Telex 29297 BRITCO P

Lisbon
Libraries
The British Institute (BC)
Rua Cecilio de Sousa 65
1294 Lisboa Codex
Tel. 369208/9, 320173, 325725, 325761, 325771, 328750
Telex 42544 BRITCO P

Biblioteca Americana (USIS)
Avenida das Forças Armadas
1507 Lisboa
(in the U.S. Embassy)
Tel. 726 66 00

Bookshops
Livraria Britannica
Rua de São Marçal 83
1200 Lisboa
Tel. 32 84 72

Also, several bookshops on Rua Garrett have some English-language books.

Newspaper
Anglo-Portuguese News, published the second and fourth Thursday each month, has news, entertainment listings, and ads. Available at newsstands.

Porto
Bookshop
Livraria Britanica
Rua Jose Falcão 188
4000 Porto
Tel. 323930

Romania

Bucharest
Libraries
Biblioteca Americana
(USIS)
Strada Alexandru Sahia
7-9
Bucuresti 70201

British Council Library
(BC)
Strada Jules Michelet
24
Bucuresti
Tel. 11 1634/6
Telex 11295 PRODM R

Soviet Union

Moscow

Library (BC)
Naberezhnaya Morisa
Yoreza 14
Moscow 109072
Tel. 2318511 (Embassy)
2334507 (Cultural
Section)
Telex 413341 BEMOS SU
Британское Посольство
(Библиотека)
Набережная Мориса
Тереза 14
109072 МОСКВА

Bookshop
U.S. Bookstore
Ulitsa Chekhova 16
103006 Moscow
Tel. 2567190
Telex MK 41160
(Behind Sovincentr, at
Zone 4A, Exhibition
Complex.) Accepts hard
currency only.
США Книжный магазин
Улица Чехова 15
103006 МОСКВА

Spain

Barcelona

Libraries
British Council Library (BC)
Calle Amigo 83
08021 Barcelona
Tel. 209 13 64
Fax 3220354 (Consulate line)
Telex 50512 BINB E

Centro de Referencias y Bibliografia
Via Augusta 123
08006 Barcelona

Madrid

Libraries
Biblioteca Washington Irving (USIS)
Centro Cultural de los Estados Unidos
Marques de Villamagna 8
28001 Madrid
Tel. 447 19 00

British Council Library (BC)
Plaza de Santa Barbara 10
28004 Madrid
Tel. 419 12 50
Fax 5213947
Telex 427699 INSBR E

Bookshop
Turner English Bookshop
Calle Génova 3
28004 Madrid
Tel. 410 4359 and 410 2915

Newspapers
Iberia Daily, sold at newsstands and hotels. Also, Guidepost Magazine, a weekly magazine, lists entertainment and cultural events.

Seville

Library
Plaza Neuva 8 DPDO
41001 Seville
Tel. 22 88 73
Telex 63281 INBV E

Valencia

Library
The British Institute (BC) General San Martín 7
46004 Valencia
Tel. 351 88 18, 352 98 74
Telex 63281 INBV E

Sweden

Stockholm

Libraries

American Reference
Center (USIS)
Strandvagen 118
S-11350 Stockholm
Tel. 783 53 00

British Council Library
Skarpögatan 6
S-11527 Stockholm
Tel. 667 01 40
Fax 63 72 71
Telex 19340 BRITEMB S

Bookshops

Almqvist & Wiksell
Bokhandel AB
G Brogade 26
Tel. 23 79 90

English Book Centre
Sorbrunnsgatan 51
Tel. 30 14 47

Fritzes Horbokhandel
AB
Regeringsgade 12
Tel. 23 89 00

Hedengrens Bokhandel
Sturepl 4
Tel. 11 43 84
or 11 43 91

Switzerland

Zurich

Bookshops

Buchhandlung Friedrich
Däniker
In Gassen 11
Tel. 211 27 04

Buchhandlung Kurt
Stäheli & Co.
Bahnhofstrasse 70
8021 Zurich
Tel. 211 33 02
Telex 813771 STAE CH

Turkey

Ankara

Library

British Council Library (BC)
Kirlangic Sokak 9
Gazi Osman Pasa
Ankara 06700
Tel. 128 31 65/6/7/8/9
Telex 42049 IBIK TR

Istanbul

Libraries
Amerikan Kutuphanesi (USIS) 104-108
Mesrutiyet Caddesi (in the American Consulate)
Tepebasi
Tel. 1436200/09

British Council Library (BC)
Cumhuriyet Caddesi 22-24 PK436 Beyoglu
Ege Han K2 Elmadag
80074 Istanbul
Tel. 1467125/6, 1463073
Telex 23283 IKIK TR

Bookshop
Redhouse Kitabevi
Rizapasa Yokusu 50 (district near the Misir Carsisi)
Tel. 5223905

Newspaper
The Turkish Daily News and Dateline Turkey (weekly), published in Ankara, are available at some newsstands and hotels.

Yugoslavia

Belgrade
Libraries
Americki Centar (USIS)
Cika Ljubina 19
11000 Beograd

British Council Library
Generala Zdanova 34, mezanin Post Fah 248
11011 Beograd
Tel. 332 441, 327 910
Telex 11032 BRIBEL YU

Ljubljana
Library
Ameriški Center (USIS)
Candarjeva 11
61000 Ljubljana
Tel. 210 910

Sarajevo
Library
Americki Centar (USIS)
Omladinska broj 1
71000 Sarajevo
Tel. 16 079 and 25 997

Skopje
Library
Amerikanski Centar (USIS)
Grandski Zid, blok IV
91000 Skopje

Titograd
Library
Americki Centar (USIS)
Bulevar Oktobarske Revolucije 100
81000 Titograd

Zagreb
Libraries
Americki Centar (USIS)
Zrinjevac 13
41000 Zagreb

British Centre (BC)
Ilica 12/1
41001 Zagreb
Tel. 425 244 Telex 22533 BRIZAG YU

Returning Home
Airports and Customs

Returning home requires some planning. You'll have to pack your belongings, get to the airport or dock, arrange for value added tax refunds if your purchases qualify, and check in.

Packing

You should pack your declarable items where they're easily available customs inspection. If you plan to ask for value-added tax refunds, you may be required to show the purchases made before the European customs officer (for non-EC countries) or British customs officer (for EC countries) stamps your refund forms, which is usually necessary to receive a refund.

Getting to the Airport

Major airports are relatively easy to get to by public transport. Quick, frequent, inexpensive trains go to airports in Brussels, Frankfurt, Amsterdam, and Zurich, among others. The rest, such as Charles de Gaulle and Orly in Paris, Schwechat in Vienna, and most of the airports in Eastern Europe are linked to their cities by frequent shuttle buses travelling from city or airline terminals.

In most cases the public transport alternatives are much cheaper and quicker than taxis. Likewise the underground and trains can be quicker than a private car, too.

See the Public Transport chapter.

Check-in and Security Checks

You must pass through security and passport control after check-in. This will take about an hour and a half, on average. While check-in is about the same the world over, security varies country by country and airport by airport, and, also, by the level of terrorist activity in the previous few weeks. Several inspection systems can be used. At some airports, all checked-in passengers must pass through a single inspection station. At others, such as Frankfurt, you are inspected by security only as you actually board the plane. (The second system is preferable for the passenger, since it means your plane is less likely to take off without you as you squeeze and jostle passengers on all other flights.)

You can ask for film to be hand inspected but the request will not always be honoured.

Value Added Tax Refunds

When you leave non-EC countries, if you want to have your value-added tax money refunded, you must have all the paperwork stamped. Be prepared to show your receipts and the merchandise. In some countries, these offices are before the security check (and before check-in). Others have them after check-in. You have to ask specifically for the office—otherwise you cannot, in most cases, receive your refund. The office name to ask for varies from country to country. Allow an extra hour or two to take care of this task. It may not take this long, but then again, it might.

Note: you can only be "de-taxed" for items purchased in the country you're leaving. See the Value-Added Tax Refunds chapter for detailed information.

Duty-Free Shops

Virtually every airport has one or more "duty-free" or "tax-free" shops. You'll encounter them after you have passed the point of no return. These shops can amount to small shopping centres, such as at Amsterdam, Copenhagen, Frankfurt, and Shannon (Ireland).

Duty-free doesn't mean you may not have to pay customs duty at the other end of the flight. Duty-free means only that you don't have to pay any national value-added tax or tariff in the country of purchase.

Compare prices carefully, and know what the items cost outside, since you may find that prices at duty-free shops are no bargain. In fact, at many airports, the only duty-free items are alcohol and tobacco products. Often you can pay less in town if you can get the VAT refunded. Some in-city stores will even deliver the goods to the airport for pickup. (This may save you from the paperwork of the VAT refund process.) Some items are even cheaper at home than at the duty-free shops.

Duty-Free Allowances for British Residents

What Purchases Can You Legally Bring Home?

You can bring home most goods purchased abroad. Some things are completely prohibited, others are restricted. In other cases, you can bring in certain amounts duty- and tax-free, and must pay tax and duty on all amounts exceeding the limit.

Prohibited Items

Generally prohibited items include those made from protected species (including many furs, ivory, and reptiles), controlled drugs, many firearms and certain other weapons, and any material deemed by Customs to be obscene.

If you are interested in attempting to bring any of these classes of things home, contact Customs before entering the U.K.

Restricted Items

Restricted goods include animal products (for example, uncooked pork is prohibited, but uncooked beef and cooked patü is admissible), plant materials, and fruit and vegetables (for example, potatoes from the Continent are prohibited but peaches are admissible). Other foods vary, depending on type and origin.

Live animals, including pets such as cats and dogs, can only be admitted to the U.K. after a quarantine period of up to six months. Contact Customs before attempting to bring any animals back to Britain (even your own pet that originated in the U.K.).

Duty-Free Allowances for U.K. Residents

You can import most types of goods duty-free for personal use (but not for resale) into the U.K., but there are limits on their value, and in some cases, the quantity. In general, you can bring much more home tax- and duty-free if purchased in the European Community (EC) than purchased outside it or at tax- and duty-free shops.

You can bring home up to £250 worth of goods purchased in the European Community, if the price you paid includes Value Added Tax (VAT) and duty. Alternatively, you can bring in up to £32 of goods duty- and tax-free if purchased outside the European Community or from a tax- or duty-free shop (such as on the Channel ferries).

Special Duty-Free Allowances

In addition to the general £250 or £32 exemption, you can bring in certain other goods tax- and duty-free. The liquor, wine, and tobacco allowances are only available to persons 17 or older.

- *Liquors:* Inside the EC: 1-1/2 litres of spirits, or 3 litres of fortified wines, sparkling wines, and liqueurs if less than 22% alcohol by volume. Outside the EC, the limit is 1 litre of spirits, or 2 litres if under 22% alcohol by volume. These beverages may be combined as long as the overall limit is not exceeded.

- *Still table wine:* Inside the EC: 5 litres. Outside the EC: 2 litres.

- *Tobacco:* Inside the EC: 300 cigarettes, 150 cigarillos, 75 cigars, or 400 grammes of loose tobacco. Outside the EC, 200 cigarettes, 100 cigarillos, 50 cigars, or 250 grammes of loose tobacco.

- *Perfume:* Inside the EC: 90 cubic centimetres (cc) or millilitres (ml). Outside the EC: 60 cc or ml.

- *Toilet Water:* Inside the EC: 375 cc or ml. Outside the EC: 250 cc or ml.

Note: In these special categories, you cannot combine duty-free and duty-paid in any classification except still wine.

Paying Tax and Duty

If you bring home goods over any of the tax- and duty-free limits, you will have to pay duty on them, and will have to pay VAT if the items were purchased outside the EC.

Your goods will not be released from Customs until all taxes and duty are paid.

Note that the tax and duty on some types of goods (spirits, perfumes, and toilet water) are very high.

Is VAT Payable?

In general, you must pay on VAT the purchase price of all goods over the tax- and duty-free allowances.

Even if you purchase goods worth over £250 in the EC, you do not have to pay VAT if:
- you are not claiming a VAT export refund from the seller.
- the purchase receipt states that the price includes VAT or shows the rate and amount of VAT.
- the rate of VAT is over the British rate on that type of goods.

If you paid less VAT than the applicable British rate (most often 15%), you must pay the difference between what you paid and the British rate.

If you're claiming a VAT refund from the seller in another country, you must pay British VAT.

If you purchased the items outside the EC, you must generally pay VAT whether that country charged you VAT or not.

Note that payment of VAT is not the same as payment of duty.

Immigration and Customs

Most British ports of entry have separate Immigration and Customs inspections.

First you clear Immigration: generally this entails showing your passport or Visitor's Passport, which takes only a minute.

Then you must clear Customs.

If your purchases are under the duty-free limits, and you have no restricted or prohibited items, go through the Green channel. Generally, at airports, you just walk through. At ferry terminals, you may be asked a few questions. Customs officials occasionally spot check people in the Green channels: co-operate fully and be courteous to speed the process along.

If your purchases are over the duty-free limits, or you have restricted or prohibited items, go to the Red channel and declare any goods you believe you may owe tax or duty on, or believe are restricted for any reason.

If tax and duty are payable, you must pay before the goods will be released to you.

Failure to declare goods to Customs may lead to forfeiture of the goods, fines, and other legal action.

Index

AA (Automobile Association)
  reservations, ferry 36
  car insurance 155
  International Driver
    Permits at 150
  emergency road service
    pamphlet 159
Airlines, British-owned 41-42
  complaints about 41
Air safety violations
  reporting 41
Airplane tickets
  bucket shops 41, 91-92
  charter 40
  discount 91
  from travel agents 15
  full fare 40
  scheduled airlines 40
  to Europe 40-42
Airports
  customs at 405
  duty-free shops 442-443
  exchanging money at 61
  getting to (see public
    transport)
  toilets at 250
Aix-en-Provence flea market
  364
A la carte meals 283-284
Albania
  business hours 325
  embassies of 26-27
  holidays 325
  tourist office in
    U.K. 11
  tours of 10
  visas to 26-27
Albergo diurno 261
American Express
  card 65
  cashing cheques
    at 66
  car sales in front
    of—Paris 154
  money sent to 67
  post at 170-171
Amsterdam
  English-language
    bookshops 393-394
  English-language library
    393
  flea markets 369
  public transport 113-115
  used car sales in 154
Andorra
  buses in 110
  telephones 198-200
  tourist office in U.K. 11
Ankara (Turkey)
  English-language library
    398
  U.K. embassy in 321
Antiquities and antiques
  fakes 308
  markets of (see also Flea
    markets)
    Aix-en-Provence 364
    Amsterdam 369
    Antwerp 363
    Arezzo 369
    Barcelos 369-370
    Birmingham 367
    Brussels 363
    Copenhagen 364
    Lisbon 370
    Liège 363
    London 367-368
    Lyon 364-365
    Munich 367
    Paris 365-366
    Rome 369
    Rotterdam 369
    Turin 369
  exportation of—
    Belgium 340
    Eastern Europe 339
    France 339-340
    Germany (West) 339-340
    Great Britain 339-340
    Greece 339-340
    Italy 339-340
    Netherlands 340
    Switzerland 340
    Spain 339-340
    Turkey 339
Antwerp
  flea markets 363
Arezzo (Italy) antiques fair
  369
Athens
  English-language
    bookshops 390
  English-language libraries
    389
  English-language
    newspaper 390
  flea market 368
  U.K. embassy in 318
Austria
  bed and breakfast 260,
    261-263
  breakfast 263, 279
  buses in 110
  business hours 325
  dry cleaners 301
  emergency road service
    160
  English-language

Index — Autobahn speed limits

bookshops 382
English-language libraries 382
farm stays 264
flea markets 363
Fremdenzimmer 262-263
holidays 325
health care, emergency 73-74
launderettes 296
rail discounts 99
postal busses 110
shopping 340
staying on a farm 264
telephones 184-186
tourist office in U.K. 11
U.K. embassy in 316
value added tax refunds 345-346
Zimmer Frei 262-263
Autobahn speed limits
  East Germany 144
  West Germany 144
Autos (see Cars)
B-Tourrail 99
Baggage
  bicycles as 44
  excess 45-46
  firearms 45
  golf clubs as 43-44
  limits
    first class 43, 91
    economy 43, 91
  skis as 43-44
Banks
  business hours 322-337
    (see also countries)
  cash advances at European 65
  commissions to cash foreign checks 64
  correspondent 60, 66, 67
  European checking accounts 66
  exchanging money at 60-61
  Holidays, Bank, Britain and Ireland 329
Barcelona (Spain)
  English-language libraries 397
  U.K. consulate in 319
Barcelos (Portugal), flea market 369-370
Bars
  breakfast at 280-281
  toilets at 253
Basel, flea market 370
Bed & Breakfast 260-264
  Austria 262-263

baths & showers at 263-264
Eastern Europe 261
France 261
Germany (West) 261
Great Britain 261-262
Ireland 261-262
Netherlands 263
Scandinavia 263
Belgium
  beer 287
  blue zones 145
  breakfast 263, 279
  business hours 325-326
  car leasing 153
  dry cleaners 300, 301
  emergency road service 160
  English-language bookshops 383
  English-language libraries 382-383
  farm stays 264
  flea markets 363
  health care, emergency 74
  farm stays 264
  holidays 325
  launderettes 296
  rail discounts 98, 99
  staying on a farm 264
  telephones 187-189
  shopping 341
  tourist office in the U.K. 11
  U.K. embassy in 316
  value added tax refunds 347
Belgrade (Yugoslavia)
  English-language libraries 399
  U.K. embassy in 321
Benelux Tourrail 98
Berlin
  access to East 29, 116
  English-language bookshops 387
  English-language libraries 386-387
  public transport-West 115-117
  public transport-East 117
  opera 372
  transit visas to 29, 116
  U.K. consulate in (West) 317
  U.K. embassy in (East) 317
Berolina Travel Ltd. 28
Bern (Switzerland)

U.K. embassy in 320
Bicycles
 as baggage 44, 95-96
Bidet 260

Biglietto Turistico di
 Libera Circolazione
 105
Biglietto Chilometrico
 105-106
Bilbao (Spain)
 U.K. consulate in 320
Bilhete Reduçao a Velhos
 108
Bilhete turistico 108
Birmingham (Great Britain)
 flea market 367
Bonn (West Germany)
 English-language
  library in 386
 U.K. embassy in 317
Bookshops
 English-language
  in Europe 380, 382-399
 for background infor-
  mation 9-10
 specializing in travel 9-10
Bordeaux
 English-language library
  385
 U.K. consulate in 316
Breakfast
 alternative to hotel
  280-281
 at bed & breakfasts
  261, 263
 Continental 263,
  279
 English 252, 278-279
 full 252, 278-279
Brighton (England), flea
 market in 367
British Council libraries
 381, 382-399
British Telecom 180, 207,
 209
Brussels
 English-language
  bookshops 383
 English-language libraries
  382
 flea markets 363
 obtaining Eastern
  European visas in 39
 public transport in
  117-119
 U.K. embassy in 316
BTW tax
 Belgium 347
 Netherlands 357
Bucharest

English-language libraries
 in 396
U.K. embassy in 319
Bucket shops (discount
 air fares) 15, 41, 91-92
Budapest
 English-language library
  in 390
 English-language news-
  paper in 391
 U.K. embassy in 318
Bulgaria
 business hours 326
 embassy in U.K. 27
 emergency road service
  160
 health care, emergency
  74
 International Drivin
  Permit 152
 holidays 326
 shopping 341
 telephones 190-191
 tourist office in U.K. 12
 U.K. embassy in 316
 visas 27
Bundes Netzkarte (West
 Germany) 101
Bundesnetzkarte (Austria)
 99
Business hours 322-337
 Albania 325
 Austria 325
 Bank Holidays
  Great Britain 329
  Ireland 331
 Belgium 325-326
 Bulgaria 326
 Czechoslovakia 326
 Denmark 327
 early closing 329, 331
 Finland 327
 France 327-328
 Germany, East 328
 Germany, West 328-329
 Great Britain 329
 Greece 330
 Hungary 330
 Ireland 331
 Italy 331
 Luxembourg 332
 Netherlands 332
 Norway 332-333
 Poland 333
 Portugal 333-334
 Romania 334
 Soviet Union 334
 Spain 335
 Sweden 335-336
 Switzerland 336
 Turkey 336

Index *Buses* 409

Yugoslavia 337
Buses
  intercity 100, 124
  local (see city names)
  long distance 124
  stations, toilets at 250
Cafes
  breakfast at 280-281
  lunch at 280-281
  toilets at 253
Cagliari, U.K. vice-consulate in 318
Camera
  film processing of 58
  protection of 57, 308-309
  writing address on 57, 308
  X ray of at airports 58-59
Camping 276-277
  Carnet 277
  guidebooks 277
Canada Direct 180-181
Caravanettes, purchase of 154-155
Cars
  buying a used car 153-155
    dealers in London 154-155
    dealers in Amsterdam 154
    dealers in Paris 154
  Country Codes Key 162-163
  country of registration key 162-163
  emergency road service calls 159-161
  flea market in Paris 153-154
  insurance 143, 150, 154-155
  leasing 143, 153
  licencing, driver 147, 150
  licencing, car (see registration)
  parts, eastern Europe 158-159
  purchasing 143
  registration, used cars 143
  rental and leasing companies in U.K. 152
  renting 143
  repairs 158-161
  road sign key 148-149
  road signs 147, 148-149
  roundabouts 145
  rules of the road 144-146
  safety checks 155
  seat belts 144-145
  street markets in
    Amsterdam 154
    London 153-154
    Frankfurt 154
    Paris 153-154
  touring, advantages of 143
  theft 306
  traffic circles 145
  Value Added Tax Rate Key 152
Carte ad'Argento 106
Cash 61-62
Charter flights 15, 40
  buying tickets on 40
Chemists 83
  symbol for 83
  words for 83
Cheques
  cashing at embassies 315
  cashing foreign currency 344
  Eurocheques 66-67
  personal 65-66
  traveller's 62-64
    commissions 62-64
    denominations 62
    in foreign currency 62
    replacement of 64
Chequetren 108
Climates
  range of 48
Closings
  early (EC) 329, 331
  holiday 322-323, 325-327
  weekend 322
Civil Aviation Authority 42
Clothes 47-56
  (Also see Laundry)
  care of 49
  layering 48
  men's 49-52
    checklist key 51-52
  three thoughts on 47-48
  wardrobes 48
  washing 293-301
  (also see Laundry)
  women's 52-56
    checklist key 45
Coffee, serving of 263, 278, 279, 280, 284, 286
Coimbra (Portugal)
  English-language library 395
Coins, left over 68
Cologne (Köln)
  English-language libraries 387
Complaints, airline 42
Concerts 373-374

Consulates
  (also see Embassies)
  duties of 311-315
  Eastern European in
    U.K. 27-32
  U.K. in Europe
    315-321
Consular responsibilities
  311-315
Copenhagen
  Card 375
  English-language
    bookshops 384
  English-language libraries
    384
  English-language
    magazine 384
  flea markets 364
  public transport 119-120
  This Week magazine 384
  U.K. embassy in 316
Country Codes
  Key 162-163
Crédit Agricole bank 375
Credit cards 65, 84
  telephone 176
Culture
  discount cards
    Copenhagen Card 373
    Göteborgskortet 378
    Great Britain Heritage
      Pass 375-376
    Historic Buildings &
      Monuments Commission 376
    Historic Houses Association Card 377
    Holland Culture Card
      377
    Malmökortet 378
    National Museum
      Card 377
    National Trust
      Card 376
    National Trust for
      Scotland Card
      376-377
    Stockholmskortet 378
  Evensong 373
  half-price theatre tickets
    372
  in summer 374
  music 373
  music festivals 374
  opera 372
  theatre
    in London 371-372
    on the Continent
      372
  tickets 371-374
Currency exchange 61

Customs 404-405
  for packages 168
Cyprus, health care,
  emergency 75
Czechoslovakia
  bed and breakfast 261
  beer 287
  business hours 326-327
  discount petrol
    coupons 156-157
  dry cleaners 301
  English-language library
    383
  embassy in U.K. 27
  export duties 341
  health care, emergency 75
  holidays 326-327
  shopping 341
  telephones 192-193
  tourist office in U.K. 12
  U.K. embassy in 316
  visas 27
Dagkaart 106
Dagretour 107
Daylight saving time 324
DDR (see East Germany)
Denmark
  business hours 327
  car insurance 155
  Copenhagen Card 375
  dry cleaning 301
  emergency road service
    160
  English-language
    bookshops 384
  English-language
    libraries 383
  English-language magazine 383
  farm stays 265
  flea markets 364
  holidays 327
  launderettes in 296
  "menus" in 282-283
  rail discounts 98, 100
  shopping 341
  staying on a farm 265
  telephones 194-195
  tourist office in U.K. 12
  U.K. embassy in 316
  value added tax refunds
    348
Department of Health and
  Human Services 70
Días Azules 109
Did you forget anything?
  Key 84-86
Dijon, market 364
Dinarcheques 64
Diner's Club 65
Dinner 282-284

Drinks
  after dinner 287
  beer 287
  coffee 278, 279, 281, 274, 285, 286
  fizzy drinks 286-287
  water 285
  wine 287
Driving (see also Cars) 143-163
  emergency road service 159-161
  in cities 143
  licence 147-150
  parking 145
  rules of the road 144-146
  speed limits 144-145
  under the influence 147
Drunk driving 147
Dry cleaning 300-301
  Dry cleaning word key 301
Dublin
  U.K. embassy in 317
Düsseldorf (West Germany)
  U.K. consulate in 317
Duty 404-405
Duty-free allowances 402-404
  prohibited items 402-403
  restricted items 403
Duty Free Shops 402
Edinburgh (Scotland)
  National Trust for Scotland office 477
Embassies
  absentee voting 314
  are not travel agencies 311
  Eastern European in U.K. 27-32
  in an emergency 311-315
  registration at 348
  repatriation loans at 67, 315
  services to citizens 311-313
  U.K. in Europe 315-321
Emergency
  death 313
  disorders and disasters 313
  embassy aid in an 311-315
  health 69, 313
  legal 313-313
  passport loss 311-312
  road service 159-161
  theft 302-310
  travelers check loss 64, 310
English-language reading in Europe 379-399
  (see also city names)

Environmental ticket 110
Europabus 110
European government tourist offices
  in U.K. 11-14
European Community nations
  health care in 70
  VAT refunds 343
European rail passes 97-110
Evening meal 282-284
Evensong 373
Farms, staying on 264-271
Fast food 285
Fermo Posta 166
Ferries, international services 34-39
Film
  Agfa developing system 58
  buying 58
  in Eastern Europe 58
  protection of from X rays 58-59
Financial Times, The 380
Finland
  business hours 327
  dry cleaners 301
  emergency road service 160
  English-language bookshops 384
  English-language libraries 384
  farm stays 265
  headlights on 146
  health care, emergency 75
  holidays 327
  launderettes 296
  rail discounts 98, 100
  shopping 341
  staying on a farm 265
  street market 364
  telephones 196-197
  tourist office in U.K. 12
  U.K. embassy in 316
  value added tax refunds 349
Finnrailpass 100
Firearms, restrictions on transporting 45
Flat rentals 273-374
Flea markets 361-370
  bargaining in 362
  cities with 363-370
  countries 363-370
Florence
  English-language bookshops 391
  English-language

library 391
U.K. consulate in 318
Floriana
(Malta), U.K. High Commission in 319
Food 261-163, 278-292, (also see drinks)
  a la carte 283-284
  appetizers 283
  breakfast 261, 263, 278-281
  courses 283-284
  dessert 283
  evening meal 282-284
  fast food 285
  luncheon 281-282
  Menu Key 288-291
  menus 282-283, 284
  picnics 281-282
  sandwiches 282
  set meals 284
  snacks 285
  sweets 283
France
  antiques and antiquities 339-340
  Appels Vert 179
  August holidays 328
  bed & breakfast 261, 263
  breakfast 279
  Blue Zones 145
  business hours 327-328
  camping 277
  car leasing 153
  cheeses 283
  Crédit Agricole bank 375
  dry cleaners 300, 301
  emergency road service 160
  English-language bookshops 385-386
  English-language libraries 385-386
  exportation of antiquities and fine arts 339-340
  farm stays 265-266
  flea markets 364-366
  food
    cheeses 283
    menu reader 288, 290
  "Gîtes rurales" 265-266
  health care, emergency 75-76
  holidays 328
  La cARTe 375
  launderettes 296
  "menus" in 282-284
  modems on telephones 182
  museum pass 375
  rail discounts 100-101
  shopping 341
  speed traps in 144
  staying on a farm 265-266
  strikes 324
  telephones 198-200
  tourist office in U.K. 12
  U.K. embassy and consulates in 316-317
  value added tax refunds 349-350
  Vacances pass 100-101
Frankfurt
  English-language bookshop 387
  English-language library 387
  flea market 366-367
  for cars 154
  public transport 121-122
  U.K. consulate in 317
Freedom of Scotland ticket 104
Freiburg
  English-language library 387
Fremdenzimmer 262-263
French
  language key 88
  menu key 288, 290
FRG (see West Germany)
Gasoline (see Petrol)
GDR (see East Germany)
Gebiets Netzkarte 101
Geneva
  flea market 370
  U.K. consulate in 320
German
  language key 89
  menu key 289, 291
Germany, East (DDR)
  business hours 328
  discount petrol coupons 157
  embassy in U.K. 29
  English-language library 386
  health care, emergency 76-77
  holidays 368
  Reisebüro der DDR 29
  speed traps in 144
  telephones 201-202
  tourist office in U.K. 12
  transit visas 29
  visas 28-29
  U.K. embassy in 317
Germany, West (BRD)
  antiques 359

Index Ghent

bed and breakfast
 262-263, 265
beer 287
breakfast 263, 278-280
business hours 328-329
car rental 151
dry cleaners 300, 301
emergency road service
 160
English-language
 bookshops 387-388
English-language
 libraries 387-388
farm stays 266-267
flea markets 366-367
health care, emer-
 gency 77
holidays 328-329
launderettes 296
rail discounts 101
shopping 341
speed limits 144
stay on a farm 266-267
telephones 203-206
tourist office in U.K. 12
U.K. embassy and
 consulates in 317
value added tax
 refunds 351-352
Ghent
 (Gand) Belgium
 street market 353
Golf clubs as baggage 43, 44,
 95
Gibraltar
 health care, emer-
  gency 78
 tourist office in U.K. 12
Gîtes rurales 265-266
Gondolas 139
Göteborg (Sweden)
 discount museum and
  transportation card 378
 U.K. consulate in 320
Government tourist offices
 benefits and drawbacks of
  10-11
 in Europe 11
 in U.K. 11-14
Great Britain
 antiques 339-340
 bank holidays 329
 bed & breakfast 261-262
 bookshops 389
 breakfasts 261-262, 278
 business hours 329
 buying used cars in
  153
 early closing 329
 emergency road service
  160

exporting fine arts and
 antiquities from 339-340
Evensong 373
farm stays 267-268
flea markets 367-368
holidays 329
home exchanges 272-273
launderettes 301
libraries 388-389
magazines 389
museum discount cards
 375-377
National Health
 Service 69
newspapers 388-389
public libraries 388-389
rail discounts 101-104
shopping 341
staying on a farm 267-268
strikes 324
telephones 207-210
value added tax
 refunds 352-353
Greece
 antiques in 339-340
 buses 110
 business hours 330
 dry cleaners 301
 emergency road service
  160
 English-language
  bookshops 390
 English-language libraries
  389-390
 English-language
  newspapers 390
 exportation of antiques
  and antiquities 339-340
 farm stays 268
 flea market 368
 health care, emer-
  gency 78
 holidays 330
 launderettes 296
 rail discounts 104
 shopping 341
 staying on a farm 268
 telephones 211-212
 tourist office in U.K. 12
 U.K. embassy in 318
Greek Prehistoric and
 Classical Antiquities
 Service 340
 export permits 339-340
Green Cards (car insurance)
 150
 health insurance with 70
Guardian, The 380
Gypsies, protection from
 304, 369, 370

Half-Price Ticket Office
  (London) 372
The Hague (Netherlands)
  English-language
    bookshop 394
  English-language
    library 394
  U.K. embassy in 319
Hamburg
  English-language libraries
    387
  U.K. consulate in 317
Hannover (West Germany)
  English-language
    library 388
Harrods 352
Health care 69-83
  European Community
    nations 70
  reciprocal agree-
    ment nations 70-71
  no-coverage nations 71
  procedures 71-72
  services, defini-
    tion of 73
  country-by-country
    coverage 73-83
  chemists 83
Heidelberg
  English-language library
    in 388
Helsinki
  English-language
    bookshops 384
  English-language
    libraries 384
  Street market 364
  U.K. embassy in 316
Historic Buildings and
  Monuments Commission
  Card 376
Historic Houses Association
  Card 377
Holidays 322-323
  Albania 325
  Austria 325
  Bank 326, 328
  Belgium 326
  Bulgaria 326
  Czechoslovakia 326
  Denmark 327
  Finland 327
  France 328
  Germany, East 328
  Germany, West 329
  Great Britain 329
  Greece 330
  Hungary 331
  Ireland 331
  Italy 331
  Luxembourg 332
  Netherlands 332
  Norway 333
  Poland 333
  Portugal 333-334
  Romania 334
  Soviet Union 334
  Spain 335
  Sweden 336
  Switzerland 336
  Turkey 336
  Yugoslavia 337
Holland
  (see Netherlands)
Holland Culture Card 377
Holland Leisure Card
  377-378
Home exchanging services
Home and flat rentals
  273-374
  271-272
Hostels 225-260
Hotels
  274-276
  baths & showers 260
  day 261
  mail held at 164, 171
  room finding
    services 259
  telephone surcharges
    177
  toilets at 251-252
Hovercraft 34
Hungary
  bed and breakfast 261
  business hours 330
  dry cleaners 301
  embassy in U.K. 30
  emergency road service
    160
  English-language library
    390
  English-language
    newspaper 391
  farm stays 268
  health care, emer-
    gency 79
  holidays 330
  launderette 296
  shopping 341
  staying on a farm 268
  telephones 213-214
  tourist office in U.K. 12
  U.K. embassy in 318
  VAT 343
  visas 30
Hygrolet 25075
Immigration 405
Insurance
  car 150, 154-155
  health 69-83
International Driving

Index   Keys   415

Permit 150
International
 ferry services 34-39
Intourist 31
Ireland
 bed & breakfast 261-262
 business hours 331
 dry cleaners 301
 early closing (EC) 331
 emergency road service 160
 farm stays 269
 health care, emergency 79
 holidays 331
 launderettes 296
 rail discounts 106
 shopping 341
 stay on a farm 269
 telephones 215-217
 tourist office in U.K. 13
 U.K. embassy in 318
 value added tax refunds 354
Ireland, Northern (see Great Britain)
Irish Overlander 105
Irish Tourist Board 13
Isle of Man
 rail discount 103
Istanbul
 English-language bookshop 399
 English-language library 399
 English-language newspaper 399
 U.K. consulate in 321
Italian
 language key 89
 menu key 289, 291
Italy
 antiques 339-340
 breakfast 279
 business hours 331
 closing days 331
 discount petrol coupons 157
 dry cleaners 301
 emergency road service 160
 English-language bookshops 391-392
 English-language libraries 391-392
 English-language newspaper 392-393
 exportation of antiquities and fine arts 339-340
 farm stays 269

 flea markets 369
 health care, emergency 79
 holidays 331
 launderettes 296
 menu key 289, 291
 rail discounts 105-106
 shopping 341
 staying on a farm 269
 strikes 324
 telephones 218-220
 tourist office in U.K. 13
 U.K. embassy and consulates in 318
 value added tax refunds 355-356
IVA (Imposto di Valore Aggiunto)—Italy 355-356
IVA (Impuesto de Valór Añadido)—Spain 355-356
Key, spare for rental car 151
Keys
 Before You Leave Checklist 84-86
 Business Hours 325-337
 Car Rental Value Added Tax 152
 Country Codes, car 162-163
 Did You Forget Anything? 84-86
 Dry Cleaner Word 301
 Eastern European embassies and consulates in U.K. 26-32
 Car origins 162-163
 English-language bookshops and libraries 382-399
 Flea and street markets 363-370
 Health claim procedures 73-83
 Hot, Warm, Cold 299
 Language (French, German, Italian) 88-89
 Launderette Word Key 296-297
 Laundry Supply Key 294-295
 Men's Clothes Checklist 51-52
 Menu (French, German, Italian) 288-291
 Passport offices in U.K. 21-22
 Postal service 172-173
 Public transport 113-142

Shopping specialities 340-341
Railpasses 98-110
Road Sign 148-149
Shopping specialties 380-381
Telephone 183-248
Toilet, word for 256-257
Tourist offices
 in U.K. 11-14
U.K. Embassies and Consulates 315-321
Value added tax
 rates on rental cars 152
Value added tax refund 345-360
Visa Requirements for Eastern Europe 26-32
Women's Clothes Checklist 56
Kosthuis 263
Krakow (Poland)
 English-language library 394
La cARTe 375
Language Key 88-89
Las Palmas, U.K. consulate in 320
Laundry 293-301
 Dry Cleaner Word Key 301
 laundromats (see launderettes)
 Launderette Word Key 296-297
 supplies for 294-295
 types of in Europe 295-301
  dry cleaners 300-301
  hotel laundry services 294
  hotel sinks 293-294
  laundries (full service) 298-300
  launderettes 295-298
Lead lined film bags 59
Leasing cars 153
Legal problems 312-313
Libraries
 as information source 8-9
  contents of 8-9
  drawback to 8-9
 British Council 381, 382-399
 English-language in Europe 381-399
 U.S. Information Agency in Europe 381, 382-399
 university and college in U.K. 8
Liechtenstein
 telephones 241-243
Liège (Belgium)
 flea market 363
Lille (France)
 English-language library 385
 U.K. consulate in 317
Lisbon
 English-language bookshops 395
 English-language libraries 395
 English-language newspaper 395
 flea market 370
 U.K. embassy in 319
Lista de correos 166
Ljubljana (Yugoslavia), English-language library in 399
Lodging 258-277
 (see also bed & breakfast, camping, farms, hotels, homes, exchanges, youth hostels)
 hints 258-259
 room-finding services 259
 room security 305-306
 trains as 260-261
London
 Auto Trader (newspaper) 153
 bookshops 9-10
 Exchange & Mart 153
 flea markets 367-368
 Half-Price Ticket Booth 372
 public transport 123-126
 theatre 371-372
 Used car sales in 154
Lunch (see Luncheon)
Luncheon 281, 282
 closing during 281
 in cafes 282
 picnic 282, 283
 rush hours around 281
Luxembourg
 business hours 332
 dry cleaners 391
 emergency road service 161
 English-language bookshop 393
 English-language newspaper 393
 health care, emergency 80
 holidays 332
 launderettes 297

rail discounts 98, 106
telephones 221-222
tourist office in U.K. 13
U.K. embassy in 319
value added tax refunds 356
LVV (Liikevaihtavero)
Finnish value added tax 349
Lyon (France)
English-language library 385
flea markets 364-365
U.K. consulate in 317
Maandnetkaarten 107
Madrid
English-language bookshop 397
English-language libraries 397
English-language newspaper 397
flea markets 370
public transport 127
U.K. embassy in 319
Magazines
The Athenian 390
English-language in Europe 379-380
Copenhagen This Week 384
Time Out 41, 389
What's On 41, 389
Mail and packages 164-173
at American Express offices 164, 167, 170-171
express documents 168
Fermo posta 166
Lista de correos 166
receiving in Europe 169-171
to Europe 164-169
Parcel post 169, 171
Post boxes 173
Postal Service Key 172-173
Postlagernd 166
post offices 164-173
Poste Restante 166, 167-170
stamps 172-173
Malmökortet 378
Malta
Health care, emergency 80
tourist office in U.K. 13
U.K. high commission in 319
Malmö (Sweden)
discount museum and transportation card 378
Maps, sources of 9
Marseille
English-language library 385
U.K. consulate in 317
MCI Call USA 180
Meals 278-292
Medical problems (see Health)
Menu
meaning of 282-283, 294
Menu Key (French, German, Italian) 288-291
Michelin guides
authorized car repair listings 158
camping 277
Milan (Milano)
English-language bookshop 392
English-language libraries 391
flea markets 369
opera 372
public transport 128-129
U.K. consulate in 318
MOMS (tax)
Denmark 348
Norway 358
Sweden 359-360
Monaco
postage stamps 344
shopping 341
telephones 198-299
tourist office in U.K. 13
Money 60-68
cash 61-62
cashing foreign checks 344
credit and charge cards 65
European bank accounts 66
Eurocheques 66-67
exchange rates 60
forms of 60
leftover 68
obtaining more 67
telegraphing 60
transferring 67
traveller's cheques 62-64
cashing 63-64
repatriation loan 315
replacing 64
where to exchange 61
Moscow
English-language bookshop 396
English-language library 396

Munich (München)
  U.K. embassy in 320
Munich (München)
  English-language bookshop 388
  English-language libraries 388
  flea market 367
  public transport 129-131
  U.K. consulate in 317
Museum passes 374-378
Music 373-374
  festivals 373-374
  annual festival guide 374
MWST (Mehrwertsteuer) (tax)
  Austria 345-346
  West Germany 351-352
Naples
  English-language library 392
  U.K. consulate in 318
National Health Insurance 69
National holidays (see Holidays)
National Museum Card (Netherlands) 377
National rail passes 97-110
National Trust Card 376
National Trust for Scotland Card 376-377
Netherlands
  bed & breakfast 263
  breakfast 279
  Bureaux de Change 61
  business hours 332
  dry cleaners 301
  emergency road service 161
  English-language bookshops 393-394
  English-language libraries 493-394
  farm stays 269
  flea markets 369
  Health care, emergency 80-81
  holidays 332
  Holland Culture Card 377
  Holland Leisure Card 377-378
  launderettes 297
  National Museum Card 377
  rail discounts 48, 106-107
  shopping 341
  stay on a farm 269
  telephones 223-225
  tourist office in U.K. 13
  U.K. embassy in 319
  value added tax refunds 357
Newspapers
  English-language
    Athens 399
    Budapest 391
    Copenhagen 388
    Eastern European 380
    Financial Times 380
    Gardian (The) 380
    Hungary 391
    Istanbul 399
    Lisbon 395
    Luxembourg 393
    Madrid 397
    Rome 392-393
    Telegraph (The) 380
    Times (The) 380
    Turkey 399
  Sunday travel sections 15
Nordturist (rail pass) 98
Northern Ireland
  tourist office in U.K. 13
  rail passes 103-104
  Irish Overlander 104
Norway
  business hours 332-333
  dry cleaners 301
  emergency road service 161
  English-language bookshops 394
  English-language library 394
  headlights on 146
  health care, emergency 81
  holidays 333
  launderettes 297
  rail discounts 98, 107
  shopping 341
  telephones 226-227
  tourist office in U.K. 13
  U.K. embassy in 319
  value added tax refunds 358
NS-Jaarkaart 107
Nürnberg
  English-language library in 388
Offenbach (W. Germany), flea market in 367
Opera 372
Oporto (see Porto)
Oslo (Norway)
  English-language bookshops 394
  English-language library

394
U.K. embassy in 319
Overlander Pass 105
Packages (see Letters and Packages)
Packing 400
Paris
  Albanian embassy in 26
  English-language bookshops and libraries 385-386
  English-language SOS line 199
  flea markets 365-366
  opera 372
  Paris Hebdo (newspaper) 153
  public transport 131-134
  used car sales in 153-154
  U.K. embassy in 316
Paso touring card (Greece) 104
Passports
  Index Card 20
  Blue 20
  Burgundy 20
  children, adding to 21
  childrens' 17
  cost and duration 19, 23-24
  countersignature 20
  declaration 20
  extending 20-21
  forms for 18
  lost, replacing 311-312
  mailing label 20
    passport offices 17, 21-22
    photos 17, 21
    proof of nationality 19
    quick issuance 22-23
  renewing 20-21, 24
  standard British 16
  Visitor's 16, 23-24
    where to apply 17-18
Personal cheques (see cheques, personal)
Petrol
  discount coupons 156-158
  in Eastern Europe 156
  stations 155-156
  types of 155-156
Photographs
  composition of 59
  prohibition of 59
Picnic lunches 281-282
Pickpockets
  at flea markets 369, 370
  at museums 374
  cons of 303-304
  foiling 304
  women's bags 55, 303

Poland
  business hours 333
  discount petrol coupons 157
  dry cleaners 301
  embassy in U.K. 30
  emergency road service 161
  English-language libraries 394-395
  farm stays 270
  health care, emergency 81
  holidays 333
  rail discounts 108
  shopping 341
  staying on a farm 270
  telephones 228-229
  tourist office in U.K. 14
  U.K. embassy in 319
  visas 30
PolRailPass 108
Porto (Portugal)
  U.K. consulate in 319
  English-language library 396
Portugal
  business hours 333-334
  dry cleaners 301
  English-language bookshops 395-396
  English-language libraries 395
  English-language newspaper 395
  farm stays 270
  flea markets 369-370
  health care, emergency 81
  holidays 333-334
  launderettes 297
  rail discounts 108
  shopping 341
  staying on a farm 270
  strikes 324
  telephones 230-232
  tourist office in U.K. 14
  U.K. embassy and consulate in 319
Postal buses
  Austria 110
  Switzerland 110
Postal Services Key 172-173
Poste Restante 170, 166, 167
Postlagernd 166
Post offices 164-173, 322
Poznan
  (Poland)

English-language library 394
Prague
  English-language library 383
  U.K. embassy in 316
Public transport 112-142
  Amsterdam 113-115
  Berlin 115-117
  Brussels 117-119
  Copenhagen 119-120
  Frankfurt 121-122
  London 123-126
  Madrid 127
  Milan 128-129
  Munich 129-131
  Paris 131-134
  Rome 135-136
  Stockholm 135-137
  Venice 138-139
  Vienna 140-142
RAC (Royal Automobile Club)
  car insurance 155
  emergency road service 160
  International Driving Permit 150
  reservations, ferry 36
Rail discounts (types of)
  Abbonement (Luxembourg) 106
  Austria 99
  Bargain Rail Pass 107
  B-Tourrail 98
  Belgium 98-99
  Benelux Tourrail 98
  Biglietto Chilometrico 105-106
  Biglietto Turistico di Libera Circolazione 105
  Bilhete Redução a Velhos 108
  Bilhete Turístico 108
  Britainshrinkers 103
  BTLC (Italy) 105
  B-Tourrail 98
  Bundes Netzkarte (West Germany) 101
  Bundesnetzkarte (Austria) 99
  Cart' ad Argento 106
  Carte d'Abonnement 106
  Chequetren 108
  Dagkaart 106
  Dagretour 107
  Day Return 102
  Denmark 98, 100
  Días Azules 109
  Disabled Persons Railcard 103
  Environment Ticket 110
  Family Railcard 102
  Finland 98-100
  Finnrailpass 99
  France Vacances 100-101
  Freedom of Scotland Ticket 104
  Gebeits Netzkarte 101
  Germany, West 101
  Great Britain 101-104
  Greece 104
  Gruppe Billet 100
  Half-price card 99
  Holland Culture Card 377
  Holland Leisure Card 377-378
  InterRail Junior 97
  Ireland 105
  Irish Overlander 103-104
  Italy 105-106
  Local Rovers 104
  Luxembourg 98, 106
  Maandnetkaarten 107
  national railpasses 98-110
  Netherlands 98, 106-107
  Network Card 102
  Nord Tourist 98
  Norway 98, 107
  NS-Jaarkaart 107
  Overlander Pass 105
  Paso 104
  Poland 108
  Polrailpass 108
  Portugal 108
  Rail and ferry combinations 140
  Rail Rover 101-102, 103
  Rail Runabout 104
  Rambler Ticket 105
  regional rail passes 98
  Reiver Rover 104
  Scandinavia (Scanrail pass) 98
  Scottish Highlands and Islands Travelpass 104
  Senior citizens discount 100, 106, 107
  Senioren-Ausweis 99
  Senioren Billet 100
  Senior Golden Card 102-103
  60+ Seniorenkaart 107
  Spain 108-109
  Sweden 98, 109
  Swiss Pass 109-110
  Switzerland 109-110
  Tarjeta Dorado 109
  Tarjeta Turistica 108
  Touristkarte 101
  Weekend Return 107

Index   *Soviet Union*   421

   Weekendretour 107
   Weeknetkaart 106
   Young Person's Railcard 122
   Youth Rambler Pass 105
   3-Dagsnetkaart 106
Railway stations 93-96
   changing money at 61
Reading
   in Europe 379-399
Reciprocal Agreement countries,
   health care in 70-71
Regional rail discounts 97
Regional rail passes 97
Reisebüro der DDR 29
Religious holidays 323
   (also see countries)
Renting
   cars 150-152
   homes 273-274
Repatriation loans 67, 315
Returning home 400-405
Ritz Hotel 252
Road signs 146-147
   key to 148-149
Romania
   business hours 334
   embassy in U.K. 30-31
   emergency road service 161
   English-language libraries 496
   health care, emergency 81-82
   holidays 334
   petrol coupons 157
   shopping 341
   telephones 233-234
   tourist office in U.K. 14
   U.K. embassy in 319
   visas 30-31
Rome
   Albanian embassy in 26-27
   English-language bookshop 392
   English-language newspaper 392-393
   English-language libraries 392
   flea market 369
   public transport 135-136
   U.K. embassy in 318
Rotterdam
   Flea market in 369
Roundabouts 145
Rules of the Road 144-146
Rungis (Paris) food market 366
Saarbrücken
   English-language library 388
Safety hazards on airplanes in U.K. 42
Sanisette 253-254
San Marino (Republic of)
   telephones 218-220
Sarajevo (Yugoslavia)
   English-language library in 399
Sarlat le Canéda (France) 361-362, 366
   street market 366
Scandinavia
   breakfast 263
Scanrailpass 98
Scotland
   buses in 123-124
   National Trust Card 376-377
   rail discounts 101-103, 104
Scottish Highlands and Islands Travelpass 103
Security
   against gypsies 369, 370
   airport 401
   checks for film 58-59, 401
   cons and swindles 303-304
   foiling pickpockets 304
   of autos 306
   of cameras 308-309
   of luggage 302-303, 305, 309
   of papers 302-303
   of hotel rooms 305-306
   reporting thefts 310
   women's bags 55, 303
Seniorenkaart 107
Skis as baggage 43-44, 95
Seville
   English-language library 397
Shopping 338-341
Skopje (Yugoslavia)
   English-language library 399
Smoking in restaurants 292
Sofia (Bulgaria)
   U.K. embassy in 316
Soviet Union
   business hours 334
   discount petrol coupons 158
   embassy in U.K. 31
   English-language bookshop 396
   English-language library 396
   International Driving Permit 150
   health care, emergency 82

Spain

- holidays 334
- launderettes 297
- telephones 235-236
- tourist office in U.K. 14
- U.K. embassy in 320
- visas 31

Spain
- antiques and antiquities 339, 340
- business hours 335
- dry cleaners 301
- English-language bookshop 397
- English-language libraries 397
- English-language magazine 397
- English-language newspaper 397
- exportation of antiques and fine arts 339, 340
- farm stays 270
- flea markets 370
- health care, emergency 82
- holidays 335
- launderettes 297
- rail discounts 108-109
- shopping 341
- staying on a farm 270
- strikes 324
- telephones 237-238
- tourist office in U.K. 14
- U.K. embassy and consulates in 319-320
- value added tax refund 358-359

Stamps
(see Letters and Packages)

Stockholm
- discount public transport card 378
- English-language bookshops 398
- English-language library 398
- public transport 136-137
- U.K. embassy in 320
- Stockholmskortet 378

Street markets (see Flea markets)

Strikes
- France 324
- Great Britain 324
- Italy 324
- Portugal 324
- Spain 324

Stuttgart (West Germany)
- English-language library 488

Sunday newspaper travel sections 15
Supabus 110
Superloo 253-254

Sweden
- business hours 335-336
- dry cleaners 301
- English-language bookshops 398
- English-language library 398
- Göteborgskortet 378
- headlights on 146
- health care, emergency 82-83
- holidays 335-336
- launderettes 297
- Malmökortet 378
- public transport discounts 109, 378
- rail discounts 98, 109
- shopping 341
- Stockholmskortet 378
- telephones 239-240
- tourist office in U.K. 14
- U.K. embassy and consulate in 320
- value added tax refunds 359-360

Swiss Pass (rail pass) 109-110

Switzerland
- banks 66
- Bureaux de Change 61
- buses 110
- business hours 336
- driving sticker 146
- dry cleaners 301
- emergency road service 161
- English-language bookshops 398
- farm stays 270-271
- flea markets 370
- health care, emergency 83
- holidays 336
- launderettes 297
- postal buses 110
- rail discounts 109-110
- shopping 341
- staying on a farm 270-271
- telephones 241-243
- tourist office in the U.K. 14
- turnover tax refunds 360
- U.K. embassy and consulate in 320

Tapas 384
Tarjeta Turistica 108
Tax-free car leasing 153

Index — Toilets

Taxis (see Public transport)
Tax refunds (see VAT)
Tea 286
Telgraph (The) 380
Telephones 174-248
  Andorra 198-200
  answering machines 279
  area codes 178
  Austria 184-186
  Belgium 187-189
  Bulgaria 190-191
  business and government offices 178
  calling cards 174
  calling Europe 181
  calling from
    businesses 178
    hotels 177
    card phones 176
    government offices 178
    pay phones 176
    private homes 176-177
    telephone offices 176
  Canada Direct 180-181
  city codes 178
  computers, using 182
  credit cards 176
  Czechoslovakia 193-193
  Denmark 194-195
  direct dialling 179-180
  directory assistance 181
    (see also countries)
  enquiries 181
  fax machines 183
  Finland 196-197
  France 198-200
  emergency road service 160-161
  Germany, East 201-202
  Germany, West 203-206
  Great Britain 207-210
  Greece 211-212
  Hungary 213-214
  international calls 175
  International directory assistance 181
  Ireland 215-217
  Italy 218-220
  Liechtenstein 241-243
  local calls 175 (see also countries)
  long distance calls 175, 178
  Luxembourg 221-222
  MCI Call USA 180
  modems, use of 182
  Monaco 198-200
  Netherlands 223-225
  Norway 226-227
  numbers, local 178
  pay phones 176
  Poland 228-229
  Portugal 230-232
  Romania 233-234
  San Marino 218-220
  Soviet Union 235-236
  Spain 237-238
  surcharges 177
  Sweden 239-240
  Switzerland 241-243
  offices 176
  tones 181-182
  Turkey 244-246
  U.K. Direct 180
  U.S.A. Direct 180
  Vatican City 218-220
  Yugoslavia 247-248
Theatre 371-372
Thefts (see Security)
Thessaloniki (Greece)
  English-language libraries 390
Tickets
  concert 373-374
  museum 374-348
  music 373-374
  parking 145
  theatre 371-372
  traffic 144-145
  transport (see public transport)
Time Out magazine 41, 389
Tipping
  at meals 292
  taxis (see public transport)
Titograd (Yugoslavia)
  English-language library 499
Toilets
  249-257
  airports 250
  bars 253
  bushes 255
  bus stations 250-251
  cafes 253
  castles 251
  churches 251
  coins for
  department stores 251
  flushing 249-250
  garages 252
  historic monuments 251
  hotels 251-252
  Hygrolet 250
  monasteries 251
  museums 251
  offices 252
  restaurants 252
  Sanisette 253-254
  squat 254-255
  Superloo 253-254
  supplies to have 249-250

train stations 250-251
Turkish 254-255
urban public 253
urinals 253
Word Key 256-257
Tours (France)
  flea market in 366
Trains
  advantages of 90
  as hotels 260-261
  baggage on 95-96
  border crossings on 92
  checked-in baggage 95-96
  classes 93, 94-95
  discount fares on 96-110
  finding your 94-95
  intermediate stops 95
  rail passes 97-110 (see also rail discounts)
  rail station 93-95
  reservations 93
  smoking seats 93
  splitting 92
  tickets 93
    penalty for no 93
  timeliness of 92
  timetables 94
  toilets at stations 250-251
Transport
  air to Europe 34, 40-42
  air inside Europe 91
  bucket shops 41
  buses 110-111
  driving 143-163 (also see Cars)
  ferries to Europe 34-39
  public 112-142
  trains 92-119 (see also Trains)
Travel Agents
  as information sources 14-15
  as ticket sellers 40
  choosing 14-15
Travel bookshops 9-10
Travel health insurance 69, 71
Traveller's cheques (see Cheques, traveller's)
Tübingen (Germany)
  English-language library 388
Turin (Torino) (Italy)
  Antique fair 369
Turkey
  buses 110
  business hours 336
  dry cleaners 301
  English-language bookstore 399
  English-language libraries 398-399
  English-language newspaper 399
  exportation of antiquities 339
  health care, emergency 83
  holidays 336
  shopping 341
  telephones 244-246
  tourist office in the U.K. 14
  U.K. embassy and consulate in 321
TVA (Taxe sur la Valeur Ajoutée)
  Belgium 347
  France 349-351
  Luxembourg 356
Tyre repair 159
U.K. Direct 180
United Kingdom (see Great Britain)
USA Direct 180
United States Information Service libraries 381
Urlaub auf dem Bauernhof 266
Used cars, buying 153-155
U.S.I.S. libraries 381, 382-399
Valencia (Spain)
  English-language library 397
Valletta (Malta)
  U.K. high commission in 319
Value added tax (see VAT)
Vans (see Cars)
VAT (value added tax) 342-350, 401
  Austria 345-346
  Belgium 347
  definition 344
  Denmark 348
  Finland 349
  France 349-351
  European Community 343
  general refund procedure 343-344, 401-405
  Germany, West 351-352
  Great Britain 342-353
  Ireland 354
  Italy 355-356
  Luxembourg 356
  Netherlands 357
  non-EC countries 343
  Norway 358
  on car rentals 152
  on used car sales 154

Index

refunds 342-360
  Spain 358-359
  Sweden 359-360
  Switzerland 360
  (see also BTW, IVA, LVV, MOMS, MWST, TVA)
Vatican City
  telephones 218-220
Venice
  gondolas 139
  public transport 138-139
  U.K. consulate in 318
Vienna
  Eastern European visas in 32
  English-language bookshops and libraries 382
  flea market 353
  opera 372
  public transport 140-142
  U.K. embassy in 316
Visas 25-33
  definition 25
  how to obtain
    in U.K. 26
    in Europe 32-33
  Countries:
    Albania 26-27
    Bulgaria 27
    Czechoslovakia 27-28
    East Germany 28-29
    Hungary 30
    Poland 30
    Romania 30-31
    Soviet Union 31
    Yugoslavia 32
Wardrobes 47-56
  men's 49-52
  women's 52-56

Warsaw
  English-language libraries 395
  U.K. embassy in 319
Weekendretour 107
Weekend Return 102
Weeknetkaart 107
What's On magazine 41, 389
Warenumsatzteuer 360
WUST (tax) 360
Youth hostels 274-276
Yugoslavia
  business hours 337
  embasssy in U.K. 32
  "dinarcheck" scrip 64
  discount petrol coupons 158
  dry cleaners 301
  emergency road service 161
  English-language libraries 499
  farm stays 271
  health care, emergency 83
  holidays 337
  shopping 341
  staying on a farm 271
  telephones 247-278
  tourist office in the U.K. 14
  U.K. embassy in 321
  visas 31-32
Zagreb (Yugoslavia)
  English language libraries 399
Zimmer Frei 262-263
Zurich
  English-language bookshops 398
  flea markets 370
  U.K. consulate in 320

Will You Help?

Time passes. Things change. Almost as soon as this book was sent to the printer, a few things became out of date. You can help, because you'll make discoveries about how to get things done. Future readers can benefit from your experiences and need to know about the changes you've found. Please fill in the blanks and send us the form. Use additional (and larger) sheets of paper if you need more space.
 Thank you!

Country:

Chapter:

What did you find different?

How did you solve the problem?

Are there any tricks for success or pitfalls to avoid?

What else did you find?

Thank you very much! Your help is appreciated not only by us but also by next year's readers.
(See over)

Mail your comments to:

Peter Manston
B.T. Batsford
4 Fitzhardinge St.
London W1H 0AH

If you'd like, please let me know your:

Name:

Address:

Telephone:

Weights

Metric:

1 Gramme = Weight (Mass) of 1 cubic Centimetre of water = 0.03 Ounce

1000 Grammes (G) = 10 Decagrammes = 1 Kilogramme (Kg) = 2.2 Pounds

1000 Kilogrammes = 1 Tonne = 2400 Pounds

1000 cubic Centimetres (cc) = 1 Litre (l) = 1.7 Imperial Pints

Imperial:

1 Ounce = 28 Grammes

16 Ounces = 1 Pound = 453 Grammes

14 Pounds = 1 Stone = 6.35 Kilogrammes

2240 Pounds = 1 Ton (U.K.)

1 Kilogramme = 2.2 Pounds

16 fluid Ounces = 1 Pint = 0.61 Litres

32 fluid Ounces = 1 Quart = 1.12 Litres (l)

128 fluid Ounces = 1 Imperial Gallon = 4.54 Litres

(Note: 1 U.S. Pint, Quart, or Gallon = 0.83 Imperial Pint, Quart, or Gallon)

(Conversions between Imperial and Metric are approximate.)

Measures

Centimetres (cm) and Inches (in) (right)

2.54 Centimetres = 1 Inch

30.5 Centimetres = 1 Foot

91.5 Centimetres = 1 Yard

1000 Millimetres = 100 Centimetres = 1 Metre = 39.5 Inches

39 Inches = 1 Metre

Imperial:

12 Inches = 1 Foot = 0.3 Metre
3 Feet = 1 Yard = 0.9 Metre
5280 Feet = 1 Statute (Land) Mile = 1600 Metres

Metric:

1000 Metres = 1 Kilometre (Km) = 0.6 Mile
1.6 Kilometres = 1 Mile

Speed:

Km/hour	Miles/hour
10	6
16	10
20	12
30	18
32	20
50	30
100	62
110	70
160	100
200	120

About the Author

Peter Manston has been travelling in Europe since he was a child. He has seen Europe by car, train, plane, bus, boat, bicycle, and on foot.

His fascination with how things work is clearly evident in his detailed coverage of subjects as diverse as public transport, toilets, and visas.

He has haunted flea markets, book stalls, and antique shops searching for the "jewels among the junk" he talks about in this and his other books.

His love of fine food has taken him to many restaurants, both famous and unknown, along the way. He's also spent early mornings at street markets, bakeries, and the many other shops for which Europe is renowned.

He has organised this book for both the seasoned traveller and the first-time traveller, whether wise in the ways of other lands or cautiously off for an exciting first venture. He wants you to enjoy travelling as much as he does.

Bon Voyage!
Buon Viaggio!
Gute Reise!